DISABILITY LAW: STATUTORY APPENDIX: FEDERAL STATUTES AND REGULATIONS

DISABILITY LAW:

STATUTORY APPENDIX:
FEDERAL STATUTES AND REGULATIONS

Fifth Edition

Laura Rothstein
*Professor of Law and
Distinguished University Scholar
University of Louisville
Louis D. Brandeis School of Law*

Ann C. McGinley
*William S. Boyd Professor of Law
William S. Boyd School of Law
University of Nevada Las Vegas*

ISBN: 978-0-7698-6885-1
ISBN: 978-0-3271-9172-8 (eBook)

NOTE TO USERS

To ensure that you are using the latest materials available in this area, please be sure to periodically check the LexisNexis Law School web site for downloadable updates and supplements at www.lexisnexis.com/lawschool.

Editorial Offices
121 Chanlon Rd., New Providence, NJ 07974 (908) 464-6800
201 Mission St., San Francisco, CA 94105-1831 (415) 908-3200
www.lexisnexis.com

MATTHEW◆BENDER

PREFACE

With ready access to the Internet, all regulations are readily available on line. Students and others, however, often find it much more usable to have a paper document to reference, so this updated Statutory Appendix has been prepared for that purpose.

In order to have an affordable appendix, the authors have edited the documents, often deleting portions relating to funding mechanisms and some (not all) federal agency enforcement and remedies. The Interpretive Guidance found in the Code of Federal Regulations is not included in this Appendix, but web link references are provided. These interpretations are often quite helpful in clarifying the intent of the regulation and the consideration of different viewpoints in deciding on a regulatory provision. Appreciation is expressed to Jeanne Price, Director of the Wiener-Rogers Law Library at the William S. Boyd School of Law, University of Nevada, Las Vegas, for assistance in preparing the list of links.

All statutes and regulations in this appendix are current as of March 2013. Inasmuch as disability law is a dynamic and changing area of law, if using statutory and regulatory references for writing papers or preparing legal documents, it is essential that the user check for any changes that might have occurred since this appendix was prepared.

Of significance since the 2006 Fourth Edition is that the Fifth Edition includes the ADA Amendments Act, with its changes to the statutory definition (and other changes). The 2008 ADAAA also amended portions of the Rehabilitation Act, and those amendments are reflected in this Appendix. Also significant are the numerous regulatory changes to the ADA for all three major titles.

SUMMARY OF CONTENTS

TABLE OF CONTENTS

TABLE OF CONTENTS

TABLE OF CONTENTS

TABLE OF CONTENTS

Chapter 4	**Regulations Implementing Title III of the Americans with Disabilities Act**
	28 C.F.R. Part 36 . . . . **101**

TABLE OF CONTENTS

TABLE OF CONTENTS

TABLE OF CONTENTS

TABLE OF CONTENTS

TABLE OF CONTENTS

Links to Interpretive Guidance

I. AMERICANS WITH DISABILITIES ACT

A. Equal Employment Opportunity Commission

1. Title I: Interpretive Guidances

29 C.F.R. Part 1630, Appendix — Interpretive Guidance on Title I of the Americans with Disabilities Act (July 1, 2011):

> http://www.gpo.gov/fdsys/pkg/CFR-2012-title29-vol4/pdf/CFR-2012-title29-vol4-part1630-app-id989.pdf

Regulations To Implement the Equal Employment Provisions of the Americans With Disabilities Act as Amended, Appendix to Part 1630 — Interpretive Guidance on Title I of the Americans With Disabilities Act Federal Register Vol. 76 No. 58 Fri., March 25, 2011 PG. 17003 [March 2011 final ADA regulations and accompanying interpretive guidances promulgated by the EEOC in order to implement the ADA Amendments Act of 2008]:

> http://www.gpo.gov/fdsys/pkg/FR-2011-03-25/pdf/2011-6056.pdf

2. Title I: Enforcement Guidances:

General:

> http://www.eeoc.gov/laws/guidance/subject.cfm#ada

EEOC Enforcement Guidance: Reasonable Accommodation and Undue Hardship under the Americans with Disabilities Act (Oct. 17, 2002):

> http://www.eeoc.gov/policy/docs/accommodation.html

EEOC Enforcement Guidance on Disability-Related Inquiries and Medical Examinations of Employees under the Americans with Disabilities Act (July 27, 2000):

> http://www.eeoc.gov/policy/docs/guidance-inquiries.html

Questions and Answers: Enforcement Guidance on Disability-Related Inquires and Medical Examinations of Employees under the Americans with Disabilities Act (July 27, 2000):

> http://www.eeoc.gov/policy/docs/qanda-inquiries.html

EEOC Enforcement Guidance on the Americans with Disabilities Act and Psychiatric Disabilities (March 25, 1997):

> http://www.eeoc.gov/policy/docs/psych.html

EEOC Enforcement Guidance on the Effect of Representations Made in Applications for Benefits on the Determination of Whether a Person is a "Qualified Individual with a Disability" under the Americans with Disabilities Act of 1990 (Feb. 12, 1997):

> http://www.eeoc.gov/policy/docs/qidreps.html

EEOC Enforcement Guidance: Workers' Compensation and the ADA (Sept. 3, 1996):

> http://www.eeoc.gov/policy/docs/workcomp.html

EEOC Enforcement Guidance: Pre-employment Disability — Related Questions and Medical Examinations (Oct. 10, 1995):

> http://www.eeoc.gov/policy/docs/preemp.html

EEOC Interim Enforcement Guidance on the Application of the Americans with Disabilities Act of

LINKS TO INTERPRETIVE GUIDANCE

1990 to Disability-Based Distinction in Employer Provided Health Insurance (June 8, 1993):

http://www.eeoc.gov/policy/docs/health.html

B. Department of Education

Questions and Answers on the ADA Amendments Act of 2008 for Students with Disabilities Attending Public Elementary and Secondary Schools (Jan. 20, 2012):

http://www2.ed.gov/about/offices/list/ocr/docs/dcl-504faq-201109.html

Transition of Students with Disabilities to Postsecondary Education: A Guide for High School Educators (Mar. 3, 2007):

http://www2.ed.gov/print/about/offices/list/ocr/transitionguide.html

C. Department of Justice

1. *Titles II & III*

ADA 2010 Revised Requirements: Accessible Pools: Means of Entry and Exit (May 24, 2012):

http://www.ada.gov/pools_2010.htm

Questions and Answers: Accessibility Requirements for Existing Swimming Pools at Hotels and Other Public Accommodations (May 24, 2012)

http://www.ada.gov/qa_existingpools_titleIII.htm

ADA Update: A Primer for Small Business (updated March 16, 2011):

http://www.ada.gov/regs2010/smallbusiness/smallbusprimer2010.htm

ADA 2010 Revised Requirements: Effective Date / Compliance Date (February 2011):

http://www.ada.gov/revised_effective_dates-2010.htm

ADA 2010 Revised Requirements: Ticket Sales (September 15, 2010):

http://www.ada.gov/ticketing_2010.htm

ADA 2010 Revised Requirements: Service Animals (September 15, 2010):

http://www.ada.gov/service_animals_2010.htm

Guidance on the 2010 ADA Standards for Accessible Design (Sept. 15, 2010):

http://www.ada.gov/regs2010/2010ADAStandards/Guidance_2010ADAStandards.pdf

ADA Title III Technical Assistance Manual Covering Public Accommodations and Commercial Facilities (1993):

http://www.ada.gov/taman3.html

D. Department of Transportation / Federal Transit Administration

1. *Disability Law Guidances*:

http://www.fta.dot.gov/12325_3886.html

Questions and Answers Regarding Wheelchairs and Bus and Rail Service. DOT Disability Law Guidance. (updated Feb. 4, 2013):

http://www.fta.dot.gov/12325_15055.html

Full-Length, Level-Boarding Platforms in New Commuter and Intercity Rail Stations (Sept. 1, 2005):

http://www.fta.dot.gov/12325_3890.html

LINKS TO INTERPRETIVE GUIDANCE

Origin-to-Destination Service (Sept. 1, 2005):

http://www.fta.dot.gov/12325_3891.html

Paratransit Requirements for § 5311-Funded Fixed-Route Service Operated by Private Entities (Sept. 1, 2005):

http://www.fta.dot.gov/12325_3892.html

Use of "Segways" on Transportation Vehicles (Sept. 1, 2005):

http://www.fta.dot.gov/12325_3893.html

II. FAMILY AND MEDICAL LEAVE ACT

A. Department of Labor / Wage and Hour Division

Administrator Interpretations Letters:

http://www.dol.gov/WHD/opinion/adminIntrprtnFMLA.htm

Opinion Letters from the Administrator:

http://www.dol.gov/WHD/opinion/fmla.htm

Non-Administrator Letters from the Wage and Hour Division:

http://www.dol.gov/WHD/opinion/fmlana.htm

III. REHABILITATION ACT

A. Department of Education

Guidance: Funds for the State Independent Living Grants Program and Independent Living Services for Older Individuals Who Are Blind Program / Title VII, Chapter 1, Part B and Title VII, Chapter 2 of the Rehabilitation Act of 1973, as amended, made available under the American Recovery and Reinvestment Act of 2009 (April 1, 2009):

http://www2.ed.gov/policy/gen/leg/recovery/guidance/ils.pdf

Transition of Students with Disabilities to Postsecondary Education: A Guide for High School Educators (Mar. 3, 2007):

http://www2.ed.gov/print/about/offices/list/ocr/transitionguide.html

Policy Directive — Whether Centers that do not Receive Title VII, Part C Grants are Included as Centers for Independent Living Under the Rehabilitation Act of 1973, as amended, and the Implications for SILC Composition, Network of Centers, and Part B and Part C Funding (Aug. 8, 2008):

http://www2.ed.gov/policy/speced/guid/rsa/pd-03-06.pdf

Employment Goal for an Individual with a Disability (Aug., 19, 1997):

http://www2.ed.gov/offices/OSERS/RSA/guidance/PD-97-04.pdf

B. Equal Employment Opportunity Commission

Policy Guidance on Executive Order 13164: Establishing Procedures to Facilitate the Provision of Reasonable Accommodation (October 20, 2000):

http://www.eeoc.gov/policy/docs/accommodation_procedures.html

C. Department of Health, Education, and Welfare

Program Instruction re: RSA Policy Statement on Interpretation of State VR Organizational Requirements of the Rehabilitation Act as Amended (June 3, 1975):

http://www2.ed.gov/policy/speced/guid/rsa/pi/pi-75-31.pdf

LINKS TO INTERPRETIVE GUIDANCE

IV. FAIR HOUSING ACT

A. Department of Housing and Urban Development

Guidance for FHEO Staff in Assisting Persons with Disabilities Transitioning from Institutions (Aug. 11, 2011):

> http://portal.hud.gov/hudportal/documents/huddoc?id=disabilitiestransitioning.PDF

Insurance Policy Restrictions as a Defense for Refusals to Make a Reasonable Accommodation (June 12, 2006):

> http://portal.hud.gov/hudportal/documents/huddoc?id=DOC_7772.doc

B. Department of Housing and Urban Development and Department of Justice

Joint Statement of the Department of Housing and Urban Development and the Department of Justice — Reasonable Modifications under the Fair Housing Act (March 5, 2008):

> http://portal.hud.gov/hudportal/documents/huddoc?id=DOC_7502.pdf

Joint Statement of the Department of Housing and Urban Development and the Department of Justice — Reasonable Accommodations under the Fair Housing Act (May 17, 2004):

> http://portal.hud.gov/hudportal/documents/huddoc?id=DOC_7771.pdf

Joint Statement of the Department of Housing and Urban Development and the Department of Justice — Group Homes, Local Land Use, And The Fair Housing Act (Aug. 18, 1999):

> http://www.justice.gov/crt/about/hce/final8_1.php

V. INDIVIDUALS WITH DISABILITIES EDUCATION ACT

A. Department of Education

Non-Regulatory Guidance on the IDEA Part B Regulations Regarding Parental Consent for the Use of Public Benefits or Insurance to Pay for Services under the IDEA, issued February 14, 2013 and effective March 18, 2013:

> http://www2.ed.gov/policy/speced/reg/idea/part-b/idea-part-b-parental-consent--qa.doc

Part B IDEA MOE Guidance for States on the Education Jobs Fund Programs (May 2011):

> http://www2.ed.gov/policy/speced/guid/idea/idea-edjobs-guidance.pdf

Questions and Answers on Individualized Education Programs: Evaluations and Reevaluations (June 2010):

> http://www2.ed.gov/policy/speced/guid/idea/iep-qa-2010.pdf

Questions and Answers on Providing Services to Children with Disabilities During an H1N1 Outbreak (Dec. 2009):

> http://www2.ed.gov/policy/speced/guid/idea/h1n1-idea-qa.pdf

Questions and Answers on Serving Children with Disabilities Eligible for Transportation (Nov. 2009):

> http://idea.ed.gov/explore/view/p/%2Croot%2Cdynamic%2CQaCorner%2C12%2C

Questions and Answers On Procedural Safeguards and Due Process Procedures For Parents and Children With Disabilities (June 2009):

> http://idea.ed.gov/explore/view/p/%2Croot%2Cdynamic%2CQaCorner%2C6%2C

Guidance: Funds for Part B of the Individuals with Disabilities Education Act Made Available under the American Recovery and Reinvestment Act of 2009 (April 1, 2009):

LINKS TO INTERPRETIVE GUIDANCE

http://www2.ed.gov/policy/gen/leg/recovery/guidance/idea-b.pdf

Guidance: Funds for Part C of the Individuals with Disabilities Education Act Made Available under the American Recovery and Reinvestment Act of 2009 (April 1, 2009):

http://www2.ed.gov/policy/gen/leg/recovery/guidance/idea-c.pdf

Questions and Answers on Special Education and Homelessness (Feb. 1, 2008):

http://www2.ed.gov/policy/speced/guid/spec-ed-homelessness-q-a.doc

Chapter 1
AMERICANS WITH DISABILITIES ACT

Americans with Disabilities Act
42 U.S.C. §§ 12101 et seq

12101. Findings and purpose

(a) Findings

The Congress finds that

(1) physical or mental disabilities in no way diminish a person's right to fully participate in all aspects of society, yet many people with physical or mental disabilities have been precluded from doing so because of discrimination; others who have a record of a disability or are regarded as having a disability also have been subjected to discrimination;

(2) historically, society has tended to isolate and segregate individuals with disabilities, and, despite some improvements, such forms of discrimination against individuals with disabilities continue to be a serious and pervasive social problem;

(3) discrimination against individuals with disabilities persists in such critical areas as employment, housing, public accommodations, education, transportation, communication, recreation, institutionalization, health services, voting, and access to public services;

(4) unlike individuals who have experienced discrimination on the basis of race, color, sex, national origin, religion, or age, individuals who have experienced discrimination on the basis of disability have often had no legal recourse to redress such discrimination;

(5) individuals with disabilities continually encounter various forms of discrimination, including outright intentional exclusion, the discriminatory effects of architectural, transportation, and communication barriers, overprotective rules and policies, failure to make modifications to existing facilities and practices, exclusionary qualification standards and criteria, segregation, and relegation to lesser services, programs, activities, benefits, jobs, or other opportunities;

(6) census data, national polls, and other studies have documented that people with disabilities, as a group, occupy an inferior status in our society, and are severely disadvantaged socially, vocationally, economically, and educationally;

(7) the Nation's proper goals regarding individuals with disabilities are to assure equality of opportunity, full participation, independent living, and economic self-sufficiency for such individuals; and

(8) the continuing existence of unfair and unnecessary discrimination and prejudice denies people with disabilities the opportunity to compete on an equal basis and to pursue those opportunities for which our free society is justifiably famous, and costs the United States billions of dollars in unnecessary expenses resulting from dependency and nonproductivity.

(b)   Purpose

It is the purpose of this chapter

(1) to provide a clear and comprehensive national mandate for the elimination of discrimination against individuals with disabilities;

(2) to provide clear, strong, consistent, enforceable standards addressing discrimination against individuals with disabilities;

(3) to ensure that the Federal Government plays a central role in enforcing the standards established in this chapter on behalf of individuals with disabilities; and

(4) to invoke the sweep of congressional authority, including the power to enforce the fourteenth amendment and to regulate commerce, in order to address the major areas of discrimination faced day-to-day by people with disabilities.

12101 note: Findings and Purposes of ADA Amendments Act of 2008, Pub. L. 110-325, § 2, Sept. 25, 2008, 122 Stat. 3553, provided that:

(a)   Findings

Congress finds that —

(1) in enacting the Americans with Disabilities Act of 1990 (ADA), Congress intended that the Act "provide a clear and comprehensive national mandate for the elimination of discrimination against individuals with disabilities" and provide broad coverage;

(2) in enacting the ADA, Congress recognized that physical and mental disabilities in no way diminish a person's right to fully participate in all aspects of society, but that people with physical or mental disabilities are frequently precluded from doing so because of prejudice, antiquated attitudes, or the failure to remove societal and institutional barriers;

(3) while Congress expected that the definition of disability under the ADA would be interpreted consistently with how courts had applied the definition of a handicapped individual under the Rehabilitation Act of 1973, that expectation has not been fulfilled;

(4) the holdings of the Supreme Court in Sutton v. United Air Lines, Inc., 527 U.S. 471 (1999) and its companion cases have narrowed the broad scope of protection intended to be afforded by the ADA, thus eliminating protection for many individuals whom Congress intended to protect;

(5) the holding of the Supreme Court in Toyota Motor Manufacturing, Kentucky, Inc. v. Williams, 534 U.S. 184 (2002) further narrowed the broad scope of protection intended to be afforded by the ADA;

(6) as a result of these Supreme Court cases, lower courts have incorrectly found in individual cases that people with a range of substantially limiting impairments are not people with disabilities;

(7) in particular, the Supreme Court, in the case of Toyota Motor

Manufacturing, Kentucky, Inc. v. Williams, 534 U.S. 184 (2002), interpreted the term "substantially limits" to require a greater degree of limitation than was intended by Congress; and

(8) Congress finds that the current Equal Employment Opportunity Commission ADA regulations defining the term "substantially limits" as "significantly restricted" are inconsistent with congressional intent, by expressing too high a standard.

(b)   Purposes

The purposes of this Act are —

(1) to carry out the ADA's objectives of providing "a clear and comprehensive national mandate for the elimination of discrimination" and "clear, strong, consistent, enforceable standards addressing discrimination" by reinstating a broad scope of protection to be available under the ADA;

(2) to reject the requirement enunciated by the Supreme Court in Sutton v. United Air Lines, Inc., 527 U.S. 471 (1999) and its companion cases that whether an impairment substantially limits a major life activity is to be determined with reference to the ameliorative effects of mitigating measures;

(3) to reject the Supreme Court's reasoning in Sutton v. United Air Lines, Inc., 527 U.S. 471 (1999) with regard to coverage under the third prong of the definition of disability and to reinstate the reasoning of the Supreme Court in School Board of Nassau County v. Arline, 480 U.S. 273 (1987) which set forth a broad view of the third prong of the definition of handicap under the Rehabilitation Act of 1973;

(4) to reject the standards enunciated by the Supreme Court in Toyota Motor Manufacturing, Kentucky, Inc. v. Williams, 534 U.S. 184 (2002), that the terms "substantially" and "major" in the definition of disability under the ADA "need to be interpreted strictly to create a demanding standard for qualifying as disabled," and that to be substantially limited in performing a major life activity under the ADA "an individual must have an impairment that prevents or severely restricts the individual from doing activities that are of central importance to most people's daily lives";

(5) to convey congressional intent that the standard created by the Supreme Court in the case of Toyota Motor Manufacturing, Kentucky, Inc. v. Williams, 534 U.S. 184 (2002) for "substantially limits", and applied by lower courts in numerous decisions, has created an inappropriately high level of limitation necessary to obtain coverage under the ADA, to convey that it is the intent of Congress that the primary object of attention in cases brought under the ADA should be whether entities covered under the ADA have complied with their obligations, and to convey that the question of whether an individual's impairment is a disability under the ADA should not demand extensive analysis; and

(6) to express Congress' expectation that the Equal Employment Opportunity Commission will revise that portion of its current regulations that

defines the term "substantially limits" as "significantly restricted" to be consistent with this Act, including the amendments made by this Act.

12102. Definition of disability

As used in this chapter:

(1) Disability

The term "disability" means, with respect to an individual

(A) a physical or mental impairment that substantially limits one or more major life activities of such individual;

(B) a record of such an impairment; or

(C) being regarded as having such an impairment (as described in paragraph (3)).

(2) Major Life Activities

(A) In general

For purposes of paragraph (1), major life activities include, but are not limited to, caring for oneself, performing manual tasks, seeing, hearing, eating, sleeping, walking, standing, lifting, bending, speaking, breathing, learning, reading, concentrating, thinking, communicating, and working.

(B) Major bodily functions

For purposes of paragraph (1), a major life activity also includes the operation of a major bodily function, including but not limited to, functions of the immune system, normal cell growth, digestive, bowel, bladder, neurological, brain, respiratory, circulatory, endocrine, and reproductive functions.

(3) Regarded as having such an impairment

For purposes of paragraph (1)(C):

(A) An individual meets the requirement of "being regarded as having such an impairment" if the individual establishes that he or she has been subjected to an action prohibited under this chapter because of an actual or perceived physical or mental impairment whether or not the impairment limits or is perceived to limit a major life activity.

(B) Paragraph (1)(C) shall not apply to impairments that are transitory and minor. A transitory impairment is an impairment with an actual or expected duration of 6 months or less.

(4) Rules of construction regarding the definition of disability

The definition of "disability" in paragraph (1) shall be construed in accordance with the following:

(A) The definition of disability in this chapter shall be construed in favor of broad coverage of individuals under this chapter, to the maximum extent permitted by the terms of this chapter.

(B) The term "substantially limits" shall be interpreted consistently with the findings and purposes of the ADA Amendments Act of 2008.

(C) An impairment that substantially limits one major life activity need not limit other major life activities in order to be considered a disability.

(D) An impairment that is episodic or in remission is a disability if it would substantially limit a major life activity when active.

(E)

(i) The determination of whether an impairment substantially limits a major life activity shall be made without regard to the ameliorative effects of mitigating measures such as

(I) medication, medical supplies, equipment, or appliances, low-vision devices (which do not include ordinary eyeglasses or contact lenses), prosthetics including limbs and devices, hearing aids and cochlear implants or other implantable hearing devices, mobility devices, or oxygen therapy equipment and supplies;

(II) use of assistive technology;

(III) reasonable accommodations or auxiliary aids or services; or

(IV) learned behavioral or adaptive neurological modifications.

(ii) The ameliorative effects of the mitigating measures of ordinary eyeglasses or contact lenses shall be considered in determining whether an impairment substantially limits a major life activity.

(iii) As used in this subparagraph

(I) the term "ordinary eyeglasses or contact lenses" means lenses that are intended to fully correct visual acuity or eliminate refractive error; and

(II) the term "low-vision devices" means devices that magnify, enhance, or otherwise augment a visual image.

12103. Additional definitions

As used in this chapter

(1)   Auxiliary aids and services

The term "auxiliary aids and services" includes

(A) qualified interpreters or other effective methods of making aurally delivered materials available to individuals with hearing impairments;

(B) qualified readers, taped texts, or other effective methods of making visually delivered materials available to individuals with visual impairments;

(C) acquisition or modification of equipment or devices; and

(D) other similar services and actions.

(2)   State

The term "State" means each of the several States, the District of Columbia, the Commonwealth of Puerto Rico, Guam, American Samoa, the Virgin Islands of the United States, the Trust Territory of the Pacific Islands, and the Commonwealth of the Northern Mariana Islands.

Title 1

SUBCHAPTER I — EMPLOYMENT

12111.   Definitions

As used in this subchapter:

(1)   Commission

The term "Commission" means the Equal Employment Opportunity Commission established by section 2000e-4 of this title.

(2)   Covered entity

The term "covered entity" means an employer, employment agency, labor organization, or joint labor-management committee.

(3)   Direct threat

The term "direct threat" means a significant risk to the health or safety of others that cannot be eliminated by reasonable accommodation.

(4)   Employee

The term "employee" means an individual employed by an employer. With respect to employment in a foreign country, such term includes an individual who is a citizen of the United States.

(5) Employer

(A)   In general

The term "employer" means a person engaged in an industry affecting commerce who has 15 or more employees for each working day in each of 20 or more calendar weeks in the current or preceding calendar year, and any agent of such person, except that, for two years following the effective date of this subchapter, an employer means a person engaged in an industry affecting commerce who has 25 or more employees for each working day in each of 20 or more calendar weeks in the current or preceding year, and any agent of such person.

(B)   Exceptions

The term "employer" does not include

(i) the United States, a corporation wholly owned by the government of the United States, or an Indian tribe; or

(ii) a bona fide private membership club (other than a labor organization) that is exempt from taxation under section 501(c) of title 26.

(6) Illegal use of drugs

(A)   In general

The term "illegal use of drugs" means the use of drugs, the possession or distribution of which is unlawful under the Controlled Substances Act [21 U.S.C. 801 et seq.]. Such term does not include the use of a drug taken under supervision by a licensed health care professional, or other uses authorized by the Controlled Substances Act or other provisions of Federal law.

(B)   Drugs

The term "drug" means a controlled substance, as defined in schedules I through V of section 202 of the Controlled Substances Act [21 U.S.C. 812].

(7) Person, etc.

The terms "person", "labor organization", "employment agency", "commerce", and "industry affecting commerce", shall have the same meaning given such terms in section 2000e of this title.

(8) Qualified individual

The term "qualified individual" means an individual who, with or without reasonable accommodation, can perform the essential functions of the employment position that such individual holds or desires. For the purposes of this subchapter, consideration shall be given to the employer's judgment as to what functions of a job are essential, and if an employer has prepared a written description before advertising or interviewing applicants for the job, this description shall be considered evidence of the essential functions of the job.

(9) Reasonable accommodation

The term "reasonable accommodation" may include

(A) making existing facilities used by employees readily accessible to and usable by individuals with disabilities; and

(B) job restructuring, part-time or modified work schedules, reassignment to a vacant position, acquisition or modification of equipment or devices, appropriate adjustment or modifications of examinations, training materials or policies, the provision of qualified readers or interpreters, and other similar accommodations for individuals with disabilities.

(10) Undue hardship

(A) In general

The term "undue hardship" means an action requiring significant difficulty or expense, when considered in light of the factors set forth in subparagraph (B).

(B) Factors to be considered

In determining whether an accommodation would impose an undue hardship on a covered entity, factors to be considered include

(i) the nature and cost of the accommodation needed under this chapter;

(ii) the overall financial resources of the facility or facilities involved in the provision of the reasonable accommodation; the number of persons employed at such facility; the effect on expenses and resources, or the impact otherwise of such accommodation upon the operation of the facility;

(iii) the overall financial resources of the covered entity; the overall size of the business of a covered entity with respect to the number of its employees; the number, type, and location of its facilities; and

(iv) the type of operation or operations of the covered entity, including the composition, structure, and functions of the workforce of such entity; the geographic separateness, administrative, or fiscal relationship of the facility or facilities in question to the covered entity.

12112. Discrimination

(a) General rule

No covered entity shall discriminate against a qualified individual on the basis of disability in regard to job application procedures, the hiring, advancement, or discharge of employees, employee compensation, job training, and other terms, conditions, and privileges of employment.

(b) Construction

As used in subsection (a) of this section, the term "discriminate against a qualified individual on the basis of disability" includes

(1) limiting, segregating, or classifying a job applicant or employee in a way that adversely affects the opportunities or status of such applicant or employee because of the disability of such applicant or employee;

(2) participating in a contractual or other arrangement or relationship that has the effect of subjecting a covered entity's qualified applicant or employee with a disability to the discrimination prohibited by this subchapter (such relationship includes a relationship with an employment or referral agency, labor union, an organization providing fringe benefits to an employee of the covered entity, or an organization providing training and apprenticeship programs);

(3) utilizing standards, criteria, or methods of administration

(A) that have the effect of discrimination on the basis of disability;

(B) that perpetuate the discrimination of others who are subject to common administrative control;

(4) excluding or otherwise denying equal jobs or benefits to a qualified individual because of the known disability of an individual with whom the qualified individual is known to have a relationship or association;

(5)

(A) not making reasonable accommodations to the known physical or mental limitations of an otherwise qualified individual with a disability who is an applicant or employee, unless such covered entity can demonstrate that the accommodation would impose an undue hardship on the operation of the business of such covered entity; or

(B) denying employment opportunities to a job applicant or employee who is an otherwise qualified individual with a disability, if such denial is based on the need of such covered entity to make reasonable accommodation to the physical or mental impairments of the employee or applicant;

(6) using qualification standards, employment tests or other selection criteria that screen out or tend to screen out an individual with a disability or a class of individuals with disabilities unless the standard, test or other selection criteria, as used by the covered entity, is shown to be job-related for the position in question

and is consistent with business necessity; and

(7) failing to select and administer tests concerning employment in the most effective manner to ensure that, when such test is administered to a job applicant or employee who has a disability that impairs sensory, manual, or speaking skills, such test results accurately reflect the skills, aptitude, or whatever other factor of such applicant or employee that such test purports to measure, rather than reflecting the impaired sensory, manual, or speaking skills of such employee or applicant (except where such skills are the factors that the test purports to measure).

(c) Covered entities in foreign countries

(1) In general

It shall not be unlawful under this section for a covered entity to take any action that constitute discrimination under this section with respect to an employee in a workplace in a foreign country if compliance with this section would cause such covered entity to violate the law of the foreign country in which such workplace is located.

(2) Control of corporation

(A) Presumption

If an employer controls a corporation whose place of incorporation is a foreign country, any practice that constitutes discrimination under this section and is engaged in by such corporation shall be presumed to be engaged in by such employer.

(B) Exception

This section shall not apply with respect to the foreign operations of an employer that is a foreign person not controlled by an American employer.

(C) Determination

For purposes of this paragraph, the determination of whether an employer controls a corporation shall be based on

(i) the interrelation of operations;

(ii) the common management;

(iii) the centralized control of labor relations; and

(iv) the common ownership or financial control of the employer and the corporation.

(d) Medical examinations and inquiries

(1) In general

The prohibition against discrimination as referred to in subsection (a) of this section shall include medical examinations and inquiries.

(2) Preemployment

(A) Prohibited examination or inquiry

Except as provided in paragraph (3), a covered entity shall not conduct a medical examination or make inquiries of a job applicant as to whether such applicant is an individual with a disability or as to the nature or severity of such disability.

(B)   Acceptable inquiry

A covered entity may make preemployment inquiries into the ability of an applicant to perform job-related functions.

(3)   Employment entrance examination

A covered entity may require a medical examination after an offer of employment has been made to a job applicant and prior to the commencement of the employment duties of such applicant, and may condition an offer of employment on the results of such examination, if

(A) all entering employees are subjected to such an examination regardless of disability;

(B) information obtained regarding the medical condition or history of the applicant is collected and maintained on separate forms and in separate medical files and is treated as a confidential medical record, except that

(i) supervisors and managers may be informed regarding necessary restrictions on the work or duties of the employee and necessary accommodations;

(ii) first aid and safety personnel may be informed, when appropriate, if the disability might require emergency treatment; and

(iii) government officials investigating compliance with this chapter shall be provided relevant information on request; and

(C) the results of such examination are used only in accordance with this subchapter.

(4)   Examination and inquiry

(A)   Prohibited examinations and inquiries

A covered entity shall not require a medical examination and shall not make inquiries of an employee as to whether such employee is an individual with a disability or as to the nature or severity of the disability, unless such examination or inquiry is shown to be job-related and consistent with business necessity.

(B)   Acceptable examinations and inquiries

A covered entity may conduct voluntary medical examinations, including voluntary medical histories, which are part of an employee health program available to employees at that work site. A covered entity may make inquiries into the ability of an employee to perform job-related functions.

(C)   Requirement

Information obtained under subparagraph (B) regarding the medical condition or history of any employee are subject to the requirements of subparagraphs (B) and (C) of paragraph (3).

12113. Defenses

(a) In general

It may be a defense to a charge of discrimination under this chapter that an alleged application of qualification standards, tests, or selection criteria that screen out or tend to screen out or otherwise deny a job or benefit to an individual with a disability has been shown to be job- related and consistent with business necessity, and such performance cannot be accomplished by reasonable accommodation, as required under this subchapter.

(b) Qualification standards " Direct threat defense "

The term "qualification standards" may include a requirement that an individual shall not pose a direct threat to the health or safety of other individuals in the workplace, or to oneself

(c) Qualification standards and tests related to uncorrected vision

Notwithstanding section 12102(4)(E)(ii), a covered entity shall not use qualification standards, employment tests, or other selection criteria based on an individual's uncorrected vision unless the standard, test, or other selection criteria, as used by the covered entity, is shown to be job-related for the position in question and consistent with business necessity.

(d) Religious entities

(1) In general

This subchapter shall not prohibit a religious corporation, association, educational institution, or society from giving preference in employment to individuals of a particular religion to perform work connected with the carrying on by such corporation, association, educational institution, or society of its activities.

(2) Religious tenets requirement

Under this subchapter, a religious organization may require that all applicants and employees conform to the religious tenets of such organization.

(e) List of infectious and communicable diseases

(1) In general

The Secretary of Health and Human Services, not later than 6 months after July 26, 1990, shall

(A) review all infectious and communicable diseases which may be transmitted through handling the food supply;

(B) publish a list of infectious and communicable diseases which are transmitted through handling the food supply;

(C) publish the methods by which such diseases are transmitted; and

(D)   widely disseminate such information regarding the list of diseases and their modes of transmissibility to the general public.

Such list shall be updated annually.

(2)   Applications

In any case in which an individual has an infectious or communicable disease that is transmitted to others through the handling of food, that is included on the list developed by the Secretary of Health and Human Services under paragraph (1), and which cannot be eliminated by reasonable accommodation, a covered entity may refuse to assign or continue to assign such individual to a job involving food handling.

(3)   Construction

Nothing in this chapter shall be construed to preempt, modify, or amend any State, county, or local law, ordinance, or regulation applicable to food handling which is designed to protect the public health from individuals who pose a significant risk to the health or safety of others, which cannot be eliminated by reasonable accommodation, pursuant to the list of infectious or communicable diseases and the modes of transmissibility published by the Secretary of Health and Human Services.

12114.   Illegal use of drugs and alcohol

(a)   Qualified individual with a disability

For purposes of this subchapter, qualified individual with a disability shall not include any employee or applicant who is currently engaging in the illegal use of drugs, when the covered entity acts on the basis of such use.

(b)   Rules of construction

Nothing in subsection (a) of this section shall be construed to exclude as a qualified individual with a disability an individual who

(1) has successfully completed a supervised drug rehabilitation program and is no longer engaging in the illegal use of drugs, or has otherwise been rehabilitated successfully and is no longer engaging in such use;

(2) is participating in a supervised rehabilitation program and is no longer engaging in such use; or

(3)   is erroneously regarded as engaging in such use, but is not engaging in such use;

except that it shall not be a violation of this chapter for a covered entity to adopt or administer reasonable policies or procedures, including but not limited to drug testing, designed to ensure that an individual described in paragraph (1) or (2) is no longer engaging in the illegal use of drugs.

(c)   Authority of covered entity

A covered entity

(1) may prohibit the illegal use of drugs and the use of alcohol at the workplace by all employees;

(2) may require that employees shall not be under the influence of alcohol or be engaging in the illegal use of drugs at the workplace;

(3) may require that employees behave in conformance with the requirements established under the Drug-Free Workplace Act of 1988 (41 U.S.C. 701 et seq.);

(4) may hold an employee who engages in the illegal use of drugs or who is an alcoholic to the same qualification standards for employment or job performance and behavior that such entity holds other employees, even if any unsatisfactory performance or behavior is related to the drug use or alcoholism of such employee; and

(5) may, with respect to Federal regulations regarding alcohol and the illegal use of drugs, require that

(A) employees comply with the standards established in such regulations of the Department of Defense, if the employees of the covered entity are employed in an industry subject to such regulations, including complying with regulations (if any) that apply to employment in sensitive positions in such an industry, in the case of employees of the covered entity who are employed in such positions (as defined in the regulations of the Department of Defense);

(B) employees comply with the standards established in such regulations of the Nuclear Regulatory Commission, if the employees of the covered entity are employed in an industry subject to such regulations, including complying with regulations (if any) that apply to employment in sensitive positions in such an industry, in the case of employees of the covered entity who are employed in such positions (as defined in the regulations of the Nuclear Regulatory Commission); and

(C) employees comply with the standards established in such regulations of the Department of Transportation, if the employees of the covered entity are employed in a transportation industry subject to such regulations, including complying with such regulations (if any) that apply to employment in sensitive positions in such an industry, in the case of employees of the covered entity who are employed in such positions (as defined in the regulations of the Department of Transportation).

(d) Drug testing

(1) In general

For purposes of this subchapter, a test to determine the illegal use of drugs shall not be considered a medical examination.

(2) Construction

Nothing in this subchapter shall be construed to encourage, prohibit, or authorize the conducting of drug testing for the illegal use of drugs by job applicants or employees or making employment decisions based on such test results.

(e) Transportation employees

Nothing in this subchapter shall be construed to encourage, prohibit, restrict, or authorize the otherwise lawful exercise by entities subject to the jurisdiction of the Department of Transportation of authority to

(1) test employees of such entities in, and applicants for, positions involving

safety-sensitive duties for the illegal use of drugs and for on-duty impairment by alcohol; and

(2) remove such persons who test positive for illegal use of drugs and on-duty impairment by alcohol pursuant to paragraph (1) from safety-sensitive duties in implementing subsection (c) of this section.

12115.   Posting notices

Every employer, employment agency, labor organization, or joint labor-management committee covered under this subchapter shall post notices in an accessible format to applicants, employees, and members describing the applicable provisions of this chapter, in the manner prescribed by section 2000e-10 of this title.

12116.   Regulations

Not later than 1 year after July 26, 1990, the Commission shall issue regulations in an accessible format to carry out this subchapter in accordance with subchapter II of chapter 5 of title 5.

12117.   Enforcement

(a)   Powers, remedies, and procedures

The powers, remedies, and procedures set forth in sections 2000e-4, 2000e-5, 2000e-6, 2000e-8, and 2000e-9 of this title shall be the powers, remedies, and procedures this subchapter provides to the Commission, to the Attorney General, or to any person alleging discrimination on the basis of disability in violation of any provision of this chapter, or regulations promulgated under section 12116 of this title, concerning employment.

(b)   Coordination

The agencies with enforcement authority for actions which allege employment discrimination under this subchapter and under the Rehabilitation Act of 1973 [29 U.S.C. 701 et seq.] shall develop procedures to ensure that administrative complaints filed under this subchapter and under the Rehabilitation Act of 1973 are dealt with in a manner that avoids duplication of effort and prevents imposition of inconsistent or conflicting standards for the same requirements under this subchapter and the Rehabilitation Act of 1973. The Commission, the Attorney General, and the Office of Federal Contract Compliance Programs shall establish such coordinating mechanisms (similar to provisions contained in the joint regulations promulgated by the Commission and the Attorney General at part 42 of title 28 and part 1691 of title 29, Code of Federal Regulations, and the Memorandum of Understanding between the Commission and the Office of Federal Contract Compliance Programs dated January 16, 1981 (46 Fed. Reg. 7435, January 23, 1981)) in regulations implementing this subchapter and Rehabilitation Act of 1973 not later than 18 months after July 26, 1990.

Title 2

SUBCHAPTER II — PUBLIC SERVICES

Part A — Prohibition Against Discrimination and Other Generally Applicable Provisions

12131. Definitions

As used in this subchapter:

(1) Public entity

The term "public entity" means

(A) any State or local government;

(B) any department, agency, special purpose district, or other instrumentality of a State or States or local government; and

(C) the National Railroad Passenger Corporation, and any commuter authority (as defined in section 24102(4) of title 49).

(2) Qualified individual with a disability

The term "qualified individual with a disability" means an individual with a disability who, with or without reasonable modifications to rules, policies, or practices, the removal of architectural, communication, or transportation barriers, or the provision of auxiliary aids and services, meets the essential eligibility requirements for the receipt of services or the participation in programs or activities provided by a public entity.

12132. Discrimination

Subject to the provisions of this subchapter, no qualified individual with a disability shall, by reason of such disability, be excluded from participation in or be denied the benefits of services, programs, or activities of a public entity, or be subjected to discrimination by any such entity.

12133. Enforcement

The remedies, procedures, and rights set forth in section 794a of title 29 shall be the remedies, procedures, and rights this subchapter provides to any person alleging discrimination on the basis of disability in violation of section 12132 of this title.

12134. Regulations

(a) In general

Not later than 1 year after July 26, 1990, the Attorney General shall promulgate regulations in an accessible format that implement this part. Such regulations shall not include any matter within the scope of the authority of the Secretary of Transportation under section 12143, 12149, or 12164 of this title.

(b) Relationship to other regulations

Except for "program accessibility, existing facilities", and "communications", regulations under subsection (a) of this section shall be consistent with this chapter and with the coordination regulations under part 41 of title 28, Code of Federal

Regulations (as promulgated by the Department of Health, Education, and Welfare on January 13, 1978), applicable to recipients of Federal financial assistance under section 794 of title 29. With respect to "program accessibility, existing facilities", and "communications", such regulations shall be consistent with regulations and analysis as in part 39 of title 28 of the Code of Federal Regulations, applicable to federally conducted activities under section 794 of title 29.

(c)   Standards

Regulations under subsection (a) of this section shall include standards applicable to facilities and vehicles covered by this part, other than facilities, stations, rail passenger cars, and vehicles covered by part B of this subchapter. Such standards shall be consistent with the minimum guidelines and requirements issued by the Architectural and Transportation Barriers Compliance Board in accordance with section 12204(a) of this title.

Part B — Actions Applicable to Public Transportation Provided by Public Entities Considered Discriminatory

Subpart I — Public Transportation Other than by Aircraft or Certain Rail Operations

12141.   Definitions

As used in this subpart:

(1)   Demand responsive system

The term "demand responsive system" means any system of providing designated public transportation which is not a fixed route system.

(2)   Designated public transportation

The term "designated public transportation" means transportation (other than public school transportation) by bus, rail, or any other conveyance (other than transportation by aircraft or intercity or commuter rail transportation (as defined in section 12161 of this title)) that provides the general public with general or special service (including charter service) on a regular and continuing basis.

(3)   Fixed route system

The term "fixed route system" means a system of providing designated public transportation on which a vehicle is operated along a prescribed route according to a fixed schedule.

(4)   Operates

The term "operates", as used with respect to a fixed route system or demand responsive system, includes operation of such system by a person under a contractual or other arrangement or relationship with a public entity.

(5)   Public school transportation

The term "public school transportation" means transportation by school bus vehicles of schoolchildren, personnel, and equipment to and from a public elementary or secondary school and school-related activities.

(6)   Secretary

The term "Secretary" means the Secretary of Transportation.

12142.   Public entities operating fixed route systems

(a)   Purchase and lease of new vehicles

It shall be considered discrimination for purposes of section which operates a fixed route system to purchase or lease a new bus, a new rapid rail vehicle, a new light rail vehicle, or any other new vehicle to be used on such system, if the solicitation for such purchase or lease is made after the 30th day following July 26, 1990, and if such bus, rail vehicle, or other vehicle is not readily accessible to and usable by individuals with disabilities, including individuals who use wheelchairs.

(b)   Purchase and lease of used vehicles

Subject to subsection (c)(1) of this section, it shall be considered discrimination for purposes of section 12132 of this title and section 794 of title 29 for a public entity which operates a fixed route system to purchase or lease, after the 30th day following July 26, 1990, a used vehicle for use on such system unless such entity makes demonstrated good faith efforts to purchase or lease a used vehicle for use on such system that is readily accessible to and usable by individuals with disabilities, including individuals who use wheelchairs.

(c) Remanufactured vehicles

(1)   General rule

Except as provided in paragraph (2), it shall be considered discrimination for purposes of section 12132 of this title and section 794 of title 29 for a public entity which operates a fixed route system

(A) to remanufacture a vehicle for use on such system so as to extend its usable life for 5 years or more, which remanufacture begins (or for which the solicitation is made) after the 30th day following July 26, 1990; or

(B) to purchase or lease for use on such system a remanufactured vehicle which has been remanufactured so as to extend its usable life for 5 years or more, which purchase or lease occurs after such 30th day and during the period in which the usable life is extended; unless, after remanufacture, the vehicle is, to the maximum extent feasible, readily accessible to and usable by individuals with disabilities, including individuals who use wheelchairs.

(2)   Exception for historic vehicles

(A)   General rule

If a public entity operates a fixed route system any segment of which is included on the National Register of Historic Places and if making a vehicle of historic character to be used solely on such segment readily accessible to and usable by individuals with disabilities would significantly alter the historic character of such vehicle, the public entity only has to make (or to purchase or lease a remanufactured vehicle with) those modifications which are necessary to meet the requirements of paragraph (1) and which do not significantly alter the historic character of such vehicle.

(B)　Vehicles of historic character defined by regulations

For purposes of this paragraph and section 12148(a) of this title, a vehicle of historic character shall be defined by the regulations issued by the Secretary to carry out this subsection.

12143.　Paratransit as a complement to fixed route service

(a)　General rule

It shall be considered discrimination for purposes of section 12132 of this title and section 794 of title 29 for a public entity which operates a fixed route system (other than a system which provides solely commuter bus service) to fail to provide with respect to the operations of its fixed route system, in accordance with this section, paratransit and other special transportation services to individuals with disabilities, including individuals who use wheelchairs that are sufficient to provide to such individuals a level of service

(1) which is comparable to the level of designated public transportation services provided to individuals without disabilities using such system; or

(2) in the case of response time, which is comparable, to the extent practicable, to the level of designated public transportation services provided to individuals without disabilities using such system.

(b)　Issuance of regulations

Not later than 1 year after July 26, 1990, the Secretary shall issue final regulations to carry out this section.

(c)　Required contents of regulations

(1)　Eligible recipients of service

The regulations issued under this section shall require each public entity which operates a fixed route system to provide the paratransit and other special transportation services required under this section

(A)

(i) to any individual with a disability who is unable, as a result of a physical or mental impairment (including a vision impairment) and without the assistance of another individual (except an operator of a wheelchair lift or other boarding assistance device), to board, ride, or disembark from any vehicle on the system which is readily accessible to and usable by individuals with disabilities;

(ii) to any individual with a disability who needs the assistance of a wheelchair lift or other boarding assistance device (and is able with such assistance) to board, ride, and disembark from any vehicle which is readily accessible to and usable by individuals with disabilities if the individual wants to travel on a route on the system during the hours of operation of the system at a time (or within a reasonable period of such time) when such a vehicle is not being used to provide designated public transportation on the route; and

(iii) to any individual with a disability who has a specific impairment-related condition which prevents such individual from traveling to a boarding location or from a disembarking location on such system;

(B) to one other individual accompanying the individual with the disability; and

(C) to other individuals, in addition to the one individual described in subparagraph (a), accompanying the individual with a disability provided that space for these additional individuals are available on the paratransit vehicle carrying the individual with a disability and that the transportation of such additional individuals will not result in a denial of service to individuals with disabilities.

For purposes of clauses (i) and (ii) of subparagraph (A), boarding or disembarking from a vehicle does not include travel to the boarding location or from the disembarking location.

(2) Service area

The regulations issued under this section shall require the provision of paratransit and special transportation services required under this section in the service area of each public entity which operates a fixed route system, other than any portion of the service area in which the public entity solely provides commuter bus service.

(3) Service criteria

Subject to paragraphs (1) and (2), the regulations issued under this section shall establish minimum service criteria for determining the level of services to be required under this section.

(4) Undue financial burden limitation

The regulations issued under this section shall provide that, if the public entity is able to demonstrate to the satisfaction of the Secretary that the provision of paratransit and other special transportation services otherwise required under this section would impose an undue financial burden on the public entity, the public entity, notwithstanding any other provision of this section (other than paragraph (5)), shall only be required to provide such services to the extent that providing such services would not impose such a burden.

(5) Additional services

The regulations issued under this section shall establish circumstances under which the Secretary may require a public entity to provide, notwithstanding paragraph (4), paratransit and other special transportation services under this section beyond the level of paratransit and other special transportation services which would otherwise be required under paragraph (4).

(6) Public participation

The regulations issued under this section shall require that each public entity which operates a fixed route system hold a public hearing, provide an opportunity for public comment, and consult with individuals with disabilities in preparing its plan under paragraph (7).

(7) Plans

The regulations issued under this section shall require that each public entity which operates a fixed route system

(A) within 18 months after July 26, 1990, submit to the Secretary, and commence implementation of, a plan for providing paratransit and other special transportation services which meets the requirements of this section; and

(B) on an annual basis thereafter, submit to the Secretary, and commence implementation of, a plan for providing such services.

(8) Provision of services by others

The regulations issued under this section shall

(A) require that a public entity submitting a plan to the Secretary under this section identify in the plan any person or other public entity which is providing a paratransit or other special transportation service for individuals with disabilities in the service area to which the plan applies; and

(B) provide that the public entity submitting the plan does not have to provide under the plan such service for individuals with disabilities.

(9) Other provisions

The regulations issued under this section shall include such other provisions and requirements as the Secretary determines are necessary to carry out the objectives of this section.

(d) Review of plan

(1) General rule

The Secretary shall review a plan submitted under this section for the purpose of determining whether or not such plan meets the requirements of this section, including the regulations issued under this section.

(2) Disapproval

If the Secretary determines that a plan reviewed under this subsection fails to meet the requirements of this section, the Secretary shall disapprove the plan and notify the public entity which submitted the plan of such disapproval and the reasons therefor.

(3) Modification of disapproved plan

Not later than 90 days after the date of disapproval of a plan under this subsection, the public entity which submitted the plan shall modify the plan to meet the requirements of this section and shall submit to the Secretary, and commence implementation of, such modified plan.

(e) "Discrimination" defined

As used in subsection (a) of this section, the term "discrimination" includes

(1) a failure of a public entity to which the regulations issued under this section apply to submit, or commence implementation of, a plan in accordance with subsections (c)(6) and (c)(7) of this section;

(2) a failure of such entity to submit, or commence implementation of, a modified plan in accordance with subsection (d) (3) of this section;

(3) submission to the Secretary of a modified plan under subsection (d)(3) of this section which does not meet the requirements of this section; or

(4) a failure of such entity to provide paratransit or other special transportation services in accordance with the plan or modified plan the public entity submitted to the Secretary under this section.

(f)   Statutory construction

Nothing in this section shall be construed as preventing a public entity

(1) from providing paratransit or other special transportation services at a level which is greater than the level of such services which are required by this section,

(2) from providing paratransit or other special transportation services in addition to those paratransit and special transportation services required by this section, or

(3) from providing such services to individuals in addition to those individuals to whom such services are required to be provided by this section.

12144.   Public entity operating a demand responsive system

If a public entity operates a demand responsive system, it shall be considered discrimination, for purposes of section 12132 of this title and section 794 of title 29, for such entity to purchase or lease a new vehicle for use on such system, for which a solicitation is made after the 30th day following July 26, 1990, that is not readily accessible to and usable by individuals with disabilities, including individuals who use wheelchairs, unless such system, when viewed in its entirety, provides a level of service to such individuals equivalent to the level of service such system provides to individuals without disabilities.

12145.   Temporary relief where lifts are unavailable

(a)   Granting

With respect to the purchase of new buses, a public entity may apply for, and the Secretary may temporarily relieve such public entity from the obligation under section 12142(a) or 12144 of this title to purchase new buses that are readily accessible to and usable by individuals with disabilities if such public entity demonstrates to the satisfaction of the Secretary

(1) that the initial solicitation for new buses made by the public entity specified that all new buses were to be lift-equipped and were to be otherwise accessible to and usable by individuals with disabilities;

(2) the unavailability from any qualified manufacturer of hydraulic, electrome-chanical, or other lifts for such new buses;

(3) that the public entity seeking temporary relief has made good faith efforts to locate a qualified manufacturer to supply the lifts to the manufacturer of such buses in sufficient time to comply with such solicitation; and

(4) that any further delay in purchasing new buses necessary to obtain such lifts would significantly impair transportation services in the community served by the public entity.

(b) Duration and notice to Congress

Any relief granted under subsection (a) of this section shall be limited in duration by a specified date, and the appropriate committees of Congress shall be notified of any such relief granted.

(c) Fraudulent application

If, at any time, the Secretary has reasonable cause to believe that any relief granted under subsection (a) of this section was fraudulently applied for, the Secretary shall

(1) cancel such relief if such relief is still in effect; and

(2) take such other action as the Secretary considers appropriate.

12146. New facilities

For purposes of section 12132 of this title and section 794 of title 29, it shall be considered discrimination for a public entity to construct a new facility to be used in the provision of designated public transportation services unless such facility is readily accessible to and usable by individuals with disabilities, including individuals who use wheelchairs.

12147. Alterations of existing facilities

(a) General rule

With respect to alterations of an existing facility or part thereof used in the provision of designated public transportation services that affect or could affect the usability of the facility or part thereof, it shall be considered discrimination, for purposes of section 12132 of this title and section 794 of title 29, for a public entity to fail to make such alterations (or to ensure that the alterations are made) in such a manner that, to the maximum extent feasible, the altered portions of the facility are readily accessible to and usable by individuals with disabilities, including individuals who use wheelchairs, upon the completion of such alterations. Where the public entity is undertaking an alteration that affects or could affect usability of or access to an area of the facility containing a primary function, the entity shall also make the alterations in such a manner that, to the maximum extent feasible, the path of travel to the altered area and the bathrooms, telephones, and drinking fountains serving the altered area, are readily accessible to and usable by individuals with disabilities, including individuals who use wheelchairs, upon completion of such alterations, where such alterations to the path of travel or the bathrooms, telephones, and drinking fountains serving the altered area are not disproportionate to the overall alterations in terms of cost and scope (as determined under criteria established by the Attorney General).

(b) Special rule for stations

(1) General rule

For purposes of section 12132 of this title and section 794 of title 29, it shall be considered discrimination for a public entity that provides designated public transportation to fail, in accordance with the provisions of this subsection, to make key stations (as determined under criteria established by the Secretary by regulation) in rapid rail and light rail systems readily accessible to and usable by individuals with disabilities, including individuals who use wheelchairs.

(2) Rapid rail and light rail key stations

(A) Accessibility

Except as otherwise provided in this paragraph, all key stations (as determined under criteria established by the Secretary by regulation] in rapid rail and light rail systems shall be made readily accessible to and usable by individuals with disabilities, including individuals who use wheelchairs, as soon as practicable but in no event later than the last day of the 3-year period beginning on July 26, 1990.

(B) Extension for extraordinarily expensive structural changes

The Secretary may extend the 3-year period under subparagraph (A) up to a 30-year period for key stations in a rapid rail or light rail system which stations need extraordinarily expensive structural changes to, or replacement of, existing facilities; except that by the last day of the 20th year following July 26, 1990, at least 2/3 of such key stations must be readily accessible to and usable by individuals with disabilities.

(3) Plans and milestones

The Secretary shall require the appropriate public entity to develop and submit to the Secretary a plan for compliance with this subsection

(A) that reflects consultation with individuals with disabilities affected by such plan and the results of a public hearing and public comments on such plan, and

(B) that establishes milestones for achievement of the requirements of this subsection.

12148. Public transportation programs and activities in existing facilities and one car per train rule

(a) Public transportation programs and activities in existing facilities

(1) In general

With respect to existing facilities used in the provision of designated public transportation services, it shall be considered discrimination, for purposes of section 12132 of this title and section 794 of title 29, for a public entity to fail to operate a designated public transportation program or activity conducted in such facilities so that, when viewed in the entirety, the program or activity is readily accessible to and usable by individuals with disabilities.

(2)   Exception

Paragraph (1) shall not require a public entity to make structural changes to existing facilities in order to make such facilities accessible to individuals who use wheelchairs, unless and to the extent required by section 12147(a) of this title (relating to alterations) or section 12147(a) of this title (relating to key stations).

(3)   Utilization

Paragraph (1) shall not require a public entity to which paragraph (2) applies, to provide to individuals who use wheelchairs services made available to the general public at such facilities when such individuals could not utilize or benefit from such services provided at such facilities.

(b)   One car per train rule

(1)   General rule

Subject to paragraph (2), with respect to 2 or more vehicles operated as a train by a light or rapid rail system, for purposes of section 12132 of this title and section 794 of title 29, it shall be considered discrimination for a public entity to fail to have at least 1 vehicle per train that is accessible to individuals with disabilities, including individuals who use wheelchairs, as soon as practicable but in no event later than the last day of the 5-year period beginning on the effective date of this section.

(2)   Historic trains

In order to comply with paragraph (1) with respect to the remanufacture of a vehicle of historic character which is to be used on a segment of a light or rapid rail system which is included on the National Register of Historic Places, if making such vehicle readily accessible to and usable by individuals with disabilities would significantly alter the historic character of such vehicle, the public entity which operates such system only has to make (or to purchase or lease a remanufactured vehicle with) those modifications which are necessary to meet the requirements of section 12142(c)(1) of this title and which do not significantly alter the historic character of such vehicle.

12149.   Regulations

(a)   In general

Not later than 1 year after July 26, 1990, the Secretary of Transportation shall issue regulations, in an accessible format, necessary for carrying out this subpart (other than section 12143 of this title).

(b)   Standards

The regulations issued under this section and section 12143 of this title shall include standards applicable to facilities and vehicles covered by this part. The standards shall be consistent with the minimum guidelines and requirements issued by the Architectural and Transportation Barriers Compliance Board in accordance with section 12204 of this title.

12150.   Interim accessibility requirements

If final regulations have not been issued pursuant to section 12149 of this title, for new construction or alterations for which a valid and appropriate State or local building permit is obtained prior to the issuance of final regulations under such section, and for which the construction or alteration authorized by such permit begins within one year of the receipt of such permit and is completed under the terms of such permit, compliance with the Uniform Federal Accessibility Standards in effect at the time the building permit is issued shall suffice to satisfy the requirement that facilities be readily accessible to and usable by persons with disabilities as required under sections 12146 and 12147 of this title, except that, if such final regulations have not been issued one year after the Architectural and Transportation Barriers Compliance Board has issued the supplemental minimum guidelines required under section 12204(a) of this title, compliance with such supplemental minimum guidelines shall be necessary to satisfy the requirement that facilities be readily accessible to and usable by persons with disabilities prior to issuance of the final regulations.

Subpart II — Public Transportation by Intercity and Commuter Rail

12161. Definitions

As used in this subpart:

(1) Commuter authority

The term "commuter authority" has the meaning given such term in section 24102(4) of title 49.

(2) Commuter rail transportation

The term "commuter rail transportation" has the meaning given the term "commuter rail passenger transportation" in section 24102(5) of title 49.

(3) Intercity rail transportation

The term "intercity rail transportation" means transportation provided by the National Railroad Passenger Corporation.

(4) Rail passenger car

The term "rail passenger car" means, with respect to intercity rail transportation, single-level and bi-level coach cars, single-level and bi-level dining cars, single- level and bi-level sleeping cars, single-level and bi-level lounge cars, and food service cars.

(5) Responsible person

The term "responsible person" means

(A) in the case of a station more than 50 percent of which is owned by a public entity, such public entity;

(B) in the case of a station more than 50 percent of which is owned by a private party, the persons providing intercity or commuter rail transportation to such station, as allocated on an equitable basis by regulation by the Secretary of Transportation; and

(C) in a case where no party owns more than 50 percent of a station, the persons providing intercity or commuter rail transportation to such station and the owners of the station, other than private party owners, as allocated on an equitable basis by regulation by the Secretary of Transportation.

(6)   Station

The term "station" means the portion of a property located appurtenant to a right-of-way on which intercity or commuter rail transportation is operated, where such portion is used by the general public and is related to the provision of such transportation, including passenger platforms, designated waiting areas, ticketing areas, restrooms, and, where a public entity providing rail transportation owns the property, concession areas, to the extent that such public entity exercises control over the selection, design, construction, or alteration of the property, but such term does not include flag stops.

12162.   Intercity and commuter rail actions considered discriminatory

(a)   Intercity rail transportation

(1)   One car per train rule

It shall be considered discrimination for purposes of section 12132 of this title and section 794 of title 29 for a person who provides intercity rail transportation to fail to have at least one passenger car per train that is readily accessible to and usable by individuals with disabilities, including individuals who use wheelchairs, in accordance with regulations issued under section 12164 of this title, as soon as practicable, but in no event later than 5 years after July 26, 1990.

(2)   New intercity cars

(A)   General rule

Except as otherwise provided in this subsection with respect to individuals who use wheelchairs, it shall be considered discrimination for purposes of section 12132 of this title and section 794 of title 29 for a person to purchase or lease any new rail passenger cars for use in intercity rail transportation, and for which a solicitation is made later than 30 days after July 26, 1990, unless all such rail cars are readily accessible to and usable by individuals with disabilities, including individuals who use wheelchairs, as prescribed by the Secretary of Transportation in regulations issued under section 12164 of this title.

(B)   Special rule for single-level passenger coaches for individuals who use wheelchairs

Single-level passenger coaches shall be required to

(i) be able to be entered by an individual who uses a wheelchair;

(ii) have space to park and secure a wheelchair;

(iii) have a seat to which a passenger in a wheelchair can transfer, and a space to fold and store such passenger's wheelchair; and

(iv) have a restroom usable by an individual who uses a wheelchair, only to the extent provided in paragraph (3).

(C)   Special rule for single-level dining cars for individuals who use wheelchairs

Single-level dining cars shall not be required to

(i) be able to be entered from the station platform by an individual who uses a wheelchair; or

(ii) have a restroom usable by an individual who uses a wheelchair if no restroom is provided in such car for any passenger.

(D) Special rule for bi-level dining cars for individuals who use wheelchairs

Bi-level dining cars shall not be required to

(i) be able to be entered by an individual who uses a wheelchair;

(ii) have space to park and secure a wheelchair;

(iii) have a seat to which a passenger in a wheelchair can transfer, or a space to fold and store such passenger's wheelchair; or

(iv) have a restroom usable by an individual who uses a wheelchair.

(3)   Accessibility of single-level coaches

(A)   General rule

It shall be considered discrimination for purposes of section 12132 of this title and section 794 of title 29 for a person who provides intercity rail transportation to fail to have on each train which includes one or more single-level rail passenger coaches

(i) a number of spaces

(I) to park and secure wheelchairs (to accommodate individuals who wish to remain in their wheelchairs) equal to not less than one-half of the number of single-level rail passenger coaches in such train; and

(II) to fold and store wheelchairs (to accommodate individuals who wish to transfer to coach seats) equal to not less than one-half of the number of single-level rail passenger coaches in such train, as soon as practicable, but in no event later than 5 years after July 26, 1990; and

(B)   Location

Spaces required by subparagraph (A) shall be located in single-level rail passenger coaches or food service cars.

(C)   Limitation

Of the number of spaces required on a train by subparagraph (A), not more than two spaces to park and secure wheelchairs nor more than two spaces to fold and store wheelchairs shall be located in any one coach or food service car.

(D)   Other accessibility features

Single-level rail passenger coaches and food service cars on which the spaces required by subparagraph (a) are located shall have a restroom usable by an individual who uses a wheelchair and shall be able to be entered from the station platform by an individual who uses a wheelchair.

(4)   Food service

(A)   Single-level dining cars

On any train in which a single-level dining car is used to provide food service

(i) if such single-level dining car was purchased after July 26, 1990, table service in such car shall be provided to a passenger who uses a wheelchair if

(I) the car adjacent to the end of the dining car through which a wheelchair may enter is itself accessible to a wheelchair;

(II) such passenger can exit to the platform from the car such passenger occupies, move down the platform, and enter the adjacent accessible car described in subclause (I) without the necessity of the train being moved within the station; and

(III) space to park and secure a wheelchair is available in the dining car at the time such passenger wishes to eat (if such passenger wishes to remain in a wheelchair), or space to store and fold a wheelchair is available in the dining car at the time such passenger wishes to eat (if such passenger wishes to transfer to a dining car seat); and

(ii) appropriate auxiliary aids and services, including a hard surface on which to eat, shall be provided to ensure that other equivalent food service is available to individuals with disabilities, including individuals who use wheelchairs, and to passengers traveling with such individuals. Unless not practicable, a person providing intercity rail transportation shall place an accessible car adjacent to the end of a dining car described in clause (I) through which an individual who uses a wheelchair may enter.

(B)   Bi-level dining cars

On any train in which a bi-level dining car is used to provide food service

(i) if such train includes a bi-level lounge car purchased after July 26, 1990, table service in such lounge car shall be provided to individuals who use wheelchairs and to other passengers; and

(ii) appropriate auxiliary aids and services, including a hard surface on which to eat, shall be provided to ensure that other equivalent food service is available to individuals with disabilities, including individuals who use wheelchairs, and to passengers traveling with such individuals.

(b)   Commuter rail transportation

(1)   One car per train rule

It shall be considered discrimination for purposes of section 12132 of this title and section 794 of title 29 for a person who provides commuter rail transportation to fail to have at least one passenger car per train that is readily accessible to and usable by individuals with disabilities, including individuals who use wheelchairs, in accordance with regulations issued under section 12164 of this title, as soon as practicable, but in no event later than 5 years after July 26, 1990.

(2) New commuter rail cars

(A)   General rule

It shall be considered discrimination for purposes of section 12132 of this title and section 794 of title 29 for a person to purchase or lease any new rail passenger cars for use in commuter rail transportation, and for which a solicitation is made later than 30 days after July 26, 1990, unless all such rail cars are readily accessible to and usable by individuals with disabilities, including individuals who use wheelchairs, as prescribed by the Secretary of Transportation in regulations issued under section 12164 of this title.

(B)   Accessibility

For purposes of section 12132 of this title and section 794 of title 29, a requirement that a rail passenger car used in commuter rail transportation be accessible to or readily accessible to and usable by individuals with disabilities, including individuals who use wheelchairs, shall not be construed to require

(i) a restroom usable by an individual who uses a wheelchair if no restroom is provided in such car for any passenger;

(ii) space to fold and store a wheelchair; or

(iii) a seat to which a passenger who uses a wheelchair can transfer.

(c)   Used rail cars

It shall be considered discrimination for purposes of section 1132 of this title and section 794 of title 29 for a person to purchase or lease a used rail passenger car for use in intercity or commuter rail transportation, unless such person makes demonstrated good faith efforts to purchase or lease a used rail car that is readily accessible to and usable by individuals with disabilities, including individuals who use wheelchairs, as prescribed by the Secretary of Transportation in regulations issued under section 12164 of this title.

(d) Remanufactured rail cars

(1)   Remanufacturing

It shall be considered discrimination for purposes of section 12132 of this title and section 794 of title 29 for a person to remanufacture a rail passenger car for use in intercity or commuter rail transportation so as to extend its usable life for 10 years or more, unless the rail car, to the maximum extent feasible, is made readily accessible to and usable by individuals with disabilities, including individuals who use wheelchairs, as prescribed by the Secretary of Transportation in regulations issued under section 12164 of this title.

(2)   Purchase or lease

It shall be considered discrimination for purposes of section 12132 of this title and section 794 of title 29 for a person to purchase or lease a remanufactured rail passenger car for use in intercity or commuter rail transportation unless such car was remanufactured in accordance with paragraph (1).

(e)   Stations

(1)   New stations

It shall be considered discrimination for purposes of section 12132 of this title and section 794 of title 29 for a person to build a new station for use in intercity or commuter rail transportation that is not readily accessible to and usable by individuals with disabilities, including individuals who use wheelchairs, as prescribed by the Secretary of Transportation in regulations issued under section 12164 of this title.

(2) Existing stations

(A) Failure to make readily accessible

(i) General rule

It shall be considered discrimination for purposes of section 12132 of this title and section 794 of title 29 for a responsible person to fail to make existing stations in the intercity rail transportation system, and existing key stations in commuter rail transportation systems, readily accessible to and usable by individuals with disabilities, including individuals who use wheelchairs, as prescribed by the Secretary of Transportation in regulations issued under section 12164 of this title.

(ii) Period for compliance

(I) Intercity rail

All stations in the intercity rail transportation system shall be made readily accessible to and usable by individuals with disabilities, including individuals who use wheelchairs, as soon as practicable, but in no event later than 20 years after July 26, 1990.

(II) Commuter rail

Key stations in commuter rail transportation systems shall be made readily accessible to and usable by individuals with disabilities, including individuals who use wheelchairs, as soon as practicable but in no event later than 3 years after July 26, 1990, except that the time limit may be extended by the Secretary of Transportation up to 20 years after July 26, 1990, in a case where the raising of the entire passenger platform is the only means available of attaining accessibility or where other extraordinarily expensive structural changes are necessary to attain accessibility.

(iii) Designation of key stations

Each commuter authority shall designate the key stations in its commuter rail transportation system, in consultation with individuals with disabilities and organizations representing such individuals, taking into consideration such factors as high ridership and whether such station serves as a transfer or feeder station. Before the final designation of key stations under this clause, a commuter authority shall hold a public hearing.

(iv) Plans and milestones

The Secretary of Transportation shall require the appropriate person to develop a plan for carrying out this subparagraph that reflects consultation with individuals with disabilities affected by such plan and that establishes milestones for achievement of the requirements of this subparagraph.

(B) Requirement when making alterations

(i) General rule

It shall be considered discrimination, for purposes of section 12132 of this title and section 794 of title 29, with respect to alterations of an existing station or part thereof in the intercity or commuter rail transportation systems that affect or could affect the usability of the station or part thereof, for the responsible person, owner, or person in control of the station to fail to make the alterations in such a manner that, to the maximum extent feasible, the altered portions of the station are readily accessible to and usable by individuals with disabilities, including individuals who use wheelchairs, upon completion of such alterations.

(ii) Alterations to a primary function area

It shall be considered discrimination, for purposes of section 12132 of this title and section 794 of title 29, with respect to alterations that affect or could affect the usability of or access to an area of the station containing a primary function, for the responsible person, owner, or person in control of the station to fail to make the alterations in such a manner that, to the maximum extent feasible, the path of travel to the altered area, and the bathrooms, telephones, and drinking fountains serving the altered area, are readily accessible to and usable by individuals with disabilities, including individuals who use wheelchairs, upon completion of such alterations, where such alterations to the path of travel or the bathrooms, telephones, and drinking fountains serving the altered area are not disproportionate to the overall alterations in terms of cost and scope (as determined under criteria established by the Attorney General).

(C) Required cooperation

It shall be considered discrimination for purposes of section 12132 of this title and section 794 of title 29 for an owner, or person in control, of a station governed by subparagraph (a) or (b) to fail to provide reasonable cooperation to a responsible person with respect to such station in that responsible person's efforts to comply with such subparagraph. An owner, or person in control, of a station shall be liable to a responsible person for any failure to provide reasonable cooperation as required by this subparagraph. Failure to receive reasonable cooperation required by this subparagraph shall not be a defense to a claim of discrimination under this chapter.

12163. Conformance of accessibility standards

Accessibility standards included in regulations issued under this subpart shall be consistent with the minimum guidelines issued by the Architectural and Transportation Barriers Compliance Board under section 504(a) of this title.

12164. Regulations

Not later than 1 year after July 26, 1990, the Secretary of Transportation shall issue regulations, in an accessible format, necessary for carrying out this subpart.

12165. Interim accessibility requirements

(a)   Stations

If final regulations have not been issued pursuant to section 12164 of this title, for new construction or alterations for which a valid and appropriate State or local building permit is obtained prior to the issuance of final regulations under such section, and for which the construction or alteration authorized by such permit begins within one year of the receipt of such permit and is completed under the terms of such permit, compliance with the Uniform Federal Accessibility Standards in effect at the time the building permit is issued shall suffice to satisfy the requirement that stations be readily accessible to and usable by persons with disabilities as required under section 12162(e) of this title, except that, if such final regulations have not been issued one year after the Architectural and Transportation Barriers Compliance Board has issued the supplemental minimum guidelines required under section 12204(a) of this title, compliance with such supplemental minimum guidelines shall be necessary to satisfy the requirement that stations be readily accessible to and usable by persons with disabilities prior to issuance of the final regulations.

(b)   Rail passenger cars

If final regulations have not been issued pursuant to section 12164 of this title, a person shall be considered to have complied with the requirements of section 12162(a) through (d) of this title that a rail passenger car be readily accessible to and usable by individuals with disabilities, if the design for such car complies with the laws and regulations (including the Minimum Guidelines and Requirements for Accessible Design and such supplemental minimum guidelines as are issued under section 12204(a) of this title) governing accessibility of such cars, to the extent that such laws and regulations are not inconsistent with this subpart and are in effect at the time such design is substantially completed.

Title 3

SUBCHAPTER III — PUBLIC ACCOMMODATIONS AND SERVICES OPERATED BY PRIVATE ENTITIES

12181. Definitions

As used in this subchapter:

(1) Commerce

The term "commerce" means travel, trade, traffic, commerce, transportation, or communications

(A) among the several States;

(B) between any foreign country or any territory or possession and any State; or

(C) between points in the same State but through another State or foreign country.

(2) Commercial facilities

The term "commercial facilities" means facilities

(A) that are intended for nonresidential use; and

(B) whose operations will affect commerce.

Such term shall not include railroad locomotives, railroad freight cars, railroad cabooses, railroad cars described in section 12162 of this title or covered under this subchapter, railroad rights-of-way, or facilities that are covered or expressly exempted from coverage under the Fair Housing Act of 1968 (42 U.S.C. 3601 et seq.).

(3) Demand responsive system

The term "demand responsive system" means any system of providing transportation of individuals by a vehicle, other than a system which is a fixed route system.

(4) Fixed route system

The term "fixed route system" means a system of providing transportation of individuals (other than by aircraft) on which a vehicle is operated along a prescribed route according to a fixed schedule.

(5) Over-the-road bus

The term "over-the-road bus" means a bus characterized by an elevated passenger deck located over a baggage compartment.

(6) Private entity

The term "private entity" means any entity other than a public entity (as defined in section 12131(1) of this title).

(7) Public accommodation

The following private entities are considered public accommodations for purposes of this subchapter, if the operations of such entities affect commerce

(A) an inn, hotel, motel, or other place of lodging, except for an establishment located within a building that contains not more than five rooms for rent or hire and that is actually occupied by the proprietor of such establishment as the residence of such proprietor;

(B) a restaurant, bar, or other establishment serving food or drink;

(C) a motion picture house, theater, concert hall, stadium, or other place of exhibition entertainment;

(D) an auditorium, convention center, lecture hall, or other place of public gathering;

(E) a bakery, grocery store, clothing store, hardware store, shopping center, or other sales or rental establishment;

(F) a laundromat, dry-cleaner, bank, barber shop, beauty shop, travel service, shoe repair service, funeral parlor, gas station, office of an accountant or lawyer, pharmacy, insurance office, professional office of a health care provider, hospital, or other service establishment;

(G) a terminal, depot, or other station used for specified public transportation;

(H) a museum, library, gallery, or other place of public display or collection;

(I) a park, zoo, amusement park, or other place of recreation;

(J) a nursery, elementary, secondary, undergraduate, or postgraduate private school, or other place of education;

(K) a day care center, senior citizen center, homeless shelter, food bank, adoption agency, or other social service center establishment; and

(L) a gymnasium, health spa, bowling alley, golf course, or other place of exercise or recreation.

(8)   Rail and railroad

The terms "rail" and "railroad" have the meaning given the term "railroad" in section 20102[1] of title 49.

(9)   Readily achievable

The term "readily achievable" means easily accomplishable and able to be carried out without much difficulty or expense. In determining whether an action is readily achievable, factors to be considered include

(A) the nature and cost of the action needed under this chapter;

(B) the overall financial resources of the facility or facilities involved in the action; the number of persons employed at such facility; the effect on expenses and resources, or the impact otherwise of such action upon the operation of the facility;

(C) the overall financial resources of the covered entity; the overall size of the business of a covered entity with respect to the number of its employees; the number, type, and location of its facilities; and

(D) the type of operation or operations of the covered entity, including the composition, structure, and functions of the workforce of such entity; the geographic separateness, administrative or fiscal relationship of the facility or facilities in question to the covered entity.

(10) Specified public transportation

The term "specified public transportation" means transportation by bus, rail, or any other conveyance (other than by aircraft) that provides the general public with general or special service (including charter service) on a regular and continuing basis.

(11) Vehicle

The term "vehicle" does not include a rail passenger car, railroad locomotive, railroad freight car, railroad caboose, or a railroad car described in section 12162 of this title or covered under this subchapter.

12182. Prohibition of discrimination by public accommodations

(a) General rule

No individual shall be discriminated against on the basis of disability in the full and equal enjoyment of the goods, services, facilities, privileges, advantages, or accommodations of any place of public accommodation by any person who owns, leases (or leases to), or operates a place of public accommodation.

(b) Construction

(1) General prohibition

(A) Activities

(i) Denial of participation

It shall be discriminatory to subject an individual or class of individuals on the basis of a disability or disabilities of such individual or class, directly, or through contractual, licensing, or other arrangements, to a denial of the opportunity of the individual or class to participate in or benefit from the goods, services, facilities, privileges, advantages, or accommodations of an entity.

(ii) Participation in unequal benefit

It shall be discriminatory to afford an individual or class of individuals, on the basis of a disability or disabilities of such individual or class, directly, or through contractual, licensing, or other arrangements with the opportunity to participate in or benefit from a good, service, facility, privilege, advantage, or accommodation that is not equal to that afforded to other individuals.

(iii) Separate benefit

It shall be discriminatory to provide an individual or class of individuals, on the basis of a disability or disabilities of such individual or class, directly, or through contractual, licensing, or other arrangements with a good, service, facility, privilege, advantage, or accommodation that is different or separate from that provided to other individuals, unless such action is necessary to provide the individual or class of individuals with a good, service, facility, privilege, advantage, or accommodation, or other opportunity that is as effective as that provided to others.

(iv) Individual or class of individuals

For purposes of clauses (i) through (iii) of this subparagraph, the term "individual or class of individuals" refers to the clients or customers of the covered public accommodation that enters into the contractual, licensing or other arrangement.

(B) Integrated settings

Goods, services, facilities, privileges, advantages, and accommodations shall be afforded to an individual with a disability in the most integrated setting appropriate to the needs of the individual.

(C) Opportunity to participate

Notwithstanding the existence of separate or different programs or activities provided in accordance with this section, an individual with a disability shall not be denied the opportunity to participate in such programs or activities that are not separate or different.

(D) Administrative methods

An individual or entity shall not, directly or through contractual or other arrangements, utilize standards or criteria or methods of administration

(i) that have the effect of discriminating on the basis of disability; or

(ii) that perpetuate the discrimination of others who are subject to common administrative control.

(E) Association

It shall be discriminatory to exclude or otherwise deny equal goods, services, facilities, privileges, advantages, accommodations, or other opportunities to an individual or entity because of the known disability of an individual with whom the individual or entity is known to have a relationship or association.

(2) Specific prohibitions

(A) Discrimination

For purposes of subsection (a) of this section, discrimination includes

(i) the imposition or application of eligibility criteria that screen out or tend to screen out an individual with a disability or any class of individuals with disabilities from fully and equally enjoying any goods, services, facilities, privileges, advantages, or accommodations, unless such criteria can be shown to be necessary for the provision of the goods, services, facilities, privileges, advantages, or accommodations being offered;

(ii) a failure to make reasonable modifications in policies, practices, or procedures, when such modifications are necessary to afford such goods, services, facilities, privileges, advantages, or accommodations to individuals with disabilities, unless the entity can demonstrate that making such modifications would fundamentally alter the nature of such goods, services, facilities, privileges, advantages, or accommodations;

(iii) a failure to take such steps as may be necessary to ensure that no individual with a disability is excluded, denied services, segregated or otherwise treated differently than other individuals because of the absence of auxiliary aids and services, unless the entity can demonstrate that taking such steps would fundamentally alter the nature of the good, service, facility, privilege, advantage, or accommodation being offered or would result in an undue burden;

(iv) a failure to remove architectural barriers, and communication barriers that are structural in nature, in existing facilities, and transportation barriers in existing vehicles and rail passenger cars used by an establishment for transporting individuals (not including barriers that can only be removed through the retrofitting of vehicles or rail passenger cars by the installation of a hydraulic or other lift), where such removal is readily achievable; and

(v) where an entity can demonstrate that the removal of a barrier under clause (iv) is not readily achievable, a failure to make such goods, services, facilities, privileges, advantages, or accommodations available through alternative methods if such methods are readily achievable.

(B) Fixed route system

(i) Accessibility

It shall be considered discrimination for a private entity which operates a fixed route system and which is not subject to section 12184 of this title to purchase or lease a vehicle with a seating capacity in excess of 16 passengers (including the driver) for use on such system, for which a solicitation is made after the 30th day following the effective date of this subparagraph, that is not readily accessible to and usable by individuals with disabilities, including individuals who use wheelchairs.

(ii) Equivalent service

If a private entity which operates a fixed route system and which is not subject to section 12184 of this title purchases or leases a vehicle with a seating capacity of 16 passengers or less (including the driver) for use on such system after the effective date of this subparagraph that is not readily accessible to or usable by individuals with disabilities, it shall be considered discrimination for such entity to fail to operate such system so that, when viewed in its entirety, such system ensures a level of service to individuals with disabilities, including individuals who use wheelchairs, equivalent to the level of service provided to individuals without disabilities.

(C) Demand responsive system

For purposes of subsection (a) of this section, discrimination includes

(i) a failure of a private entity which operates a demand responsive system and which is not subject to section 12184 of this title to operate such system so that, when viewed in its entirety, such system ensures a level of service to individuals with disabilities, including individuals who use wheelchairs, equivalent to the level of service provided to individuals without disabilities; and

(ii) the purchase or lease by such entity for use on such system of a vehicle with a seating capacity in excess of 16 passengers (including the driver), for which solicitations are made after the 30th day following the effective date of this subparagraph, that is not readily accessible to and usable by individuals with disabilities (including individuals who use wheelchairs) unless such entity can demonstrate that such system, when viewed in its entirety, provides a level of service to individuals with disabilities equivalent to that provided to individuals without disabilities.

(D) Over-the-road buses

(i)   Limitation on applicability

Subparagraphs (B) and (C) do not apply to over-the-road buses.

(ii)   Accessibility requirements

For purposes of subsection (a) of this section, discrimination includes

(I) the purchase or lease of an over-the-road bus which does not comply with the regulations issued under section 12186(a)(2) of this title by a private entity which provides transportation of individuals and which is not primarily engaged in the business of transporting people, and

(II) any other failure of such entity to comply with such regulations.

(3)   Specific construction

Nothing in this subchapter shall require an entity to permit an individual to participate in or benefit from the goods, services, facilities, privileges, advantages and accommodations of such entity where such individual poses a direct threat to the health or safety of others. The term "direct threat" means a significant risk to the health or safety of others that cannot be eliminated by a modification of policies, practices, or procedures or by the provision of auxiliary aids or services.

12183.   New construction and alterations in public accommodations and commercial facilities

(a)   Application of term

Except as provided in subsection (b) of this section, as applied to public accommodations and commercial facilities, discrimination for purposes of section 12182(a) of this title includes

(1) a failure to design and construct facilities for first occupancy later than 30 months after July 26, 1990, that are readily accessible to and usable by individuals with disabilities, except where an entity can demonstrate that it is structurally impracticable to meet the requirements of such subsection in accordance with standards set forth or incorporated by reference in regulations issued under this subchapter; and

(2) with respect to a facility or part thereof that is altered by, on behalf of, or

for the use of an establishment in a manner that affects or could affect the usability of the facility or part thereof, a failure to make alterations in such a manner that, to the maximum extent feasible, the altered portions of the facility are readily accessible to and usable by individuals with disabilities, including individuals who use wheelchairs. Where the entity is undertaking an alteration that affects or could affect usability of or access to an area of the facility containing a primary function, the entity shall also make the alterations in such a manner that, to the maximum extent feasible, the path of travel to the altered area and the bathrooms, telephones, and drinking fountains serving the altered area, are readily accessible to and usable by individuals with disabilities where such alterations to the path of travel or the bathrooms, telephones, and drinking fountains serving the altered area are not disproportionate to the overall alterations in terms of cost and scope (as determined under criteria established by the Attorney General).

(b)   Elevator

Subsection (a) of this section shall not be construed to require the installation of an elevator for facilities that are less than three stories or have less than 3,000 square feet per story unless the building is a shopping center, a shopping mall, or the professional office of a health care provider or unless the Attorney General determines that a particular category of such facilities requires the installation of elevators based on the usage of such facilities.

12184.   Prohibition of discrimination in specified public transportation services provided by private entities

(a)   General rule

No individual shall be discriminated against on the basis of disability in the full and equal enjoyment of specified public transportation services provided by a private entity that is primarily engaged in the business of transporting people and whose operations affect commerce.

(b)   Construction

For purposes of subsection (a) of this section, discrimination includes

(1) the imposition or application by an entity described in subsection (a) of eligibility criteria that screen out or tend to screen out an individual with a disability or any class of individuals with disabilities from fully enjoying the specified public transportation services provided by the entity, unless such criteria can be shown to be necessary for the provision of the services being offered;

(2) the failure of such entity to

(A) make reasonable modifications consistent with those required under section 12182(b)(2)(A)(ii) of this title;

(B) provide auxiliary aids and services consistent with the requirements of section 12182(b)(2)(A)(iii) of this title; and

(C) remove barriers consistent with the requirements of section 12182(b)(2)(A) of this title and with the requirements of section 12183(a)(2) of this title;

(3) the purchase or lease by such entity of a new vehicle (other than an automobile, a van with a seating capacity of less than 8 passengers, including the driver, or an over- the-road bus) which is to be used to provide specified public transportation and for which a solicitation is made after the 30th day following the effective date of this section, that is not readily accessible to and usable by individuals with disabilities, including individuals who use wheelchairs; except that the new vehicle need not be readily accessible to and usable by such individuals if the new vehicle is to be used solely in a demand responsive system and if the entity can demonstrate that such system, when viewed in its entirety, provides a level of service to such individuals equivalent to the level of service provided to the general public;

(4)

(A) the purchase or lease by such entity of an over-the-road bus which does not comply with the regulations issued under section 12186(a)(2) of this title; and

(B) any other failure of such entity to comply with such regulations; and

(5) the purchase or lease by such entity of a new van with a seating capacity of less than 8 passengers, including the driver, which is to be used to provide specified public transportation and for which a solicitation is made after the 30th day following the effective date of this section that is not readily accessible to or usable by individuals with disabilities, including individuals who use wheelchairs; except that the new van need not be readily accessible to and usable by such individuals if the entity can demonstrate that the system for which the van is being purchased or leased, when viewed in its entirety, provides a level of service to such individuals equivalent to the level of service provided to the general public;

(6) the purchase or lease by such entity of a new rail passenger car that is to be used to provide specified public transportation, and for which a solicitation is made later than 30 days after the effective date of this paragraph, that is not readily accessible to and usable by individuals with disabilities, including individuals who use wheelchairs; and

(7) the remanufacture by such entity of a rail passenger car that is to be used to provide specified public transportation so as to extend its usable life for 10 years or more, or the purchase or lease by such entity of such a rail car, unless the rail car, to the maximum extent feasible, is made readily accessible to and usable by individuals with disabilities, including individuals who use wheelchairs.

(c)   Historical or antiquated cars

(1)   Exception

To the extent that compliance with subsection (a)(2)© or (a)(7) of this section would significantly alter the historic or antiquated character of a historical or antiquated rail passenger car, or a rail station served exclusively by such cars, or would result in violation of any rule, regulation, standard, or order issued by the

Secretary of Transportation under the Federal Railroad Safety Act of 1970, such compliance shall not be required.

(2) Definition

As used in this subsection, the term "historical or antiquated rail passenger car" means a rail passenger car

(A) which is not less than 30 years old at the time of its use for transporting individuals;

(B) the manufacturer of which is no longer in the business of manufacturing rail passenger cars; and

(C) which

(i) has a consequential association with events or persons significant to the past; or

(ii) embodies, or is being restored to embody, the distinctive characteristics of a type of rail passenger car used in the past, or to represent a time period which has passed.

12185. Study

(a) Purposes

The Office of Technology Assessment shall undertake a study to determine

(1) the access needs of individuals with disabilities to over-the-road buses and over-the- road bus service; and

(2) the most cost-effective methods for providing access to over-the-road buses and over-the-road bus service to individuals with disabilities, particularly individuals who use wheelchairs, through all forms of boarding options.

(b) Contents

The study shall include, at a minimum, an analysis of the following:

(1) The anticipated demand by individuals with disabilities for accessible over-the-road buses and over-the-road bus service.

(2) The degree to which such buses and service, including any service required under sections 12184(a)(4) and 12186(a)(2) of this title, are readily accessible to and usable by individuals with disabilities.

(3) The effectiveness of various methods of providing accessibility to such buses and service to individuals with disabilities.

(4) The cost of providing accessible over-the-road buses and bus service to individuals with disabilities, including consideration of recent technological and cost saving developments in equipment and devices.

(5) Possible design changes in over-the-road buses that could enhance accessibility, including the installation of accessible restrooms which do not result in a loss of seating capacity.

(6) The impact of accessibility requirements on the continuation of over-the-

road bus service, with particular consideration of the impact of such requirements on such service to rural communities.

(c)   Advisory committee

In conducting the study required by subsection (a) of this section, the Office of
Technology Assessment shall establish an advisory committee, which shall consist of

(1) members selected from among private operators and manufacturers of
over-the-road buses;

(2) members selected from among individuals with disabilities, particularly
individuals who use wheelchairs, who are potential riders of such buses; and

(3)   members selected for their technical expertise on issues included in the
study, including manufacturers of boarding assistance equipment and devices.

The number of members selected under each of paragraphs (1) and (2) shall be
equal, and the total number of members selected under paragraphs (1) and (2)
shall exceed the number of members selected under paragraph (3).

(d)   Deadline

The study required by subsection (a) of this section, along with recommendations
by the Office of Technology Assessment, including any policy options for legislative
action, shall be submitted to the President and Congress within 36 months after
July 26, 1990. If the President determines that compliance with the regulations
issued pursuant to section 12186(a)(2)(B) of this title on or before the applicable
deadlines specified in section 12186(a)(2)(B) of this title will result in a significant
reduction in intercity over-the-road bus service, the President shall extend each
such deadline by 1 year.

(e)   Review

In developing the study required by subsection (a) of this section, the Office of
Technology Assessment shall provide a preliminary draft of such study to the
Architectural and Transportation Barriers Compliance Board established under
section 792 of title 29. The Board shall have an opportunity to comment on such
draft study, and any such comments by the Board made in writing within 120 days
after the Board's receipt of the draft study shall be incorporated as part of the final
study required to be submitted under subsection (d) of this section.

12186.   Regulations

(a)   Transportation provisions

(1)   General rule

Not later than 1 year after July 26, 1990, the Secretary of Transportation shall
issue regulations in an accessible format to carry out sections 12182 (a)(2)(a) and
(C) of this title and to carry out section 12184 of this title (other than subsection
(a)(4)).

(2) Special rules for providing access to over-the-road buses

(A)   Interim requirements

(i)   Issuance

Not later than 1 year after July 26, 1990, the Secretary of Transportation shall issue regulations in an accessible format to carry out sections 12184(b)(4) and 12182(b)(2)(D)(ii) of this title that require each private entity which uses an over-the-road bus to provide transportation of individuals to provide accessibility to such bus; except that such regulations shall not require any structural changes in over-the-road buses in order to provide access to individuals who use wheelchairs during the effective period of such regulations and shall not require the purchase of boarding assistance devices to provide access to such individuals.

(ii)   Effective period

The regulations issued pursuant to this subparagraph shall be effective until the effective date of the regulations issued under subparagraph (a).

(B)   Final requirement

(i)   Review of study and interim requirements

The Secretary shall review the study submitted under section 12185 of this title and the regulations issued pursuant to subparagraph (A).

(ii)   Issuance

Not later than 1 year after the date of the submission of the study under section 12185 of this title, the Secretary shall issue in an accessible format new regulations to carry out sections 12184(b)(4) and 12182(b)(2)(D)(ii) of this title that require, taking into account the purposes of the study under section 12185 of this title and any recommendations resulting from such study, each private entity which uses an over-the-road bus to provide transportation to individuals to provide accessibility to such bus to individuals with disabilities, including individuals who use wheelchairs.

(iii)   Effective period

Subject to section 12185(d) of this title, the regulations issued pursuant to this subparagraph shall take effect

(I) with respect to small providers of transportation (as defined by the Secretary), 3 years after the date of issuance of final regulations under clause (ii); and

(II) with respect to other providers of transportation, 2 years after the date of issuance of such final regulations.

(C)   Limitation on requiring installation of accessible restrooms

The regulations issued pursuant to this paragraph shall not require the installation of accessible restrooms in over-the-road buses if such installation would result in a loss of seating capacity.

(3)   Standards

The regulations issued pursuant to this subsection shall include standards applicable to facilities and vehicles covered by sections 12182(b) (2) and 12184 of this title.

(b)   Other provisions

Not later than 1 year after July 26, 1990, the Attorney General shall issue regulations in an accessible format to carry out the provisions of this subchapter not referred to in subsection (a) of this section that include standards applicable to facilities and vehicles covered under section 12182 of this title.

(c)   Consistency with ATBCB guidelines

Standards included in regulations issued under subsections (a) and (b) of this section shall be consistent with the minimum guidelines and requirements issued by the Architectural and Transportation Barriers Compliance Board in accordance with section 12204 of this title.

(d)   Interim accessibility standards

(1)   Facilities

If final regulations have not been issued pursuant to this section, for new construction or alterations for which a valid and appropriate State or local building permit is obtained prior to the issuance of final regulations under this section, and for which the construction or alteration authorized by such permit begins within one year of the receipt of such permit and is completed under the terms of such permit, compliance with the Uniform Federal Accessibility Standards in effect at the time the building permit is issued shall suffice to satisfy the requirement that facilities be readily accessible to and usable by persons with disabilities as required under section 12183 of this title, except that, if such final regulations have not been issued one year after the Architectural and Transportation Barriers Compliance Board has issued the supplemental minimum guidelines required under section 12204(a) of this title, compliance with such supplemental minimum guidelines shall be necessary to satisfy the requirement that facilities be readily accessible to and usable by persons with disabilities prior to issuance of the final regulations.

(2)   Vehicles and rail passenger cars

If final regulations have not been issued pursuant to this section, a private entity shall be considered to have complied with the requirements of this subchapter, if any, that a vehicle or rail passenger car be readily accessible to and usable by individuals with disabilities, if the design for such vehicle or car complies with the laws and regulations (including the Minimum Guidelines and Requirements for Accessible Design and such supplemental minimum guidelines as are issued under section 12204(a) of this title) governing accessibility of such vehicles or cars, to the extent that such laws and regulations are not inconsistent with this subchapter and are in effect at the time such design is substantially completed.

12187.   Exemptions for private clubs and religious organizations

The provisions of this subchapter shall not apply to private clubs or establishments exempted from coverage under title II of the Civil Rights Act of 1964 (42 U.S.C. 2000-a(e)) or to religious organizations or entities controlled by religious organizations, including places of worship.

12188.   Enforcement

(a)   In general

(1)   Availability of remedies and procedures

The remedies and procedures set forth in section 2000a-3(a) of this title are the remedies and procedures this subchapter provides to any person who is being subjected to discrimination on the basis of disability in violation of this subchapter or who has reasonable grounds for believing that such person is about to be subjected to discrimination in violation of section 12183 of this title. Nothing in this section shall require a person with a disability to engage in a futile gesture if such person has actual notice that a person or organization covered by this subchapter does not intend to comply with its provisions.

(2)   Injunctive relief

In the case of violations of sections 12182(b)(2)(A)(iv) and Section 12183(a) of this title, injunctive relief shall include an order to alter facilities to make such facilities readily accessible to and usable by individuals with disabilities to the extent required by this subchapter. Where appropriate, injunctive relief shall also include requiring the provision of an auxiliary aid or service, modification of a policy, or provision of alternative methods, to the extent required by this subchapter.

(b)   Enforcement by Attorney General

(1)   Denial of rights

(A)   Duty to investigate

(i)   In general

The Attorney General shall investigate alleged violations of this subchapter, and shall undertake periodic reviews of compliance of covered entities under this subchapter.

(ii)   Attorney General certification

On the application of a State or local government, the Attorney General may, in consultation with the Architectural and Transportation Barriers Compliance Board, and after prior notice and a public hearing at which persons, including individuals with disabilities, are provided an opportunity to testify against such certification, certify that a State law or local building code or similar ordinance that establishes accessibility requirements meets or exceeds the minimum requirements of this chapter for the accessibility and usability of covered facilities under this subchapter. At any enforcement proceeding under this section, such certification by the Attorney General shall be rebuttable evidence that such State law or local ordinance does meet or exceed the minimum requirements of this chapter.

(B)   Potential violation

If the Attorney General has reasonable cause to believe that

(i) any person or group of persons is engaged in a pattern or practice of discrimination under this subchapter; or

(ii) any person or group of persons has been discriminated against under this subchapter and such discrimination raises an issue of general public importance, the Attorney General may commence a civil action in any appropriate United States district court.

(2)   Authority of court

In a civil action under paragraph (1) (B), the court

(A) may grant any equitable relief that such court considers to be appropriate, including, to the extent required by this subchapter

(i) granting temporary, preliminary, or permanent relief;

(ii) providing an auxiliary aid or service, modification of policy, practice, or procedure, or alternative method; and

(iii) making facilities readily accessible to and usable by individuals with disabilities;

(B) may award such other relief as the court considers to be appropriate, including monetary damages to persons aggrieved when requested by the Attorney General; and

(C) may, to vindicate the public interest, assess a civil penalty against the entity in an amount

(i) not exceeding $50,000 for a first violation; and

(ii) not exceeding $100,000 for any subsequent violation.

(3)   Single violation

For purposes of paragraph (2) (C), in determining whether a first or subsequent violation has occurred, a determination in a single action, by judgment or settlement, that the covered entity has engaged in more than one discriminatory act shall be counted as a single violation.

(4)   Punitive damages

For purposes of subsection (b) (2) (B) of this section, the term "monetary damages" and "such other relief" does not include punitive damages.

(5)   Judicial consideration

In a civil action under paragraph (1)(B), the court, when considering what amount of civil penalty, if any, is appropriate, shall give consideration to any good faith effort or attempt to comply with this chapter by the entity. In evaluating good faith, the court shall consider, among other factors it deems relevant, whether the entity could have reasonably anticipated the need for an appropriate type of auxiliary aid needed to accommodate the unique needs of a particular individual with a disability.

12189.   Examinations and courses

Any person that offers examinations or courses related to applications, licensing, certification, or credentialing for secondary or postsecondary education, professional, or trade purposes shall offer such examinations or courses in a place and manner accessible to persons with disabilities or offer alternative accessible arrangements for such individuals.

SUBCHAPTER IV — MISCELLANEOUS PROVISIONS

12201.   Construction

(a)   In general

Except as otherwise provided in this chapter, nothing in this chapter shall be construed to apply a lesser standard than the standards applied under title V of the Rehabilitation Act of 1973 (29 U.S.C. 790 et seq.) or the regulations issued by Federal agencies pursuant to such title.

(b)   Relationship to other laws

Nothing in this chapter shall be construed to invalidate or limit the remedies, rights, and procedures of any Federal law or law of any State or political subdivision of any State or jurisdiction that provides greater or equal protection for the rights of individuals with disabilities than are afforded by this chapter. Nothing in this chapter shall be construed to preclude the prohibition of, or the imposition of restrictions on, smoking in places of employment covered by subchapter I of this chapter, in transportation covered by subchapter II or III of this chapter, or in places of public accommodation covered by subchapter III of this chapter.

(c)   Insurance

Subchapters I through III of this chapter and title IV of this Act shall not be construed to prohibit or restrict

    (1) an insurer, hospital or medical service company, health maintenance organization, or any agent, or entity that administers benefit plans, or similar organizations from underwriting risks, classifying risks, or administering such risks that are based on or not inconsistent with State law; or

    (2) a person or organization covered by this chapter from establishing, sponsoring, observing or administering the terms of a bona fide benefit plan that are based on underwriting risks, classifying risks, or administering such risks that are based on or not inconsistent with State law; or

    (3) a person or organization covered by this chapter from establishing, sponsoring, observing or administering the terms of a bona fide benefit plan that is not subject to State laws that regulate insurance.

    Paragraphs (1), (2), and (3) shall not be used as a subterfuge to evade the purposes of subchapter I and III of this chapter.

(d)   Accommodations and services

Nothing in this chapter shall be construed to require an individual with a disability to accept an accommodation, aid, service, opportunity, or benefit which such individual chooses not to accept.

(e)   Benefits under State worker's compensation laws

Nothing in this chapter alters the standards for determining eligibility for benefits under State worker's compensation laws or under State and Federal disability benefit programs.

(f)   Fundamental alteration

Nothing in this chapter alters the provision of section 12182(b)(2)(A)(ii), specifying that reasonable modifications in policies, practices, or procedures shall be required, unless an entity can demonstrate that making such modifications in policies, practices, or procedures, including academic requirements in postsecondary education, would fundamentally alter the nature of the goods, services, facilities, privileges, advantages, or accommodations involved.

(g)   Claims of no disability

Nothing in this chapter shall provide the basis for a claim by an individual without a disability that the individual was subject to discrimination because of the individual's lack of disability.

(h)   Reasonable accommodations and modifications

A covered entity under subchapter I, a public entity under subchapter II, and any person who owns, leases (or leases to), or operates a place of public accommodation under subchapter III, need not provide a reasonable accommodation or a reasonable modification to policies, practices, or procedures to an individual who meets the definition of disability in section 12102(1) solely under subparagraph (C) of such section.

12202.   State immunity

A State shall not be immune under the eleventh amendment to the Constitution of the United States from an action in Federal or State court of competent jurisdiction for a violation of this chapter. In any action against a State for a violation of the requirements of this chapter, remedies (including remedies both at law and in equity) are available for such a violation to the same extent as such remedies are available for such a violation in an action against any public or private entity other than a State.

12203.   Prohibition against retaliation and coercion

(a)   Retaliation

No person shall discriminate against any individual because such individual has opposed any act or practice made unlawful by this chapter or because such individual made a charge, testified, assisted, or participated in any manner in an investigation, proceeding, or hearing under this chapter.

(b)   Interference, coercion, or intimidation

It shall be unlawful to coerce, intimidate, threaten, or interfere with any individual in the exercise or enjoyment of, or on account of his or her having exercised or enjoyed, or on account of his or her having aided or encouraged any other individual in the exercise or enjoyment of, any right granted or protected by this chapter.

(c)   Remedies and procedures

The remedies and procedures available under sections 12117, 12133, and 12188 of this title shall be available to aggrieved persons for violations of subsections (a) and (b) of this section, with respect to subchapter I, subchapter II and subchapter III of this chapter, respectively.

[Section 12204 Regulations by Architectural and Transportation Barriers Compliance Board omitted in this Statutory Supplement.]

12205. Attorney's fees

In any action or administrative proceeding commenced pursuant to this chapter, the court or agency, in its discretion, may allow the prevailing party, other than the United States, a reasonable attorney's fee, including litigation expenses, and costs, and the United States shall be liable for the foregoing the same as a private individual.

12205a. Rule of Construction Regarding Regulatory Authority [Omitted from Statutory Supplement]

The authority to issue regulations granted to the Equal Employment Opportunity Commission, the Attorney General, and the Secretary of Transportation under this chapter includes the authority to issue regulations implementing the definitions of disability in section 12102 (including rules of construction) and the definitions in section 12103, consistent with the ADA Amendments Act of 2008.

12206. Technical assistance

[Omitted from Statutory Supplement]

12207. Federal wilderness areas

[Omitted from Statutory Supplement]

12208. Transvestites

For the purposes of this chapter, the term "disabled" or "disability" shall not apply to an individual solely because that individual is a transvestite.

12209. Instrumentalities of Congress

[Omitted from Statutory Supplement. Basically this places Congress subject to the ADA, but provides for internal enforcement only.]

12210. Illegal use of drugs

(a) In general

For purposes of this chapter, the term "individual with a disability" does not include an individual who is currently engaging in the illegal use of drugs, when the covered entity acts on the basis of such use.

(b) Rules of construction

Nothing in subsection (a) of this section shall be construed to exclude as an individual with a disability an individual who

(1) has successfully completed a supervised drug rehabilitation program and is no longer engaging in the illegal use of drugs, or has otherwise been rehabilitated successfully and is no longer engaging in such use;

(2) is participating in a supervised rehabilitation program and is no longer engaging in such use; or

(3) is erroneously regarded as engaging in such use, but is not engaging in

such use;

except that it shall not be a violation of this chapter for a covered entity to adopt or administer reasonable policies or procedures, including but not limited to drug testing, designed to ensure that an individual described in paragraph (1) or (2) is no longer engaging in the illegal use of drugs; however, nothing in this section shall be construed to encourage, prohibit, restrict, or authorize the conducting of testing for the illegal use of drugs.

(c)   Health and other services

Notwithstanding subsection (a) of this section and section 12211(b)(3) of this subchapter, an individual shall not be denied health services, or services provided in connection with drug rehabilitation, on the basis of the current illegal use of drugs if the individual is otherwise entitled to such services.

(d) "Illegal use of drugs" defined

(1)   In general

The term "illegal use of drugs" means the use of drugs, the possession or distribution of which is unlawful under the Controlled Substances Act (21 U.S.C. 801 et seq.). Such term does not include the use of a drug taken under supervision by a licensed health care professional, or other uses authorized by the Controlled Substances Act or other provisions of Federal law.

(2)   Drugs

The term "drug" means a controlled substance, as defined in schedules I through V of section 202 of the Controlled Substances Act (21 U.S.C. 812).

12211.   Definitions

(a)   Homosexuality and bisexuality

For purposes of the definition of "disability" in section 12102(2) of this title, homosexuality and bisexuality are not impairments and as such are not disabilities under this chapter.

(b)   Certain conditions

Under this chapter, the term "disability" shall not include

(1) transvestism, transsexualism, pedophilia, exhibitionism, voyeurism, gender identity disorders not resulting from physical impairments, or other sexual behavior disorders;

(2) compulsive gambling, kleptomania, or pyromania; or

(3) psychoactive substance use disorders resulting from current illegal use of drugs.

12212.   Alternative means of dispute resolution

Where appropriate and to the extent authorized by law, the use of alternative means of dispute resolution, including settlement negotiations, conciliation, facilitation, mediation, fact-finding, minitrials, and arbitration, is encouraged to resolve disputes arising under this chapter.

12213. Severability

Should any provision in this chapter be found to be unconstitutional by a court of law, such provision shall be severed from the remainder of the chapter, and such action shall not affect the enforceability of the remaining provisions of the chapter.

Chapter 2
REGULATIONS IMPLEMENTING TITLE I OF THE AMERICANS WITH DISABILITIES ACT

Regulations Implementing Title I of the Americans with Disabilities Act
29 C.F.R. Part 1630

EEOC Title I Regulations

1630.1   Purpose, applicability, and construction

(a) Purpose. The purpose of this part is to implement title I of the Americans with Disabilities Act (42 U.S.C. 12101, et seq.) (ADA), requiring equal employment opportunities for qualified individuals with disabilities, and sections 3(2), 3(3), 501, 503, 506(e), 508, 510, and 511 of the ADA as those sections pertain to the employment of qualified individuals with disabilities.

(b) Applicability. This part applies to covered entities as defined at section 1630.2(b).

(c) Construction. —

   (1) In general. Except as otherwise provided in this part, this part does not apply a lesser standard than the standards applied under title V of the Rehabilitation Act of 1973 (29 U.S.C. 790-794a), or the regulations issued by Federal agencies pursuant to that title.

   (2) Relationship to other laws. This part does not invalidate or limit the remedies, rights, and procedures of any Federal law or law of any State or political subdivision of any State or jurisdiction that provides greater or equal protection for the rights of individuals with disabilities than are afforded by this part.

1630.2   Definitions

(a) *Commission* means the Equal Employment Opportunity Commission established by Section 705 of the Civil Rights Act of 1964 (42 U.S.C. 2000e-4).

(b) *Covered Entity* means an employer, employment agency, labor organization, or joint labor management committee.

(c) *Person, labor organization, employment agency, commerce and industry affecting commerce* shall have the same meaning given those terms in Section 701 of the Civil Rights Act of 1964 (42 U.S.C. 2000e).

(d) *State* means each of the several States, the District of Columbia, the Commonwealth of Puerto Rico, Guam, American Samoa, the Virgin Islands, the Trust Territory of the Pacific Islands, and the Commonwealth of the Northern Mariana Islands.

(e) *Employer.* —

(1) In general. The term *employer* means a person engaged in an industry affecting commerce who has 15 or more employees for each working day in each of 20 or more calendar weeks in the current or preceding calendar year, and any agent of such person, except that, from July 26, 1992 through July 25, 1994, an employer means a person engaged in an industry affecting commerce who has 25 or more employees for each working day in each of 20 or more calendar weeks in the current or preceding year and any agent of such person.

(2) Exceptions. The term *employer* does not include —

(I) the United States, a corporation wholly owned by the government of the United States, or an Indian tribe; or

(II) a bona fide private membership club (other than a labor organization) that is exempt from taxation under Section 501(c) of the Internal Revenue Code of 1986.

(f) *Employee* means an individual employed by an employer.

(g) *Disability* means, with respect to an individual —

(1) a physical or mental impairment that substantially limits one or more of the major life activities of such individual;

(2) a record of such an impairment; or

(3) being regarded as having such an impairment.

(See section 1630.3 for exceptions to this definition).

(h) *Physical or mental impairment* means:

(1) Any physiological disorder, or condition, cosmetic disfigurement or anatomical loss affecting one or more of the following body systems: neurological, musculoskeletal, special sense organs, respiratory (including speech organs), cardiovascular, reproductive, digestive, genito-urinary, hemic and lymphatic, skin, and endocrine; or

(2) Any mental or psychological disorder, such as mental retardation, organic brain syndrome, emotional or mental illness, and specific learning disabilities.

(i) *Major Life Activities* means functions such as caring for oneself, performing manual tasks, walking, seeing, hearing, speaking, breathing, learning, and working.

(j) *Substantially limits.* —

(1) The term *substantially limits* means:

(I) Unable to perform a major life activity that the average person in the general population can perform; or

(II) Significantly restricted as to the condition, manner or duration under which an individual can perform a particular major life activity as compared to the condition, manner, or duration under which the average person in the general population can perform that same major life activity.

(2) The following factors should be considered in determining whether an

individual is substantially limited in a major life activity:

(I) The nature and severity of the impairment;

(II) The duration or expected duration of the impairment; and

(III) The permanent or long term impact, or the expected permanent or long term impact of or resulting from the impairment.

(3) With respect to the major life activity of working —

(I) The term *substantially limits* means significantly restricted in the ability to perform either a class of jobs or a broad range of jobs in various classes as compared to the average person having comparable training, skills and abilities. The inability to perform a single, particular job does not constitute a substantial limitation in the major life activity of working.

(II) In addition to the factors listed in paragraph (j)(2) of this section, the following factors may be considered in determining whether an individual is substantially limited in the major life activity of working:

(A) The geographical area to which the individual has reasonable access;

(B) The job from which the individual has been disqualified because of an impairment, and the number and types of jobs utilizing similar training, knowledge, skills or abilities, within that geographical area, from which the individual is also disqualified because of the impairment (class of jobs); and/or

(C) The job from which the individual has been disqualified because of an impairment, and the number and types of other jobs not utilizing similar training, knowledge, skills or abilities, within that geographical area, from which the individual is also disqualified because of the impairment (broad range of jobs in various classes).

(k) *Has a record of such impairment* means has a history of, or has been misclassified as having, a mental or physical impairment that substantially limits one or more major life activities.

(l) Is regarded as having such an impairment means:

(1) Has a physical or mental impairment that does not substantially limit major life activities but is treated by a covered entity as constituting such limitation;

(2) Has a physical or mental impairment that substantially limits major life activities only as a result of the attitudes of others toward such impairment; or

(3) Has none of the impairments defined in paragraphs (h)(1) or (2) of this section but is treated by a covered entity as having a substantially limiting impairment.

(m) *Qualified individual with a disability* means an individual with a disability who satisfies the requisite skill, experience, education and other job-related requirements of the employment position such individual holds or desires, and who, with or without reasonable accommodation, can perform the essential functions of such position. (See section 1630.3 for exceptions to this definition).

(n) *Essential functions.* —

(1) In general, the term *essential functions* means the fundamental job duties of the employment position the individual with a disability holds or desires. The term essential functions does not include the marginal functions of the position.

(2) A job function may be considered essential for any of several reasons, including but not limited to the following:

(I) The function may be essential because the reason the position exists is to perform that function;

(II) The function may be essential because of the limited number of employees available among whom the performance of that job function can be distributed; and/or

(III) The function may be highly specialized so that the incumbent in the position is hired for his or her expertise or ability to perform the particular function.

(3) Evidence of whether a particular function is essential includes, but is not limited to:

(I) The employer's judgment as to which functions are essential;

(III) Written job descriptions prepared before advertising or interviewing applicants for the job;

(III) The amount of time spent on the job performing the function;

(IV) The consequences of not requiring the incumbent to perform the function;

(V) The terms of a collective bargaining agreement;

(VI) The work experience of past incumbents in the job; and/or

(VII) The current work experience of incumbents in similar jobs.

(o) *Reasonable accommodation.* —

(1) The term *reasonable accommodation* means:

(I) Modifications or adjustments to a job application process that enable a qualified applicant with a disability to be considered for the position such qualified applicant desires; or

(II) Modifications or adjustments to the work environment, or to the manner or circumstances under which the position held or desired is customarily performed, that enable a qualified individual with a disability to perform the essential functions of that position; or

(III) Modifications or adjustments that enable a covered entity's employee with a disability to enjoy equal benefits and privileges of employment as are enjoyed by its other similarly situated employees without disabilities.

(2) Reasonable accommodation may include but is not limited to:

(I) Making existing facilities used by employees readily accessible to and usable by individuals with disabilities; and

(II) Job restructuring; part-time or modified work schedules; reassignment to a vacant position; acquisition or modifications of equipment or devices; appropriate adjustment or modifications of examinations, training materials, or policies; the provision of qualified readers or interpreters; and other similar accommodations for individuals with disabilities.

(3) To determine the appropriate reasonable accommodation it may be necessary for the covered entity to initiate an informal, interactive process with the qualified individual with a disability in need of the accommodation. This process should identify the precise limitations resulting from the disability and potential reasonable accommodations that could overcome those limitations.

(p) *Undue hardship.* —

(1)   In general.

Undue hardship means, with respect to the provision of an accommodation, significant difficulty or expense incurred by a covered entity, when considered in light of the factors set forth in paragraph (p)(2) of this section.

(2) Factors to be considered. In determining whether an accommodation would impose an undue hardship on a covered entity, factors to be considered include:

(I) The nature and net cost of the accommodation needed under this part, taking into consideration the availability of tax credits and deductions, and/or outside funding;

(II) The overall financial resources of the facility or facilities involved in the provision of the reasonable accommodation, the number of persons employed at such facility, and the effect on expenses and resources;

(III) The overall financial resources of the covered entity, the overall size of the business of the covered entity with respect to the number of its employees, and the number, type and location of its facilities;

(IV) The type of operation or operations of the covered entity, including the composition, structure and functions of the workforce of such entity, and the geographic separateness and administrative or fiscal relationship of the facility or facilities in question to the covered entity; and

(V) The impact of the accommodation upon the operation of the facility, including the impact on the ability of other employees to perform their duties and the impact on the facility's ability to conduct business.

(q) *Qualification standards* means the personal and professional attributes including the skill, experience, education, physical, medical, safety and other requirements established by a covered entity as requirements which an individual must meet in order to be eligible for the position held or desired.

(r) *Direct Threat* means a significant risk of substantial harm to the health or safety of the individual or others that cannot be eliminated or reduced by reasonable accommodation. The determination that an individual poses a direct threat shall be based on an individualized assessment of the individual's present ability to safely perform the essential functions of the job. This assessment shall be based on a reasonable medical judgment that relies on the most current medical knowledge and/or on the best available objective evidence. In determining whether an individual would pose a direct threat, the factors to be considered include:

(1) The duration of the risk;

(2) The nature and severity of the potential harm;

(3) The likelihood that the potential harm will occur; and

(4) The imminence of the potential harm.

1630.3 Exceptions to the definitions of Disability and Qualified Individual with a Disability

(a) The terms disability and qualified individual with a disability do not include individuals currently engaging in the illegal use of drugs, when the covered entity acts on the basis of such use.

(1) *Drug* means a controlled substance, as defined in schedules I through V of Section 202 of the Controlled Substances Act (21 U.S.C 812).

(2) *Illegal use of drugs* means the use of drugs the possession or distribution of which is unlawful under the Controlled Substances Act, as periodically updated by the Food and Drug Administration. This term does not include the use of a drug taken under the supervision of a licensed health care professional, or other uses authorized by the Controlled Substances Act or other provisions of Federal law.

(b) However, the terms disability and qualified individual with a disability may not exclude an individual who:

(1) Has successfully completed a supervised drug rehabilitation program and is no longer engaging in the illegal use of drugs, or has otherwise been rehabilitated successfully and is no longer engaging in the illegal use of drugs; or

(2) Is participating in a supervised rehabilitation program and is no longer engaging in such use; or

(3) Is erroneously regarded as engaging in such use, but is not engaging in such use.

(c) It shall not be a violation of this part for a covered entity to adopt or administer reasonable policies or procedures, including but not limited to drug testing, designed to ensure that an individual described in paragraph (b)(1) or (2) of this section is no longer engaging in the illegal use of drugs. (See section 1630.16(c) Drug testing).

(d) Disability does not include:

(1) Transvestism, transsexualism, pedophilia, exhibitionism, voyeurism, gender identity disorders not resulting from physical impairments, or other sexual behavior disorders;

(2) Compulsive gambling, kleptomania, or pyromania; or

(3) Psychoactive substance use disorders resulting from current illegal use of drugs.

(e) Homosexuality and bisexuality are not impairments and so are not disabilities as defied in this part.

1630.4 Discrimination prohibited

It is unlawful for a covered entity to discriminate on the basis of disability against a qualified individual with a disability in regard to:

(a) Recruitment, advertising, and job application procedures;

(b) Hiring, upgrading, promotion, award of tenure, demotion, transfer, layoff, termination, right of return from layoff, and rehiring;

(c) Rates of pay or any other form of compensation and changes in compensation;

(d) Job assignments, job classifications, organizational structures, position descriptions, lines of progression, and seniority lists;

(e) Leaves of absence, sick leave, or any other leave;

(f) Fringe benefits available by virtue of employment, whether or not administered by the covered entity;

(g) Selection and financial support for training, including: apprenticeships, professional meetings, conferences and other related activities, and selection for leaves of absence to pursue training;

(h) Activities sponsored by a covered entity including social and recreational programs; and

(i) Any other term, condition, or privilege of employment.

The term discrimination includes, but is not limited to, the acts described in sections 1630.5 through 1630.13 of this part.

1630.5 Limiting, segregating, and classifying

It is unlawful for a covered entity to limit, segregate, or classify a job applicant or employee in a way that adversely affects his or her employment opportunities or status on the basis of disability.

1630.6 Contractual or other arrangements

(a) In general. It is unlawful for a covered entity to participate in a contractual or other arrangement or relationship that has the effect of subjecting the covered entity's own qualified applicant or employee with a disability to the discrimination prohibited by this part.

(b) Contractual or other arrangement defined. The phrase contractual or other arrangement or relationship includes, but is not limited to, a relationship with an employment or referral agency; labor union, including collective bargaining agreements; an organization providing fringe benefits to an employee of the covered entity; or an organization providing training and apprenticeship programs.

(c) Application. This section applies to a covered entity, with respect to its own applicants or employees, whether the entity offered the contract or initiated the relationship, or whether the entity accepted the contract or acceded to the relationship. A covered entity is not liable for the actions of the other party or parties to the contract which only affect that other party's employees or applicants.

1630.7   Standards, criteria, or methods of administration

It is unlawful for a covered entity to use standards, criteria, or methods of administration, which are not job-related and consistent with business necessity, and:

(a) That have the effect of discriminating on the basis of disability; or

(b) That perpetuate the discrimination of others who are subject to common administrative control.

1630.8   Relationship or association with an individual with a disability

It is unlawful for a covered entity to exclude or deny equal jobs or benefits to, or otherwise discriminate against, a qualified individual because of the known disability of an individual with whom the qualified individual is known to have a family, business, social or other relationship or association.

1630.9   Not making reasonable accommodation

(a) It is unlawful for a covered entity not to make reasonable accommodation to the known physical or mental limitations of an otherwise qualified applicant or employee with a disability, unless such covered entity can demonstrate that the accommodation would impose an undue hardship on the operation of its business.

(b) It is unlawful for a covered entity to deny employment opportunities to an otherwise qualified job applicant or employee with a disability based on the need of such covered entity to make reasonable accommodation to such individuals physical or mental impairments.

(c) A covered entity shall not be excused from the requirements of this part because of any failure to receive technical assistance authorized by section 506 of the ADA, including any failure in the development or dissemination of any technical assistance manual authorized by that Act.

(d) A qualified individual with a disability is not required to accept an accommodation, aid, service, opportunity or benefit which such qualified individual chooses not to accept. However, if such individual rejects a reasonable accommodation, aid, service, opportunity or benefit that is necessary to enable the individual to perform the essential functions of the position held or desired, and cannot, as a result of that rejection, perform the essential functions of the position, the individual will not be considered a qualified individual with a disability.

1630.10   Qualification standards, tests, and other selection criteria

It is unlawful for a covered entity to use qualification standards, employment tests or other selection criteria that screen out or tend to screen out an individual with a disability or a class of individuals with disabilities, on the basis of disability, unless the standard, test or other selection criteria, as used by the covered entity, is shown to be job-related for the position in question and is consistent with business necessity.

1630.11   Administration of tests

It is unlawful for a covered entity to fail to select and administer tests concerning employment in the most effective manner to ensure that, when a test is administered to a job applicant or employee who has a disability that impairs sensory, manual or speaking skills, the test results accurately reflect the skills, aptitude, or whatever other factor of the applicant or employee that the test purports to measure, rather than reflecting the impaired sensory, manual, or speaking skills of such employee or applicant (except where such skills are the factors that the test purports to measure).

1630.12   Retaliation and coercion

(a) Retaliation. It is unlawful to discriminate against any individual because that individual has opposed any act or practice made unlawful by this part or because that individual made a charge, testified, assisted, or participated in any manner in an investigation, proceeding, or hearing to enforce any provision contained in this part.

(b) Coercion, interference or intimidation. It is unlawful to coerce, intimidate, threaten, harass or interfere with any individual in the exercise or enjoyment of, or because that individual aided or encouraged any other individual in the exercise of, any right granted or protected by this part.

1630.13   Prohibited medical examinations and inquiries

(a) Pre-employment examination or inquiry. Except as permitted by section 1630.14, it is unlawful for a covered entity to conduct a medical examination of an applicant or to make inquiries as to whether an applicant is an individual with a disability or as to the nature or severity of such disability.

(b) Examination or inquiry of employees. Except as permitted by section 1630.14, it is unlawful for a covered entity to require a medical examination of an employee or to make inquiries as to whether an employee is an individual with a disability or as to the nature or severity of such disability.

1630.14   Medical examinations and inquiries specifically permitted

(a) Acceptable pre-employment inquiry. A covered entity may make pre-employment inquiries into the ability of an applicant to perform job-related functions, and/or may ask an applicant to describe or to demonstrate how, with or without reasonable accommodation, the applicant will be able to perform job-related functions.

(b) Employment entrance examination. A covered entity may require a medical examination (and/or inquiry) after making an offer of employment to a job applicant and before the applicant begins his or her employment duties, and may condition an offer of employment on the results of such examination (and/or inquiry), if all entering employees in the same job category are subjected to such an examination (and/or inquiry) regardless of disability.

(1) Information obtained under paragraph (b) of this section regarding the medical condition or history of the applicant shall be collected and maintained on separate forms and in separate medical files and be treated as a confidential medical record, except that:

(I) Supervisors and managers may be informed regarding necessary restrictions on the work or duties of the employee and necessary accommodations;

(II) First aid and safety personnel may be informed, when appropriate, if the disability might require emergency treatment; and

(III) Government officials investigating compliance with this part shall be provided relevant information on request.

(2) The results of such examination shall not be used for any purpose inconsistent with this part.

(3) Medical examinations conducted in accordance with this section do not have to be job-related and consistent with business necessity. However, if certain criteria are used to screen out an employee or employees with disabilities as a result of such an examination or inquiry, the exclusionary criteria must be job-related and consistent with business necessity, and performance of the essential job functions cannot be accomplished with reasonable accommodation as required in this part. (See section 1630.15(b) Defenses to charges of discriminatory application of selection criteria).

(c) Examination of employees. A covered entity may require a medical examination (and/or inquiry) of an employee that is job-related and consistent with business necessity. A covered entity may make inquiries into the ability of an employee to perform job-related functions.

(1) Information obtained under paragraph (c) of this section regarding the medical condition or history of any employee shall be collected and maintained on separate forms and in separate medical files and be treated as a confidential medical record, except that:

(I) Supervisors and managers may be informed regarding necessary restrictions on the work or duties of the employee and necessary accommodations;

(II) First aid and safety personnel may be informed, when appropriate, if the disability might require emergency treatment; and

(III) Government officials investigating compliance with this part shall be provided relevant information on request.

(2) Information obtained under paragraph (c) of this section regarding the medical condition or history of any employee shall not be used for any purpose inconsistent with this part.

(d) Other acceptable examinations and inquiries. A covered entity may conduct voluntary medical examinations and activities, including voluntary medical histories, which are part of an employee health program available to employees at the work site.

(1) Information obtained under paragraph (d) of this section regarding the medical condition or history of any employee shall be collected and maintained on separate forms and in separate medical files and be treated as a confidential medical record, except that:

(I) Supervisors and managers may be informed regarding necessary restrictions on the work or duties of the employee and necessary accommodations;

(II) First aid and safety personnel may be informed, when appropriate, if the disability might require emergency treatment; and

(III) Government officials investigating compliance with this part shall be provided relevant information on request.

(2) Information obtained under paragraph (d) of this section regarding the medical condition or history of any employee shall not be used for any purpose inconsistent with this part.

1630.15 Defenses

Defenses to an allegation of discrimination under this part may include, but are not limited to, the following:

(a) Disparate treatment charges. It may be a defense to a charge of disparate treatment brought under sections 1630.4 through 1630.8 and 1630.11 through 1630.12 that the challenged action is justified by a legitimate, nondiscriminatory reason.

(b) Charges of discriminatory application of selection criteria. —

(1) In general. It may be a defense to a charge of discrimination, as described in section 1630.10, that an alleged application of qualification standards, tests, or selection criteria that screens out or tends to screen out or otherwise denies a job or benefit to an individual with a disability has been shown to be job-related and consistent with business necessity, and such performance cannot be accomplished with reasonable accommodation, as required in this part.

(2) Direct threat as a qualification standard. The term qualification standard may include a requirement that an individual shall not pose a direct threat to the health or safety of the individual or others in the workplace. (See section 1630.2(r) defining direct threat).

(c) Other disparate impact charges. It may be a defense to a charge of discrimination brought under this part that a uniformly applied standard, criterion, or policy has a disparate impact on an individual with a disability or a class of individuals with disabilities that the challenged standard, criterion or policy has been shown to be job-related and consistent with business necessity, and such performance cannot be accomplished with reasonable accommodation, as required in this part.

(d) Charges of not making reasonable accommodation. It may be a defense to a charge of discrimination, as described in section 1630.9, that a requested or necessary accommodation would impose an undue hardship on the operation of the covered entity's business.

(e) Conflict with other federal laws. It may be a defense to a charge of discrimination under this part that a challenged action is required or necessitated by another Federal law or regulation, or that another Federal law or regulation prohibits an action (including the provision of a particular reasonable accommodation) that would otherwise be required by this part.

(f) Additional defenses. It may be a defense to a charge of discrimination under this part that the alleged discriminatory action is specifically permitted by sections 1630.14 or 1630.16.

1630.16 Specific activities permitted

(a) Religious entities. A religious corporation, association, educational institution, or society is permitted to give preference in employment to individuals of a particular religion to perform work connected with the carrying on by that corporation, association, educational institution, or society of its activities. A religious entity may require that all applicants and employees conform to the religious tenets of such organization. However, a religious entity may not discriminate against a qualified individual, who satisfies the permitted religious criteria, because of his or her disability.

(b) Regulation of alcohol and drugs. A covered entity:

(1) May prohibit the illegal use of drugs and the use of alcohol at the workplace by all employees;

(2) May require that employees not be under the influence of alcohol or be engaging in the illegal use of drugs at the workplace;

(3) May require that all employees behave in conformance with the requirements established under the Drug-Free Workplace Act of 1988 (41 U.S.C. 701 et seq.);

(4) May hold an employee who engages in the illegal use of drugs or who is an alcoholic to the same qualification standards for employment or job performance and behavior to which the entity holds its other employees, even if any unsatisfactory performance or behavior is related to the employees drug use or alcoholism;

(5) May require that its employees employed in an industry subject to such regulations comply with the standards established in the regulations (if any) of the Departments of Defense and Transportation, and of the Nuclear Regulatory Commission, regarding alcohol and the illegal use of drugs; and

(6) May require that employees employed in sensitive positions comply with the regulations (if any) of the Departments of Defense and Transportation and of the Nuclear Regulatory Commission that apply to employment in sensitive

positions subject to such regulations.

(c) Drug testing. —

(1) General policy. For purposes of this part, a test to determine the illegal use of drugs is not considered a medical examination. Thus, the administration of such drug tests by a covered entity to its job applicants or employees is not a violation of section 1630.13 of this part. However, this part does not encourage, prohibit, or authorize a covered entity to conduct drug tests of job applicants or employees to determine the illegal use of drugs or to make employment decisions based on such test results.

(2) Transportation Employees. This part does not encourage, prohibit, or authorize the otherwise lawful exercise by entities subject to the jurisdiction of the Department of Transportation of authority to:

(i) Test employees of entities in, and applicants for, positions involving safety sensitive duties for the illegal use of drugs or for on-duty impairment by alcohol; and

(ii) Remove from safety-sensitive positions persons who test positive for illegal use of drugs or on-duty impairment by alcohol pursuant to paragraph (c)(2)(i) of this section.

(3) Confidentiality. Any information regarding the medical condition or history of any employee or applicant obtained from a test to determine the illegal use of drugs, except information regarding the illegal use of drugs, is subject to the requirements of section 1630.14(b)(2) and (3) of this part.

(d) Regulation of smoking. A covered entity may prohibit or impose restrictions on smoking in places of employment. Such restrictions do not violate any provision of this part.

(e) Infectious and communicable diseases; food handling jobs. —

(1) In general. Under title I of the ADA, section 103(d)(1), the Secretary of Health and Human Services is to prepare a list, to be updated annually, of infectious and communicable diseases which are transmitted through the handling of food. If an individual with a disability is disabled by one of the infectious or communicable diseases included on this list, and if the risk of transmitting the disease associated with the handling of food cannot be eliminated by reasonable accommodation, a covered entity may refuse to assign or continue to assign such individual to a job involving food handling. However, if the individual with a disability is a current employee, the employer must consider whether he or she can be accommodated by reassignment to a vacant position not involving food handling.

(2) Effect on state or other laws. This part does not preempt, modify, or amend any State, county, or local law, ordinance or regulation applicable to food handling which:

(i) Is in accordance with the list, referred to in paragraph (e)(1) of this section, of infectious or communicable diseases and the modes of transmissibility published by the Secretary of Health and Human Services; and

(ii) Is designed to protect the public health from individuals who pose a significant risk to the health or safety of others, where that risk cannot be eliminated by reasonable accommodation.

(f) Health insurance, life insurance, and other benefit plans. —

(1) An insurer, hospital, or medical service company, health maintenance organization, or any agent or entity that administers benefit plans, or similar organizations may underwrite risks, classify risks, or administer such risks that are based on or not inconsistent with State law.

(2) A covered entity may establish, sponsor, observe or administer the terms of a bona fide benefit plan that are based on underwriting risks, classifying risks, or administering such risks that are based on or not inconsistent with State law.

(3) A covered entity may establish, sponsor, observe, or administer the terms of a bona fide benefit plan that is not subject to State laws that regulate insurance.

(4) The activities described in paragraphs (f)(1),(2), and (3) of this section are permitted unless these activities are being used as a subterfuge to evade the purposes of this part.

Chapter 3

REGULATIONS IMPLEMENTING TITLE II OF THE AMERICANS WITH DISABILITIES ACT

**Regulations Implementing Title II of the Americans with Disabilities Act
28 C.F.R. Part 35
(as amended by the final rule published on September 15, 2010)**

Subpart A — General

35.101   Purpose

The purpose of this part is to effectuate subtitle A of title II of the Americans with Disabilities Act of 1990 (42 U. S. C. 12131), which prohibits discrimination on the basis of disability by public entities.

35.102   Application

(a) Except as provided in paragraph (b) of this section, this part applies to all services, programs, and activities provided or made available by public entities.

(b) To the extent that public transportation services, programs, and activities of public entities are covered by subtitle B of title II of the ADA, they are not subject to the requirements of this part.

35.103   Relationship to other laws

(a) *Rule of interpretation.* Except as otherwise provided in this part, this part shall not be construed to apply a lesser standard than the standards applied under title V of the Rehabilitation Act of 1973 or the regulations issued by Federal agencies pursuant to that title.

(b) *Other laws.* This part does not invalidate or limit the remedies, rights, and procedures of any other Federal laws, or State or local laws (including State common law) that provide greater or equal protection for the rights of individuals with disabilities or individuals associated with them.

35.104   Definitions

For purposes of this part, the term —

1991 Standards means the requirements set forth in the ADA Standards for Accessible Design, originally published on July 26, 1991, and republished as Appendix D to 28 CFR part 36.

2004 ADAAG means the requirements set forth in appendices B and D to 36 CFR part 1191 (2009).

2010 Standards means the 2010 ADA Standards for Accessible Design, which consist of the 2004 ADAAG and the requirements contained in § 35.151.

Act means the Americans with Disabilities Act (Pub. L. 101-336, 104 Stat. 327, 42 U.S.C. 12101-12213 and 47 U.S.C. 225 and 611).

Assistant Attorney General means the Assistant Attorney General, Civil Rights Division, United States Department of Justice.

Auxiliary aids and services includes —

(1) Qualified interpreters on-site or through video remote interpreting (VRI) services; notetakers; real-time computer-aided transcription services; written materials; exchange of written notes; telephone handset amplifiers; assistive listening devices; assistive listening systems; telephones compatible with hearing aids; closed caption decoders; open and closed captioning, including real-time captioning; voice, text, and video-based telecommunications products and systems, including text telephones (TTYs), videophones, and captioned telephones, or equally effective telecommunications devices; videotext displays; accessible electronic and information technology; or other effective methods of making aurally delivered information available to individuals who are deaf or hard of hearing;

(2) Qualified readers; taped texts; audio recordings; Brailled materials and displays; screen reader software; magnification software; optical readers; secondary auditory programs (SAP); large print materials; accessible electronic and information technology; or other effective methods of making visually delivered materials available to individuals who are blind or have low vision;

(3) Acquisition or modification of equipment or devices; and

(4) Other similar services and actions.

Complete complaint means a written statement that contains the complainant's name and address and describes the public entity's alleged discriminatory action in sufficient detail to inform the agency of the nature and date of the alleged violation of this part. It shall be signed by the complainant or by someone authorized to do so on his or her behalf. Complaints filed on behalf of classes or third parties shall describe or identify (by name, if possible) the alleged victims of discrimination.

Current illegal use of drugs means illegal use of drugs that occurred recently enough to justify a reasonable belief that a person's drug use is current or that continuing use is a real and ongoing problem.

Designated agency means the Federal agency designated under subpart G of this part to oversee compliance activities under this part for particular components of State and local governments.

Direct threat means a significant risk to the health or safety of others that cannot be eliminated by a modification of policies, practices or procedures, or by the provision of auxiliary aids or services as provided in § 35.139.

Disability means, with respect to an individual, a physical or mental impairment that substantially limits one or more of the major life activities of such individual; a record of such an impairment; or being regarded as having such an impairment.

(1)

(i) The phrase *physical or mental impairment* means —

(A) Any physiological disorder or condition, cosmetic disfigurement, or anatomical loss affecting one or more of the following body systems:

neurological, musculoskeletal, special sense organs, respiratory (including speech organs), cardiovascular, reproductive, digestive, genitourinary, hemic and lymphatic, skin, and endocrine;

(B) Any mental or psychological disorder such as mental retardation, organic brain syndrome, emotional or mental illness, and specific learning disabilities.

(ii) The phrase *physical or mental impairment* includes, but is not limited to, such contagious and noncontagious diseases and conditions as orthopedic, visual, speech and hearing impairments, cerebral palsy, epilepsy, muscular dystrophy, multiple sclerosis, cancer, heart disease, diabetes, mental retardation, emotional illness, specific learning disabilities, HIV disease (whether symptomatic or asymptomatic), tuberculosis, drug addiction, and alcoholism.

(iii) The phrase *physical or mental impairment* does not include homosexuality or bisexuality.

(2) The phrase *major life activities* means functions such as caring for one's self, performing manual tasks, walking, seeing, hearing, speaking, breathing, learning, and working.

(3) The phrase *has a record of such an impairment* means has a history of, or has been misclassified as having, a mental or physical impairment that substantially limits one or more major life activities.

(4) The phrase *is regarded as having an impairment* means —

(i) Has a physical or mental impairment that does not substantially limit major life activities but that is treated by a public entity as constituting such a limitation;

(ii) Has a physical or mental impairment that substantially limits major life activities only as a result of the attitudes of others toward such impairment; or

(iii) Has none of the impairments defined in paragraph (1) of this definition but is treated by a public entity as having such an impairment.

(5) The term *disability* does not include —

(i) Transvestism, transsexualism, pedophilia, exhibitionism, voyeurism, gender identity disorders not resulting from physical impairments, or other sexual behavior disorders;

(ii) Compulsive gambling, kleptomania, or pyromania; or

(iii) Psychoactive substance use disorders resulting from current illegal use of drugs.

Drug means a controlled substance, as defined in schedules I through V of section 202 of the Controlled Substances Act (21 U.S.C. 812).

Existing facility means a facility in existence on any given date, without regard to whether the facility may also be considered newly constructed or altered under this part.

Facility means all or any portion of buildings, structures, sites, complexes, equipment, rolling stock or other conveyances, roads, walks, passageways, parking lots, or other real or personal property, including the site where the building, property, structure, or equipment is located.

Historic preservation programs means programs conducted by a public entity that have preservation of historic properties as a primary purpose.

Historic properties means those properties that are listed or eligible for listing in the National Register of Historic Places or properties designated as historic under State or local law.

Housing at a place of education means housing operated by or on behalf of an elementary, secondary, undergraduate, or postgraduate school, or other place of education, including dormitories, suites, apartments, or other places of residence.

Illegal use of drugs means the use of one or more drugs, the possession or distribution of which is unlawful under the Controlled Substances Act (21 U.S.C. 812). The term illegal use of drugs does not include the use of a drug taken under supervision by a licensed health care professional, or other uses authorized by the Controlled Substances Act or other provisions of Federal law.

Individual with a disability means a person who has a disability. The term individual with a disability does not include an individual who is currently engaging in the illegal use of drugs, when the public entity acts on the basis of such use.

Other power-driven mobility device means any mobility device powered by batteries, fuel, or other engines — whether or not designed primarily for use by individuals with mobility disabilities — that is used by individuals with mobility disabilities for the purpose of locomotion, including golf cars, electronic personal assistance mobility devices (EPAMDs), such as the Segway® PT, or any mobility device designed to operate in areas without defined pedestrian routes, but that is not a wheelchair within the meaning of this section. This definition does not apply to Federal wilderness areas; wheelchairs in such areas are defined in section 508(c)(2) of the ADA, 42 U.S.C. 12207(c)(2).

Public entity means —

(1) Any State or local government;

(2) Any department, agency, special purpose district, or other instrumentality of a State or States or local government; and

(3) The National Railroad Passenger Corporation, and any commuter authority (as defined in section 103(8) of the Rail Passenger Service Act).

Qualified individual with a disability means an individual with a disability who, with or without reasonable modifications to rules, policies, or practices, the removal of architectural, communication, or transportation barriers, or the provision of auxiliary aids and services, meets the essential eligibility requirements for the receipt of services or the participation in programs or activities provided by a public entity.

Qualified interpreter means an interpreter who, via a video remote interpreting (VRI) service or an on-site appearance, is able to interpret effectively, accurately, and impartially, both receptively and expressively, using any necessary specialized vocabulary. Qualified interpreters include, for example, sign language interpreters, oral transliterators, and cued-language transliterators.

Qualified reader means a person who is able to read effectively, accurately, and impartially using any necessary specialized vocabulary.

Section 504 means section 504 of the Rehabilitation Act of 1973 (Pub. L. 93-112, 87 Stat. 394 (29 U.S.C. 794), as amended.

Service animal means any dog that is individually trained to do work or perform tasks for the benefit of an individual with a disability, including a physical, sensory, psychiatric, intellectual, or other mental disability. Other species of animals, whether wild or domestic, trained or untrained, are not service animals for the purposes of this definition. The work or tasks performed by a service animal must be directly related to the individual's disability. Examples of work or tasks include, but are not limited to, assisting individuals who are blind or have low vision with navigation and other tasks, alerting individuals who are deaf or hard of hearing to the presence of people or sounds, providing non-violent protection or rescue work, pulling a wheelchair, assisting an individual during a seizure, alerting individuals to the presence of allergens, retrieving items such as medicine or the telephone, providing physical support and assistance with balance and stability to individuals with mobility disabilities, and helping persons with psychiatric and neurological disabilities by preventing or interrupting impulsive or destructive behaviors. The crime deterrent effects of an animal's presence and the provision of emotional support, well-being, comfort, or companionship do not constitute work or tasks for the purposes of this definition.

State means each of the several States, the District of Columbia, the Commonwealth of Puerto Rico, Guam, American Samoa, the Virgin Islands, the Trust Territory of the Pacific Islands, and the Commonwealth of the Northern Mariana Islands.

Video remote interpreting (VRI) service means an interpreting service that uses video conference technology over dedicated lines or wireless technology offering high-speed, wide-bandwidth video connection that delivers high-quality video images as provided in § 35.160(d).

Wheelchair means a manually-operated or power-driven device designed primarily for use by an individual with a mobility disability for the main purpose of indoor, or of both indoor and outdoor locomotion. This definition does not apply to Federal wilderness areas; wheelchairs in such areas are defined in section 508(c)(2) of the ADA, 42 U.S.C. 12207 (c)(2).

35.105   Self-evaluation

(a) A public entity shall, within one year of the effective date of this part, evaluate its current services, policies, and practices, and the effects thereof, that do not or may not meet the requirements of this part and, to the extent modification of any such services, policies, and practices is required, the public entity shall proceed to make the necessary modifications.

(b) A public entity shall provide an opportunity to interested persons, including individuals with disabilities or organizations representing individuals with disabilities, to participate in the self-evaluation process by submitting comments.

(c) A public entity that employs 50 or more persons shall, for at least three years following completion of the self-evaluation, maintain on file and make available for public inspection:

(1) A list of the interested persons consulted;

(2) A description of areas examined and any problems identified; and

(3) A description of any modifications made.

(d) If a public entity has already complied with the self-evaluation requirement of a regulation implementing section 504 of the Rehabilitation Act of 1973, then the requirements of this section shall apply only to those policies and practices that were not included in the previous self- evaluation.

35.106   Notice

A public entity shall make available to applicants, participants, beneficiaries, and other interested persons information regarding the provisions of this part and its applicability to the services, programs, or activities of the public entity, and make such information available to them in such manner as the head of the entity finds necessary to apprise such persons of the protections against discrimination assured them by the Act and this part.

35.107   Designation of responsible employee and adoption of grievance procedures

(a) *Designation of responsible employee.* A public entity that employs 50 or more persons shall designate at least one employee to coordinate its efforts to comply with and carry out its responsibilities under this part, including any investigation of any complaint communicated to it alleging its noncompliance with this part or alleging any actions that would be prohibited by this part. The public entity shall make available to all interested individuals the name, office address, and telephone number of the employee or employees designated pursuant to this paragraph.

(b) *Complaint procedure.* A public entity that employs 50 or more persons shall adopt and publish grievance procedures providing for prompt and equitable resolution of complaints alleging any action that would be prohibited by this part.

35.108–35.129   [Reserved]

Subpart B — General Requirements

35.130   General prohibitions against discrimination

(a) No qualified individual with a disability shall, on the basis of disability, be excluded from participation in or be denied the benefits of the services, programs, or activities of a public entity, or be subjected to discrimination by any public entity.

(b)

(1) A public entity, in providing any aid, benefit, or service, may not, directly or through contractual, licensing, or other arrangements, on the basis of disability —

(i) Deny a qualified individual with a disability the opportunity to participate in or benefit from the aid, benefit, or service;

(ii) Afford a qualified individual with a disability an opportunity to participate in or benefit from the aid, benefit, or service that is not equal to that afforded others;

(iii) Provide a qualified individual with a disability with an aid, benefit, or service that is not as effective in affording equal opportunity to obtain the same result, to gain the same benefit, or to reach the same level of achievement as that provided to others;

(iv) Provide different or separate aids, benefits, or services to individuals with disabilities or to any class of individuals with disabilities than is provided to others unless such action is necessary to provide qualified individuals with disabilities with aids, benefits, or services that are as effective as those provided to others;

(v) Aid or perpetuate discrimination against a qualified individual with a disability by providing significant assistance to an agency, organization, or person that discriminates on the basis of disability in providing any aid, benefit, or service to beneficiaries of the public entity's program;

(vi) Deny a qualified individual with a disability the opportunity to participate as a member of planning or advisory boards;

(vii) Otherwise limit a qualified individual with a disability in the enjoyment of any right, privilege, advantage, or opportunity enjoyed by others receiving the aid, benefit, or service.

(2) A public entity may not deny a qualified individual with a disability the opportunity to participate in services, programs, or activities that are not separate or different, despite the existence of permissibly separate or different programs or activities.

(3) A public entity may not, directly or through contractual or other arrangements, utilize criteria or methods of administration —

(i) That have the effect of subjecting qualified individuals with disabilities to discrimination on the basis of disability;

(ii) That have the purpose or effect of defeating or substantially impairing accomplishment of the objectives of the public entity's program with respect to individuals with disabilities; or

(iii) That perpetuate the discrimination of another public entity if both public entities are subject to common administrative control or are agencies of the same State.

(4) A public entity may not, in determining the site or location of a facility, make selections —

(i) That have the effect of excluding individuals with disabilities from, denying them the benefits of, or otherwise subjecting them to discrimination; or

(ii) That have the purpose or effect of defeating or substantially impairing the accomplishment of the objectives of the service, program, or activity with respect to individuals with disabilities.

(5) A public entity, in the selection of procurement contractors, may not use criteria that subject qualified individuals with disabilities to discrimination on the basis of disability.

(6) A public entity may not administer a licensing or certification program in a manner that subjects qualified individuals with disabilities to discrimination on the basis of disability, nor may a public entity establish requirements for the programs or activities of licensees or certified entities that subject qualified individuals with disabilities to discrimination on the basis of disability. The programs or activities of entities that are licensed or certified by a public entity are not, themselves, covered by this part.

(7) A public entity shall make reasonable modifications in policies, practices, or procedures when the modifications are necessary to avoid discrimination on the basis of disability, unless the public entity can demonstrate that making the modifications would fundamentally alter the nature of the service, program, or activity.

(8) A public entity shall not impose or apply eligibility criteria that screen out or tend to screen out an individual with a disability or any class of individuals with disabilities from fully and equally enjoying any service, program, or activity, unless such criteria can be shown to be necessary for the provision of the service, program, or activity being offered.

(c) Nothing in this part prohibits a public entity from providing benefits, services, or advantages to individuals with disabilities, or to a particular class of individuals with disabilities beyond those required by this part.

(d) A public entity shall administer services, programs, and activities in the most integrated setting appropriate to the needs of qualified individuals with disabilities.

(e)

(1) Nothing in this part shall be construed to require an individual with a disability to accept an accommodation, aid, service, opportunity, or benefit provided under the ADA or this part which such individual chooses not to accept.

(2) Nothing in the Act or this part authorizes the representative or guardian of an individual with a disability to decline food, water, medical treatment, or medical services for that individual.

(f) A public entity may not place a surcharge on a particular individual with a disability or any group of individuals with disabilities to cover the costs of measures, such as the provision of auxiliary aids or program accessibility, that are required to provide that individual or group with the nondiscriminatory treatment required by the Act or this part.

(g) A public entity shall not exclude or otherwise deny equal services, programs, or activities to an individual or entity because of the known disability of an individual with whom the individual or entity is known to have a relationship or association.

(h) A public entity may impose legitimate safety requirements necessary for the safe operation of its services, programs, or activities. However, the public entity must ensure that its safety requirements are based on actual risks, not on mere speculation, stereotypes, or generalizations about individuals with disabilities.

35.131   Illegal use of drugs

(a)   *General.*

(1) Except as provided in paragraph (b) of this section, this part does not prohibit discrimination against an individual based on that individual's current illegal use of drugs.

(2) A public entity shall not discriminate on the basis of illegal use of drugs against an individual who is not engaging in current illegal use of drugs and who —

(i) Has successfully completed a supervised drug rehabilitation program or has otherwise been rehabilitated successfully;

(ii) Is participating in a supervised rehabilitation program; or

(iii) Is erroneously regarded as engaging in such use.

(b)   *Health and drug rehabilitation services.*

(1) A public entity shall not deny health services, or services provided in connection with drug rehabilitation, to an individual on the basis of that individual's current illegal use of drugs, if the individual is otherwise entitled to such services.

(2) A drug rehabilitation or treatment program may deny participation to individuals who engage in illegal use of drugs while they are in the program.

(c)   *Drug testing.*

(1) This part does not prohibit a public entity from adopting or administering reasonable policies or procedures, including but not limited to drug testing, designed to ensure that an individual who formerly engaged in the illegal use of drugs is not now engaging in current illegal use of drugs.

(2) Nothing in paragraph (c) of this section shall be construed to encourage,

prohibit, restrict, or authorize the conduct of testing for the illegal use of drugs.

35.132   Smoking

This part does not preclude the prohibition of, or the imposition of restrictions on, smoking in transportation covered by this part.

35.133   Maintenance of accessible features

(a) A public entity shall maintain in operable working condition those features of facilities and equipment that are required to be readily accessible to and usable by persons with disabilities by the Act or this part.

(b) This section does not prohibit isolated or temporary interruptions in service or access due to maintenance or repairs.

(c) If the 2010 Standards reduce the technical requirements or the number of required accessible elements below the number required by the 1991 Standards, the technical requirements or the number of accessible elements in a facility subject to this part may be reduced in accordance with the requirements of the 2010 Standards.

35.134   Retaliation or coercion

(a) No private or public entity shall discriminate against any individual because that individual has opposed any act or practice made unlawful by this part, or because that individual made a charge, testified, assisted, or participated in any manner in an investigation, proceeding, or hearing under the Act or this part.

(b) No private or public entity shall coerce, intimidate, threaten, or interfere with any individual in the exercise or enjoyment of, or on account of his or her having exercised or enjoyed, or on account of his or her having aided or encouraged any other individual in the exercise or enjoyment of, any right granted or protected by the Act or this part.

35.135   Personal devices and services

This part does not require a public entity to provide to individuals with disabilities personal devices, such as wheelchairs; individually prescribed devices, such as prescription eyeglasses or hearing aids; readers for personal use or study; or services of a personal nature including assistance in eating, toileting, or dressing.

35.136   Service animals

(a)   *General.* Generally, a public entity shall modify its policies, practices, or procedures to permit the use of a service animal by an individual with a disability.

(b)   *Exceptions.* A public entity may ask an individual with a disability to remove a service animal from the premises if —

(1) The animal is out of control and the animal's handler does not take effective action to control it; or

(2) The animal is not housebroken.

(c)   *If an animal is properly excluded.* If a public entity properly excludes a service animal under § 35.136(b), it shall give the individual with a disability the opportunity to participate in the service, program, or activity without having the service animal on the premises.

(d) *Animal under handler's control.* A service animal shall be under the control of its handler. A service animal shall have a harness, leash, or other tether, unless either the handler is unable because of a disability to use a harness, leash, or other tether, or the use of a harness, leash, or other tether would interfere with the service animal's safe, effective performance of work or tasks, in which case the service animal must be otherwise under the handler's control (*e.g.*, voice control, signals, or other effective means).

(e) *Care or supervision.* A public entity is not responsible for the care or supervision of a service animal.

(f) *Inquiries.* A public entity shall not ask about the nature or extent of a person's disability, but may make two inquiries to determine whether an animal qualifies as a service animal. A public entity may ask if the animal is required because of a disability and what work or task the animal has been trained to perform. A public entity shall not require documentation, such as proof that the animal has been certified, trained, or licensed as a service animal. Generally, a public entity may not make these inquiries about a service animal when it is readily apparent that an animal is trained to do work or perform tasks for an individual with a disability (*e.g.*, the dog is observed guiding an individual who is blind or has low vision, pulling a person's wheelchair, or providing assistance with stability or balance to an individual with an observable mobility disability).

(g) *Access to areas of a public entity.* Individuals with disabilities shall be permitted to be accompanied by their service animals in all areas of a public entity's facilities where members of the public, participants in services, programs or activities, or invitees, as relevant, are allowed to go.

(h) *Surcharges.* A public entity shall not ask or require an individual with a disability to pay a surcharge, even if people accompanied by pets are required to pay fees, or to comply with other requirements generally not applicable to people without pets. If a public entity normally charges individuals for the damage they cause, an individual with a disability may be charged for damage caused by his or her service animal.

(i) *Miniature horses.*

(1) *Reasonable modifications.* A public entity shall make reasonable modifications in policies, practices, or procedures to permit the use of a miniature horse by an individual with a disability if the miniature horse has been individually trained to do work or perform tasks for the benefit of the individual with a disability.

(2) *Assessment factors.* In determining whether reasonable modifications in policies, practices, or procedures can be made to allow a miniature horse into a specific facility, a public entity shall consider —

(i) The type, size, and weight of the miniature horse and whether the facility can accommodate these features;

(ii) Whether the handler has sufficient control of the miniature horse;

(iii) Whether the miniature horse is housebroken; and

(iv) Whether the miniature horse's presence in a specific facility compromises legitimate safety requirements that are necessary for safe operation.

(3) *Other requirements.* Paragraphs 35.136 (c) through (h) of this section, which apply to service animals, shall also apply to miniature horses.

35.137 Mobility devices

(a) *Use of wheelchairs and manually-powered mobility aids.* A public entity shall permit individuals with mobility disabilities to use wheelchairs and manually-powered mobility aids, such as walkers, crutches, canes, braces, or other similar devices designed for use by individuals with mobility disabilities in any areas open to pedestrian use.

(b)

(1) *Use of other power-driven mobility devices.* A public entity shall make reasonable modifications in its policies, practices, or procedures to permit the use of other power-driven mobility devices by individuals with mobility disabilities, unless the public entity can demonstrate that the class of other power-driven mobility devices cannot be operated in accordance with legitimate safety requirements that the public entity has adopted pursuant to § 35.130(h).

(2) *Assessment factors.* In determining whether a particular other power-driven mobility device can be allowed in a specific facility as a reasonable modification under paragraph (b)(1) of this section, a public entity shall consider —

(i) The type, size, weight, dimensions, and speed of the device;

(ii) The facility's volume of pedestrian traffic (which may vary at different times of the day, week, month, or year);

(iii) The facility's design and operational characteristics (*e.g.*, whether its service, program, or activity is conducted indoors, its square footage, the density and placement of stationary devices, and the availability of storage for the device, if requested by the user);

(iv) Whether legitimate safety requirements can be established to permit the safe operation of the other power-driven mobility device in the specific facility; and

(v) Whether the use of the other power-driven mobility device creates a substantial risk of serious harm to the immediate environment or natural or cultural resources, or poses a conflict with Federal land management laws and regulations.

(c)

(1) *Inquiry about disability.* A public entity shall not ask an individual using a wheelchair or other power-driven mobility device questions about the nature and extent of the individual's disability.

(2) *Inquiry into use of other power-driven mobility device.* A public entity may ask a person using an other power-driven mobility device to provide a credible assurance that the mobility device is required because of the person's disability. A public entity that permits the use of an other power-driven mobility device by an individual with a mobility disability shall accept the presentation of a valid, State-issued, disability parking placard or card, or other State-issued proof of disability as a credible assurance that the use of the other power-driven mobility device is for the individual's mobility disability. In lieu of a valid, State-issued disability parking placard or card, or State-issued proof of disability, a public entity shall accept as a credible assurance a verbal representation, not contradicted by observable fact, that the other power-driven mobility device is being used for a mobility disability. A "valid" disability placard or card is one that is presented by the individual to whom it was issued and is otherwise in compliance with the State of issuance's requirements for disability placards or cards.

35.138   Ticketing

(a)

(1) For the purposes of this section, "accessible seating" is defined as wheelchair spaces and companion seats that comply with sections 221 and 802 of the 2010 Standards along with any other seats required to be offered for sale to the individual with a disability pursuant to paragraph (d) of this section.

(2) *Ticket sales.* A public entity that sells tickets for a single event or series of events shall modify its policies, practices, or procedures to ensure that individuals with disabilities have an equal opportunity to purchase tickets for accessible seating —

(i) During the same hours;

(ii) During the same stages of ticket sales, including, but not limited to, pre-sales, promotions, lotteries, wait-lists, and general sales;

(iii) Through the same methods of distribution;

(iv) In the same types and numbers of ticketing sales outlets, including telephone service, in-person ticket sales at the facility, or third-party ticketing services, as other patrons; and

(v) Under the same terms and conditions as other tickets sold for the same event or series of events.

(b) *Identification of available accessible seating.* A public entity that sells or distributes tickets for a single event or series of events shall, upon inquiry —

(1) Inform individuals with disabilities, their companions, and third parties purchasing tickets for accessible seating on behalf of individuals with disabilities of the locations of all unsold or otherwise available accessible seating for any ticketed event or events at the facility;

(2) Identify and describe the features of available accessible seating in enough detail to reasonably permit an individual with a disability to assess independently

whether a given accessible seating location meets his or her accessibility needs; and

(3) Provide materials, such as seating maps, plans, brochures, pricing charts, or other information, that identify accessible seating and information relevant thereto with the same text or visual representations as other seats, if such materials are provided to the general public.

(c) *Ticket prices.* The price of tickets for accessible seating for a single event or series of events shall not be set higher than the price for other tickets in the same seating section for the same event or series of events. Tickets for accessible seating must be made available at all price levels for every event or series of events. If tickets for accessible seating at a particular price level are not available because of inaccessible features, then the percentage of tickets for accessible seating that should have been available at that price level (determined by the ratio of the total number of tickets at that price level to the total number of tickets in the assembly area) shall be offered for purchase, at that price level, in a nearby or similar accessible location.

(d) *Purchasing multiple tickets.*

(1) *General.* For each ticket for a wheelchair space purchased by an individual with a disability or a third-party purchasing such a ticket at his or her request, a public entity shall make available for purchase three additional tickets for seats in the same row that are contiguous with the wheelchair space, provided that at the time of purchase there are three such seats available. A public entity is not required to provide more than three contiguous seats for each wheelchair space. Such seats may include wheelchair spaces.

(2) *Insufficient additional contiguous seats available.* If patrons are allowed to purchase at least four tickets, and there are fewer than three such additional contiguous seat tickets available for purchase, a public entity shall offer the next highest number of such seat tickets available for purchase and shall make up the difference by offering tickets for sale for seats that are as close as possible to the accessible seats.

(3) *Sales limited to less than four tickets.* If a public entity limits sales of tickets to fewer than four seats per patron, then the public entity is only obligated to offer as many seats to patrons with disabilities, including the ticket for the wheelchair space, as it would offer to patrons without disabilities.

(4) *Maximum number of tickets patrons may purchase exceeds four.* If patrons are allowed to purchase more than four tickets, a public entity shall allow patrons with disabilities to purchase up to the same number of tickets, including the ticket for the wheelchair space.

(5) *Group sales.* If a group includes one or more individuals who need to use accessible seating because of a mobility disability or because their disability requires the use of the accessible features that are provided in accessible seating, the group shall be placed in a seating area with accessible seating so that, if possible, the group can sit together. If it is necessary to divide the group, it should be divided so that the individuals in the group who use wheelchairs are not

isolated from their group.

(e) *Hold-and-release of tickets for accessible seating.*

(1) *Tickets for accessible seating may be released for sale in certain limited circumstances.* A public entity may release unsold tickets for accessible seating for sale to individuals without disabilities for their own use for a single event or series of events only under the following circumstances —

(i) When all non-accessible tickets (excluding luxury boxes, club boxes, or suites) have been sold;

(ii) When all non-accessible tickets in a designated seating area have been sold and the tickets for accessible seating are being released in the same designated area; or

(iii) When all non-accessible tickets in a designated price category have been sold and the tickets for accessible seating are being released within the same designated price category.

(2) *No requirement to release accessible tickets.* Nothing in this paragraph requires a facility to release tickets for accessible seating to individuals without disabilities for their own use.

(3) *Release of series-of-events tickets on a series-of-events basis.*

(i) *Series-of-events tickets sell-out when no ownership rights are attached.* When series-of-events tickets are sold out and a public entity releases and sells accessible seating to individuals without disabilities for a series of events, the public entity shall establish a process that prevents the automatic reassignment of the accessible seating to such ticket holders for future seasons, future years, or future series so that individuals with disabilities who require the features of accessible seating and who become newly eligible to purchase tickets when these series-of-events tickets are available for purchase have an opportunity to do so.

(ii) *Series-of-events tickets when ownership rights are attached.* When series-of-events tickets with an ownership right in accessible seating areas are forfeited or otherwise returned to a public entity, the public entity shall make reasonable modifications in its policies, practices, or procedures to afford individuals with mobility disabilities or individuals with disabilities that require the features of accessible seating an opportunity to purchase such tickets in accessible seating areas.

(f) *Ticket transfer.* Individuals with disabilities who hold tickets for accessible seating shall be permitted to transfer tickets to third parties under the same terms and conditions and to the same extent as other spectators holding the same type of tickets, whether they are for a single event or series of events.

(g) *Secondary ticket market.*

(1) A public entity shall modify its policies, practices, or procedures to ensure that an individual with a disability may use a ticket acquired in the secondary ticket market under the same terms and conditions as other individuals who hold

a ticket acquired in the secondary ticket market for the same event or series of events.

(2) If an individual with a disability acquires a ticket or series of tickets to an inaccessible seat through the secondary market, a public entity shall make reasonable modifications to its policies, practices, or procedures to allow the individual to exchange his ticket for one to an accessible seat in a comparable location if accessible seating is vacant at the time the individual presents the ticket to the public entity.

(h) *Prevention of fraud in purchase of tickets for accessible seating.* A public entity may not require proof of disability, including, for example, a doctor's note, before selling tickets for accessible seating.

(1) *Single-event tickets.* For the sale of single-event tickets, it is permissible to inquire whether the individual purchasing the tickets for accessible seating has a mobility disability or a disability that requires the use of the accessible features that are provided in accessible seating, or is purchasing the tickets for an individual who has a mobility disability or a disability that requires the use of the accessible features that are provided in the accessible seating.

(2) *Series-of-events tickets.* For series-of-events tickets, it is permissible to ask the individual purchasing the tickets for accessible seating to attest in writing that the accessible seating is for a person who has a mobility disability or a disability that requires the use of the accessible features that are provided in the accessible seating.

(3) *Investigation of fraud.* A public entity may investigate the potential misuse of accessible seating where there is good cause to believe that such seating has been purchased fraudulently.

35.139   Direct threat

(a) This part does not require a public entity to permit an individual to participate in or benefit from the services, programs, or activities of that public entity when that individual poses a direct threat to the health or safety of others.

(b) In determining whether an individual poses a direct threat to the health or safety of others, a public entity must make an individualized assessment, based on reasonable judgment that relies on current medical knowledge or on the best available objective evidence, to ascertain: the nature, duration, and severity of the risk; the probability that the potential injury will actually occur; and whether reasonable modifications of policies, practices, or procedures or the provision of auxiliary aids or services will mitigate the risk.

Subpart C   — Employment

35.140   Employment discrimination prohibited

(a) No qualified individual with a disability shall, on the basis of disability, be subjected to discrimination in employment under any service, program, or activity conducted by a public entity.

(b)

(1) For purposes of this part, the requirements of title I of the Act, as established by the regulations of the Equal Employment Opportunity Commission in 29 CFR part 1630, apply to employment in any service, program, or activity conducted by a public entity if that public entity is also subject to the jurisdiction of title I.

(2) For the purposes of this part, the requirements of section 504 of the Rehabilitation Act of 1973, as established by the regulations of the Department of Justice in 28 CFR part 41, as those requirements pertain to employment, apply to employment in any service, program, or activity conducted by a public entity if that public entity is not also subject to the jurisdiction of title I.

35.141–35.148   [Reserved]

Subpart D — Program Accessibility

35.149   Discrimination prohibited

Except as otherwise provided in § 35.150, no qualified individual with a disability shall, because a public entity's facilities are inaccessible to or unusable by individuals with disabilities, be excluded from participation in, or be denied the benefits of the services, programs, or activities of a public entity, or be subjected to discrimination by any public entity.

35.150   Existing facilities

(a) *General.* A public entity shall operate each service, program, or activity so that the service, program, or activity, when viewed in its entirety, is readily accessible to and usable by individuals with disabilities. This paragraph does not —

(1) Necessarily require a public entity to make each of its existing facilities accessible to and usable by individuals with disabilities;

(2) Require a public entity to take any action that would threaten or destroy the historic significance of an historic property; or

(3) Require a public entity to take any action that it can demonstrate would result in a fundamental alteration in the nature of a service, program, or activity or in undue financial and administrative burdens. In those circumstances where personnel of the public entity believe that the proposed action would fundamentally alter the service, program, or activity or would result in undue financial and administrative burdens, a public entity has the burden of proving that compliance with §35.150(a) of this part would result in such alteration or burdens. The decision that compliance would result in such alteration or burdens must be made by the head of a public entity or his or her designee after considering all resources available for use in the funding and operation of the service, program, or activity, and must be accompanied by a written statement of the reasons for reaching that conclusion. If an action would result in such an alteration or such burdens, a public entity shall take any other action that would not result in such an alteration or such burdens but would nevertheless ensure that individuals with disabilities receive the benefits or services provided by the public entity.

(b) *Methods.*

(1) *General.* A public entity may comply with the requirements of this section through such means as redesign or acquisition of equipment, reassignment of services to accessible buildings, assignment of aides to beneficiaries, home visits, delivery of services at alternate accessible sites, alteration of existing facilities and construction of new facilities, use of accessible rolling stock or other conveyances, or any other methods that result in making its services, programs, or activities readily accessible to and usable by individuals with disabilities. A public entity is not required to make structural changes in existing facilities where other methods are effective in achieving compliance with this section. A public entity, in making alterations to existing buildings, shall meet the accessibility requirements of § 35.151. In choosing among available methods for meeting the requirements of this section, a public entity shall give priority to those methods that offer services, programs, and activities to qualified individuals with

disabilities in the most integrated setting appropriate.

(2)

(i) *Safe harbor.* Elements that have not been altered in existing facilities on or after March 15, 2012, and that comply with the corresponding technical and scoping specifications for those elements in either the 1991 Standards or in the Uniform Federal Accessibility Standards (UFAS), Appendix A to 41 CFR part 101–19.6 (July 1, 2002 ed.), 49 FR 31528, app. A (Aug. 7, 1984) are not required to be modified in order to comply with the requirements set forth in the 2010 Standards.

(ii) The safe harbor provided in § 35.150(b)(2)(i) does not apply to those elements in existing facilities that are subject to supplemental requirements (*i.e.,* elements for which there are neither technical nor scoping specifications in the 1991 Standards). Elements in the 2010 Standards not eligible for the element-by-element safe harbor are identified as follows —

(A) *Residential facilities dwelling units,* sections 233 and 809.

(B) *Amusement rides,* sections 234 and 1002; 206.2.9; 216.12.

(C) *Recreational boating facilities,* sections 235 and 1003; 206.2.10.

(D) *Exercise machines and equipment,* sections 236 and 1004; 206.2.13.

(E) *Fishing piers and platforms,* sections 237 and 1005; 206.2.14.

(F) *Golf facilities,* sections 238 and 1006; 206.2.15.

(G) *Miniature golf facilities,* sections 239 and 1007; 206.2.16.

(H) *Play areas,* sections 240 and 1008; 206.2.17.

(I) *Saunas and steam rooms,* sections 241 and 612.

(J) *Swimming pools, wading pools, and spas,* sections 242 and 1009.

(K) *Shooting facilities with firing positions,* sections 243 and 1010.

(L) *Miscellaneous.*

(1) *Team or player seating, section 221.2.1.4.*

(2) *Accessible route to bowling lanes, section. 206.2.11.*

(3) *Accessible route in court sports facilities, section 206.2.12.*

(3) *Historic preservation programs.* In meeting the requirements of § 35.150(a) in historic preservation programs, a public entity shall give priority to methods that provide physical access to individuals with disabilities. In cases where a physical alteration to an historic property is not required because of paragraph (a)(2) or (a)(3) of this section, alternative methods of achieving program accessibility include —

(i) Using audio-visual materials and devices to depict those portions of an historic property that cannot otherwise be made accessible;

(ii) Assigning persons to guide individuals with handicaps into or through portions of historic properties that cannot otherwise be made accessible; or

(iii) Adopting other innovative methods.

(c) *Time period for compliance.* Where structural changes in facilities are undertaken to comply with the obligations established under this section, such changes shall be made within three years of January 26, 1992, but in any event as expeditiously as possible.

(d) *Transition plan.*

(1) In the event that structural changes to facilities will be undertaken to achieve program accessibility, a public entity that employs 50 or more persons shall develop, within six months of January 26, 1992, a transition plan setting forth the steps necessary to complete such changes. A public entity shall provide an opportunity to interested persons, including individuals with disabilities or organizations representing individuals with disabilities, to participate in the development of the transition plan by submitting comments. A copy of the transition plan shall be made available for public inspection.

(2) If a public entity has responsibility or authority over streets, roads, or walkways, its transition plan shall include a schedule for providing curb ramps or other sloped areas where pedestrian walks cross curbs, giving priority to walkways serving entities covered by the Act, including State and local government offices and facilities, transportation, places of public accommodation, and employers, followed by walkways serving other areas.

(3) The plan shall, at a minimum —

(i) Identify physical obstacles in the public entity's facilities that limit the accessibility of its programs or activities to individuals with disabilities;

(ii) Describe in detail the methods that will be used to make the facilities accessible;

(iii) Specify the schedule for taking the steps necessary to achieve compliance with this section and, if the time period of the transition plan is longer than one year, identify steps that will be taken during each year of the transition period; and

(iv) Indicate the official responsible for implementation of the plan.

(4) If a public entity has already complied with the transition plan requirement of a Federal agency regulation implementing section 504 of the Rehabilitation Act of 1973, then the requirements of this paragraph (d) shall apply only to those policies and practices that were not included in the previous transition plan.

35.151 New construction and alterations

(a) *Design and construction.*

(1) Each facility or part of a facility constructed by, on behalf of, or for the use of a public entity shall be designed and constructed in such manner that the facility or part of the facility is readily accessible to and usable by individuals with disabilities, if the construction was commenced after January 26, 1992.

(2) *Exception for structural impracticability.*

(i) Full compliance with the requirements of this section is not required where a public entity can demonstrate that it is structurally impracticable to meet the requirements. Full compliance will be considered structurally impracticable only in those rare circumstances when the unique characteristics of terrain prevent the incorporation of accessibility features.

(ii) If full compliance with this section would be structurally impracticable, compliance with this section is required to the extent that it is not structurally impracticable. In that case, any portion of the facility that can be made accessible shall be made accessible to the extent that it is not structurally impracticable.

(iii) If providing accessibility in conformance with this section to individuals with certain disabilities (*e.g.*, those who use wheelchairs) would be structurally impracticable, accessibility shall nonetheless be ensured to persons with other types of disabilities, (*e.g.*, those who use crutches or who have sight, hearing, or mental impairments) in accordance with this section.

(b) *Alterations.*

(1) Each facility or part of a facility altered by, on behalf of, or for the use of a public entity in a manner that affects or could affect the usability of the facility or part of the facility shall, to the maximum extent feasible, be altered in such manner that the altered portion of the facility is readily accessible to and usable by individuals with disabilities, if the alteration was commenced after January 26, 1992.

(2) The path of travel requirements of § 35.151(b)(4) shall apply only to alterations undertaken solely for purposes other than to meet the program accessibility requirements of § 35.150.

(3)

(i) Alterations to historic properties shall comply, to the maximum extent feasible, with the provisions applicable to historic properties in the design standards specified in § 35.151(c).

(ii) If it is not feasible to provide physical access to an historic property in a manner that will not threaten or destroy the historic significance of the building or facility, alternative methods of access shall be provided pursuant to the requirements of § 35.150.

(4) *Path of travel.* An alteration that affects or could affect the usability of or access to an area of a facility that contains a primary function shall be made so as to ensure that, to the maximum extent feasible, the path of travel to the altered area and the restrooms, telephones, and drinking fountains serving the altered area are readily accessible to and usable by individuals with disabilities, including individuals who use wheelchairs, unless the cost and scope of such alterations is disproportionate to the cost of the overall alteration.

(i) *Primary function.* A "primary function" is a major activity for which the facility is intended. Areas that contain a primary function include, but are not limited to, the dining area of a cafeteria, the meeting rooms in a conference center, as well as offices and other work areas in which the activities of the public entity using the facility are carried out.

(A) Mechanical rooms, boiler rooms, supply storage rooms, employee lounges or locker rooms, janitorial closets, entrances, and corridors are not areas containing a primary function. Restrooms are not areas containing a primary function unless the provision of restrooms is a primary purpose of the area, *e.g.*, in highway rest stops.

(B) For the purposes of this section, alterations to windows, hardware, controls, electrical outlets, and signage shall not be deemed to be alterations that affect the usability of or access to an area containing a primary function.

(ii) A "path of travel" includes a continuous, unobstructed way of pedestrian passage by means of which the altered area may be approached, entered, and exited, and which connects the altered area with an exterior approach (including sidewalks, streets, and parking areas), an entrance to the facility, and other parts of the facility.

(A) An accessible path of travel may consist of walks and sidewalks, curb ramps and other interior or exterior pedestrian ramps; clear floor paths through lobbies, corridors, rooms, and other improved areas; parking access aisles; elevators and lifts; or a combination of these elements.

(B) For the purposes of this section, the term "path of travel" also includes the restrooms, telephones, and drinking fountains serving the altered area.

(C) *Safe harbor.* If a public entity has constructed or altered required elements of a path of travel in accordance with the specifications in either the 1991 Standards or the Uniform Federal Accessibility Standards before March 15, 2012, the public entity is not required to retrofit such elements to reflect incremental changes in the 2010 Standards solely because of an alteration to a primary function area served by that path of travel.

(iii) *Disproportionality.*

(A) Alterations made to provide an accessible path of travel to the altered area will be deemed disproportionate to the overall alteration when the cost exceeds 20 % of the cost of the alteration to the primary function area.

(B) Costs that may be counted as expenditures required to provide an accessible path of travel may include:

(1) Costs associated with providing an accessible entrance and an accessible route to the altered area, for example, the cost of widening doorways or installing ramps;

(2) Costs associated with making restrooms accessible, such as installing grab bars, enlarging toilet stalls, insulating pipes, or installing accessible faucet controls;

(3) Costs associated with providing accessible telephones, such as relocating the telephone to an accessible height, installing amplification devices, or installing a text telephone (TTY); and

(4) Costs associated with relocating an inaccessible drinking fountain.

(iv) *Duty to provide accessible features in the event of disproportionality.*

(A) When the cost of alterations necessary to make the path of travel to the altered area fully accessible is disproportionate to the cost of the overall alteration, the path of travel shall be made accessible to the extent that it can be made accessible without incurring disproportionate costs.

(B) In choosing which accessible elements to provide, priority should be given to those elements that will provide the greatest access, in the following order —

(1) An accessible entrance;

(2) An accessible route to the altered area;

(3) At least one accessible restroom for each sex or a single unisex restroom;

(4) Accessible telephones;

(5) Accessible drinking fountains; and

(6) When possible, additional accessible elements such as parking, storage, and alarms.

(v) *Series of smaller alterations.*

(A) The obligation to provide an accessible path of travel may not be evaded by performing a series of small alterations to the area served by a single path of travel if those alterations could have been performed as a single undertaking.

(B)

(1) If an area containing a primary function has been altered without providing an accessible path of travel to that area, and subsequent alterations of that area, or a different area on the same path of travel, are undertaken within three years of the original alteration, the total cost of alterations to the primary function areas on that path of travel during the preceding three-year period shall be considered in determining whether the cost of making that path of travel accessible is disproportionate.

(2) Only alterations undertaken on or after March 15, 2011, shall be considered in determining if the cost of providing an accessible path of travel is disproportionate to the overall cost of the alterations.

(c) *Accessibility standards and compliance date.*

(1) If physical construction or alterations commence after July 26, 1992, but prior to September 15, 2010, then new construction and alterations subject to this section must comply with either the UFAS or the 1991 Standards except that the

elevator exemption contained at section 4.1.3(5) and section 4.1.6(1)(k) of the 1991 Standards shall not apply. Departures from particular requirements of either standard by the use of other methods shall be permitted when it is clearly evident that equivalent access to the facility or part of the facility is thereby provided.

(2) If physical construction or alterations commence on or after September 15, 2010, and before March 15, 2012, then new construction and alterations subject to this section may comply with one of the following: the 2010 Standards, UFAS, or the 1991 Standards except that the elevator exemption contained at section 4.1.3(5) and section 4.1.6(1)(k) of the 1991 Standards shall not apply. Departures from particular requirements of either standard by the use of other methods shall be permitted when it is clearly evident that equivalent access to the facility or part of the facility is thereby provided.

(3) If physical construction or alterations commence on or after March 15, 2012, then new construction and alterations subject to this section shall comply with the 2010 Standards.

(4) For the purposes of this section, ceremonial groundbreaking or razing of structures prior to site preparation do not commence physical construction or alterations.

(5) *Noncomplying new construction and alterations.*

(i) Newly constructed or altered facilities or elements covered by §§ 35.151(a) or (b) that were constructed or altered before March 15, 2012, and that do not comply with the 1991 Standards or with UFAS shall before March 15, 2012, be made accessible in accordance with either the 1991 Standards, UFAS, or the 2010 Standards.

(ii) Newly constructed or altered facilities or elements covered by §§ 35.151(a) or (b) that were constructed or altered before March 15, 2012 and that do not comply with the 1991 Standards or with UFAS shall, on or after March 15, 2012, be made accessible in accordance with the 2010 Standards.

Appendix to § 35.151(c)

Compliance Date for New Construction or Alterations	Applicable Standards
Before September 15, 2010	1991 Standards or UFAS
On or after September 15, 2010, and before March 15, 2012	1991 Standards, UFAS, or 2010 Standards
On or after March 15, 2012	2010 Standards

(d) *Scope of coverage.* The 1991 Standards and the 2010 Standards apply to fixed or built-in elements of buildings, structures, site improvements, and pedestrian routes or vehicular ways located on a site. Unless specifically stated otherwise, the advisory notes, appendix notes, and figures contained in the 1991 Standards and the 2010 Standards explain or illustrate the requirements of the rule; they do not establish enforceable requirements.

(e) *Social service center establishments.* Group homes, halfway houses, shelters, or similar social service center establishments that provide either temporary sleeping accommodations or residential dwelling units that are subject to this section shall comply with the provisions of the 2010 Standards applicable to residential facilities, including, but not limited to, the provisions in sections 233 and 809.

(1) In sleeping rooms with more than 25 beds covered by this section, a minimum of 5% of the beds shall have clear floor space complying with section 806.2.3 of the 2010 Standards.

(2) Facilities with more than 50 beds covered by this section that provide common use bathing facilities, shall provide at least one roll-in shower with a seat that complies with the relevant provisions of section 608 of the 2010 Standards. Transfer-type showers are not permitted in lieu of a roll-in shower with a seat, and the exceptions in sections 608.3 and 608.4 for residential dwelling units are not permitted. When separate shower facilities are provided for men and for women, at least one roll-in shower shall be provided for each group.

(f) *Housing at a place of education.* Housing at a place of education that is subject to this section shall comply with the provisions of the 2010 Standards applicable to transient lodging, including, but not limited to, the requirements for transient lodging guest rooms in sections 224 and 806 subject to the following exceptions. For the purposes of the application of this section, the term "sleeping room" is intended to be used interchangeably with the term "guest room" as it is used in the transient lodging standards.

(1) Kitchens within housing units containing accessible sleeping rooms with mobility features (including suites and clustered sleeping rooms) or on floors containing accessible sleeping rooms with mobility features shall provide turning spaces that comply with section 809.2.2 of the 2010 Standards and kitchen work surfaces that comply with section 804.3 of the 2010 Standards.

(2) Multi-bedroom housing units containing accessible sleeping rooms with mobility features shall have an accessible route throughout the unit in accordance with section 809.2 of the 2010 Standards.

(3) Apartments or townhouse facilities that are provided by or on behalf of a place of education, which are leased on a year-round basis exclusively to graduate students or faculty, and do not contain any public use or common use areas available for educational programming, are not subject to the transient lodging standards and shall comply with the requirements for residential facilities in sections 233 and 809 of the 2010 Standards.

(g) *Assembly areas.* Assembly areas subject to this section shall comply with the provisions of the 2010 Standards applicable to assembly areas, including, but not limited to, sections 221 and 802. In addition, assembly areas shall ensure that —

(1) In stadiums, arenas, and grandstands, wheelchair spaces and companion seats are dispersed to all levels that include seating served by an accessible route;

(2) Assembly areas that are required to horizontally disperse wheelchair spaces and companion seats by section 221.2.3.1 of the 2010 Standards and have seating encircling, in whole or in part, a field of play or performance area shall disperse wheelchair spaces and companion seats around that field of play or

performance area;

(3) Wheelchair spaces and companion seats are not located on (or obstructed by) temporary platforms or other movable structures, except that when an entire seating section is placed on temporary platforms or other movable structures in an area where fixed seating is not provided, in order to increase seating for an event, wheelchair spaces and companion seats may be placed in that section. When wheelchair spaces and companion seats are not required to accommodate persons eligible for those spaces and seats, individual, removable seats may be placed in those spaces and seats;

(4) Stadium-style movie theaters shall locate wheelchair spaces and companion seats on a riser or cross-aisle in the stadium section that satisfies at least one of the following criteria —

(i) It is located within the rear 60% of the seats provided in an auditorium; or

(ii) It is located within the area of an auditorium in which the vertical viewing angles (as measured to the top of the screen) are from the 40th to the 100th percentile of vertical viewing angles for all seats as ranked from the seats in the first row (1st percentile) to seats in the back row (100th percentile).

(h) *Medical care facilities.* Medical care facilities that are subject to this section shall comply with the provisions of the 2010 Standards applicable to medical care facilities, including, but not limited to, sections 223 and 805. In addition, medical care facilities that do not specialize in the treatment of conditions that affect mobility shall disperse the accessible patient bedrooms required by section 223.2.1 of the 2010 Standards in a manner that is proportionate by type of medical specialty.

(i) *Curb ramps.*

(1) Newly constructed or altered streets, roads, and highways must contain curb ramps or other sloped areas at any intersection having curbs or other barriers to entry from a street level pedestrian walkway.

(2) Newly constructed or altered street level pedestrian walkways must contain curb ramps or other sloped areas at intersections to streets, roads, or highways.

(j) *Facilities with residential dwelling units for sale to individual owners.*

(1) Residential dwelling units designed and constructed or altered by public entities that will be offered for sale to individuals shall comply with the requirements for residential facilities in the 2010 Standards including sections 233 and 809.

(2) The requirements of paragraph (1) also apply to housing programs that are operated by public entities where design and construction of particular residential dwelling units take place only after a specific buyer has been identified. In such programs, the covered entity must provide the units that comply with the requirements for accessible features to those pre-identified buyers with disabilities who have requested such a unit.

(k) *Detention and correctional facilities.*

(1) New construction of jails, prisons, and other detention and correctional facilities shall comply with the 2010 Standards except that public entities shall provide accessible mobility features complying with section 807.2 of the 2010 Standards for a minimum of 3%, but no fewer than one, of the total number of cells in a facility. Cells with mobility features shall be provided in each classification level.

(2) *Alterations to detention and correctional facilities.* Alterations to jails, prisons, and other detention and correctional facilities shall comply with the 2010 Standards except that public entities shall provide accessible mobility features complying with section 807.2 of the 2010 Standards for a minimum of 3%, but no fewer than one, of the total number of cells being altered until at least 3%, but no fewer than one, of the total number of cells in a facility shall provide mobility features complying with section 807.2. Altered cells with mobility features shall be provided in each classification level. However, when alterations are made to specific cells, detention and correctional facility operators may satisfy their obligation to provide the required number of cells with mobility features by providing the required mobility features in substitute cells (cells other than those where alterations are originally planned), provided that each substitute cell —

(i) Is located within the same prison site;

(ii) Is integrated with other cells to the maximum extent feasible;

(iii) Has, at a minimum, equal physical access as the altered cells to areas used by inmates or detainees for visitation, dining, recreation, educational programs, medical services, work programs, religious services, and participation in other programs that the facility offers to inmates or detainees; and,

(iv) If it is technically infeasible to locate a substitute cell within the same prison site, a substitute cell must be provided at another prison site within the corrections system.

(3) With respect to medical and long-term care facilities in jails, prisons, and other detention and correctional facilities, public entities shall apply the 2010 Standards technical and scoping requirements for those facilities irrespective of whether those facilities are licensed.

35.152 Jails, detention and correctional facilities, and community correctional facilities

(a) *General.* This section applies to public entities that are responsible for the operation or management of adult and juvenile justice jails, detention and correctional facilities, and community correctional facilities, either directly or through contractual, licensing, or other arrangements with public or private entities, in whole or in part, including private correctional facilities.

(b) *Discrimination prohibited.*

(1) Public entities shall ensure that qualified inmates or detainees with disabilities shall not, because a facility is inaccessible to or unusable by individuals with disabilities, be excluded from participation in, or be denied the benefits of, the services, programs, or activities of a public entity, or be subjected

to discrimination by any public entity.

(2) Public entities shall ensure that inmates or detainees with disabilities are housed in the most integrated setting appropriate to the needs of the individuals. Unless it is appropriate to make an exception, a public entity–

(i) Shall not place inmates or detainees with disabilities in inappropriate security classifications because no accessible cells or beds are available;

(ii) Shall not place inmates or detainees with disabilities in designated medical areas unless they are actually receiving medical care or treatment;

(iii) Shall not place inmates or detainees with disabilities in facilities that do not offer the same programs as the facilities where they would otherwise be housed; and

(iv) Shall not deprive inmates or detainees with disabilities of visitation with family members by placing them in distant facilities where they would not otherwise be housed.

(3) Public entities shall implement reasonable policies, including physical modifications to additional cells in accordance with the 2010 Standards, so as to ensure that each inmate with a disability is housed in a cell with the accessible elements necessary to afford the inmate access to safe, appropriate housing.

35.153–35.159   [Reserved]

Subpart E   — Communications

35.160   General

(a)

(1) A public entity shall take appropriate steps to ensure that communications with applicants, participants, members of the public, and companions with disabilities are as effective as communications with others.

(2) For purposes of this section, "companion" means a family member, friend, or associate of an individual seeking access to a service, program, or activity of a public entity, who, along with such individual, is an appropriate person with whom the public entity should communicate.

(b)

(1) A public entity shall furnish appropriate auxiliary aids and services where necessary to afford qualified individuals with disabilities, including applicants, participants, companions, and members of the public, an equal opportunity to participate in, and enjoy the benefits of, a service, program, or activity of a public entity.

(2) The type of auxiliary aid or service necessary to ensure effective communication will vary in accordance with the method of communication used by the individual; the nature, length, and complexity of the communication involved; and the context in which the communication is taking place. In determining what types of auxiliary aids and services are necessary, a public entity shall give primary consideration to the requests of individuals with disabilities. In order to be effective, auxiliary aids and services must be provided in accessible formats, in a timely manner, and in such a way as to protect the privacy and independence of the individual with a disability.

(c)

(1) A public entity shall not require an individual with a disability to bring another individual to interpret for him or her.

(2) A public entity shall not rely on an adult accompanying an individual with a disability to interpret or facilitate communication except —

(i) In an emergency involving an imminent threat to the safety or welfare of an individual or the public where there is no interpreter available; or

(ii) Where the individual with a disability specifically requests that the accompanying adult interpret or facilitate communication, the accompanying adult agrees to provide such assistance, and reliance on that adult for such assistance is appropriate under the circumstances.

(3) A public entity shall not rely on a minor child to interpret or facilitate communication, except in an emergency involving an imminent threat to the safety or welfare of an individual or the public where there is no interpreter available.

(d) *Video remote interpreting (VRI) services.* A public entity that chooses to provide qualified interpreters via VRI services shall ensure that it provides —

(1) Real-time, full-motion video and audio over a dedicated high-speed, wide-bandwidth video connection or wireless connection that delivers high-quality video images that do not produce lags, choppy, blurry, or grainy images, or irregular pauses in communication;

(2) A sharply delineated image that is large enough to display the interpreter's face, arms, hands, and fingers, and the participating individual's face, arms, hands, and fingers, regardless of his or her body position;

(3) A clear, audible transmission of voices; and

(4) Adequate training to users of the technology and other involved individuals so that they may quickly and efficiently set up and operate the VRI.

35.161 Telecommunications

(a) Where a public entity communicates by telephone with applicants and beneficiaries, text telephones (TTYs) or equally effective telecommunications systems shall be used to communicate with individuals who are deaf or hard of hearing or have speech impairments.

(b) When a public entity uses an automated-attendant system, including, but not limited to, voice mail and messaging, or an interactive voice response system, for receiving and directing incoming telephone calls, that system must provide effective real-time communication with individuals using auxiliary aids and services, including TTYs and all forms of FCC-approved telecommunications relay system, including Internet-based relay systems.

(c) A public entity shall respond to telephone calls from a telecommunications relay service established under title IV of the ADA in the same manner that it responds to other telephone calls.

35.162 Telephone emergency services

Telephone emergency services, including 911 services, shall provide direct access to individuals who use TDD's and computer modems.

35.163 Information and signage

(a) A public entity shall ensure that interested persons, including persons with impaired vision or hearing, can obtain information as to the existence and location of accessible services, activities, and facilities.

(b) A public entity shall provide signage at all inaccessible entrances to each of its facilities, directing users to an accessible entrance or to a location at which they can obtain information about accessible facilities. The international symbol for accessibility shall be used at each accessible entrance of a facility.

35.164 Duties

This subpart does not require a public entity to take any action that it can demonstrate would result in a fundamental alteration in the nature of a service, program, or activity or in undue financial and administrative burdens. In those circumstances where personnel of the public entity believe that the proposed action would fundamentally alter the service, program, or activity or would result in undue financial and administrative burdens, a public entity has the burden of proving that compliance with this subpart would result in such alteration or burdens. The decision that compliance would result in such alteration or burdens must be made by the head of the public entity or his or her designee after considering all resources available for use in the funding and operation of the service, program, or activity and must be accompanied by a written statement of the reasons for reaching that conclusion. If an action required to comply with this subpart would result in such an alteration or such burdens, a public entity shall take any other action that would not result in such an alteration or such burdens but would nevertheless ensure that, to the maximum extent possible, individuals with disabilities receive the benefits or services provided by the public entity.

35.165–35.169   [Reserved]

Subpart F   — Compliance Procedures

[Omitted in Statutory Supplement]

Chapter 4

REGULATIONS IMPLEMENTING TITLE III OF THE AMERICANS WITH DISABILITIES ACT

Regulations Implementing Title III of the Americans with Disabilities Act
28 C.F.R. Part 36
(as amended by the final rule published on September 15, 2010)

Subpart A — General

36.101 Purpose

The purpose of this part is to implement title III of the Americans with Disabilities Act of 1990 (42 U.S.C. 12181), which prohibits discrimination on the basis of disability by public accommodations and requires places of public accommodation and commercial facilities to be designed, constructed, and altered in compliance with the accessibility standards established by this part.

36.102 Application

(a) *General.* This part applies to any —

(1) Public accommodation;

(2) Commercial facility; or

(3) Private entity that offers examinations or courses related to applications, licensing, certification, or credentialing for secondary or postsecondary education, professional, or trade purposes.

(b) *Public accommodations.*

(1) The requirements of this part applicable to public accommodations are set forth in subparts B, C, and D of this part.

(2) The requirements of subparts B and C of this part obligate a public accommodation only with respect to the operations of a place of public accommodation.

(3) The requirements of subpart D of this part obligate a public accommodation only with respect to —

(i) A facility used as, or designed or constructed for use as, a place of public accommodation; or

(ii) A facility used as, or designed and constructed for use as, a commercial facility.

(c) Commercial facilities. The requirements of this part applicable to commercial facilities are set forth in subpart D of this part.

(d) *Examinations and courses.* The requirements of this part applicable to private entities that offer examinations or courses as specified in paragraph (a) of this section are set forth in § 36.309.

(e) *Exemptions and exclusions.* This part does not apply to any private club (except to the extent that the facilities of the private club are made available to customers or patrons of a place of public accommodation), or to any religious entity or public entity.

36.103   Relationship to other laws

(a) *Rule of interpretation.* Except as otherwise provided in this part, this part shall not be construed to apply a lesser standard than the standards applied under title V of the Rehabilitation Act of 1973 (29 U.S.C. 791) or the regulations issued by Federal agencies pursuant to that title.

(b) *Section 504.* This part does not affect the obligations of a recipient of Federal financial assistance to comply with the requirements of section 504 of the Rehabilitation Act of 1973 (29 U.S.C. 794) and regulations issued by Federal agencies implementing section 504.

(c) *Other laws.* This part does not invalidate or limit the remedies, rights, and procedures of any other Federal laws, or State or local laws (including State common law) that provide greater or equal protection for the rights of individuals with disabilities or individuals associated with them.

36.104   Definitions

For purposes of this part, the term —

1991 Standards means requirements set forth in the ADA Standards for Accessible Design, originally published on July 26, 1991, and republished as Appendix D to this part.

2004 ADAAG means the requirements set forth in appendices B and D to 36 CFR part 1191 (2009).

2010 Standards means the 2010 ADA Standards for Accessible Design, which consist of the 2004 ADAAG and the requirements contained in subpart D of this part.

Act means the Americans with Disabilities Act of 1990 (Pub. L. 101-336, 104 Stat. 327, 42 U.S.C. 12101-12213 and 47 U.S.C. 225 and 611).

Commerce means travel, trade, traffic, commerce, transportation, or communication —

(1) Among the several States;

(2) Between any foreign country or any territory or possession and any State; or

(3) Between points in the same State but through another State or foreign country.

Commercial facilities means facilities —

(1) Whose operations will affect commerce;

(2) That are intended for nonresidential use by a private entity; and

(3) That are not —

(i) Facilities that are covered or expressly exempted from coverage under the Fair Housing Act of 1968, as amended (42 U.S.C. 3601 - 3631);

(ii) Aircraft; or

(iii) Railroad locomotives, railroad freight cars, railroad cabooses, commuter or intercity passenger rail cars (including coaches, dining cars, sleeping cars, lounge cars, and food service cars), any other railroad cars described in section 242 of the Act or covered under title II of the Act, or railroad rights-of-way. For purposes of this definition, "rail" and "railroad" have the meaning given the term "railroad" in section 202(e) of the Federal Railroad Safety Act of 1970 (45 U.S.C. 431(e)).

Current illegal use of drugs means illegal use of drugs that occurred recently enough to justify a reasonable belief that a person's drug use is current or that continuing use is a real and ongoing problem.

Direct threat means a significant risk to the health or safety of others that cannot be eliminated by a modification of policies, practices, or procedures, or by the provision of auxiliary aids or services, as provided in § 36.208.

Disability means, with respect to an individual, a physical or mental impairment that substantially limits one or more of the major life activities of such individual; a record of such an impairment; or being regarded as having such an impairment.

(1) The phrase *physical or mental impairment* means —

(i) Any physiological disorder or condition, cosmetic disfigurement, or anatomical loss affecting one or more of the following body systems: neurological; musculoskeletal; special sense organs; respiratory, including speech organs; cardiovascular; reproductive; digestive; genitourinary; hemic and lymphatic; skin; and endocrine;

(ii) Any mental or psychological disorder such as mental retardation, organic brain syndrome, emotional or mental illness, and specific learning disabilities;

(iii) The phrase physical or mental impairment includes, but is not limited to, such contagious and noncontagious diseases and conditions as orthopedic, visual, speech, and hearing impairments, cerebral palsy, epilepsy, muscular dystrophy, multiple sclerosis, cancer, heart disease, diabetes, mental retardation, emotional illness, specific learning disabilities, HIV disease (whether symptomatic or asymptomatic), tuberculosis, drug addiction, and alcoholism;

(iv) The phrase physical or mental impairment does not include homosexuality or bisexuality.

(2) The phrase *major life activities* means functions such as caring for one's self, performing manual tasks, walking, seeing, hearing, speaking, breathing, learning, and working.

(3) The phrase *has a record of such an impairment* means has a history of, or has been misclassified as having, a mental or physical impairment that substantially limits one or more major life activities.

(4) The phrase *is regarded as having an impairment* means —

(i) Has a physical or mental impairment that does not substantially limit major life activities but that is treated by a private entity as constituting such a limitation;

(ii) Has a physical or mental impairment that substantially limits major life activities only as a result of the attitudes of others toward such impairment; or

(iii) Has none of the impairments defined in paragraph (1) of this definition but is treated by a private entity as having such an impairment.

(5) The term disability does not include —

(i) Transvestism, transsexualism, pedophilia, exhibitionism, voyeurism, gender identity disorders not resulting from physical impairments, or other sexual behavior disorders;

(ii) Compulsive gambling, kleptomania, or pyromania; or

(iii) Psychoactive substance use disorders resulting from current illegal use of drugs.

Drug means a controlled substance, as defined in schedules I through V of section 202 of the Controlled Substances Act (21 U.S.C. 812).

Existing facility means a facility in existence on any given date, without regard to whether the facility may also be considered newly constructed or altered under this part.

Facility means all or any portion of buildings, structures, sites, complexes, equipment, rolling stock or other conveyances, roads, walks, passageways, parking lots, or other real or personal property, including the site where the building, property, structure, or equipment is located.

Housing at a *place of education* means housing operated by or on behalf of an elementary, secondary, undergraduate, or postgraduate school, or other place of education, including dormitories, suites, apartments, or other places of residence.

Illegal use of drugs means the use of one or more drugs, the possession or distribution of which is unlawful under the Controlled Substances Act (21 U.S.C. 812). The term "illegal use of drugs" does not include the use of a drug taken under supervision by a licensed health care professional, or other uses authorized by the Controlled Substances Act or other provisions of Federal law.

Individual with a disability means a person who has a disability. The term "individual with a disability" does not include an individual who is currently engaging in the illegal use of drugs, when the private entity acts on the basis of such use.

Other power-driven mobility device means any mobility device powered by batteries, fuel, or other engines — whether or not designed primarily for use by individuals with mobility disabilities — that is used by individuals with mobility disabilities for the purpose of locomotion, including golf cars, electronic personal assistance mobility devices (EPAMDs), such as the Segway® PT, or any mobility device designed to operate in areas without defined pedestrian routes, but that is not a wheelchair within the meaning of this section. This definition does not apply to Federal wilderness areas; wheelchairs in such areas are defined in section

508(c)(2) of the ADA, 42 U.S.C. 12207(c)(2).

Place of public accommodation means a facility operated by a private entity whose operations affect commerce and fall within at least one of the following categories —

(1) Place of lodging, except for an establishment located within a facility that contains not more than five rooms for rent or hire and that actually is occupied by the proprietor of the establishment as the residence of the proprietor. For purposes of this part, a facility is a "place of lodging" if it is —

(i) An inn, hotel, or motel; or

(ii) A facility that —

(A) Provides guest rooms for sleeping for stays that primarily are short-term in nature (generally 30 days or less) where the occupant does not have the right to return to a specific room or unit after the conclusion of his or her stay; and

(B) Provides guest rooms under conditions and with amenities similar to a hotel, motel, or inn, including the following —

(1) On- or off-site management and reservations service;

(2) Rooms available on a walk-up or call-in basis;

(3) Availability of housekeeping or linen service; and

(4) Acceptance of reservations for a guest room type without guaranteeing a particular unit or room until check-in, and without a prior lease or security deposit.

(2) A restaurant, bar, or other establishment serving food or drink;

(3) A motion picture house, theater, concert hall, stadium, or other place of exhibition or entertainment;

(4) An auditorium, convention center, lecture hall, or other place of public gathering;

(5) A bakery, grocery store, clothing store, hardware store, shopping center, or other sales or rental establishment;

(6) A laundromat, dry-cleaner, bank, barber shop, beauty shop, travel service, shoe repair service, funeral parlor, gas station, office of an accountant or lawyer, pharmacy, insurance office, professional office of a health care provider, hospital, or other service establishment;

(7) A terminal, depot, or other station used for specified public transportation;

(8) A museum, library, gallery, or other place of public display or collection;

(9) A park, zoo, amusement park, or other place of recreation;

(10) A nursery, elementary, secondary, undergraduate, or postgraduate private school, or other place of education;

(11) A day care center, senior citizen center, homeless shelter, food bank, adoption agency, or other social service center establishment; and

(12) A gymnasium, health spa, bowling alley, golf course, or other place of exercise or recreation.

Private club means a private club or establishment exempted from coverage under title II of the Civil Rights Act of 1964 (42 U.S.C. 2000a(e)).

Private entity means a person or entity other than a public entity.

Public accommodation means a private entity that owns, leases (or leases to), or operates a place of public accommodation.

Public entity means —

(1) Any State or local government;

(2) Any department, agency, special purpose district, or other instrumentality of a State or States or local government; and

(3) The National Railroad Passenger Corporation, and any commuter authority (as defined in section 103(8) of the Rail Passenger Service Act). (45 U.S.C. 541)

Qualified interpreter means an interpreter who, via a video remote interpreting (VRI) service or an on-site appearance, is able to interpret effectively, accurately, and impartially, both receptively and expressively, using any necessary specialized vocabulary. Qualified interpreters include, for example, sign language interpreters, oral transliterators, and cued-language transliterators.

Qualified reader means a person who is able to read effectively, accurately, and impartially using any necessary specialized vocabulary.

Readily achievable means easily accomplishable and able to be carried out without much difficulty or expense. In determining whether an action is readily achievable factors to be considered include —

(1) The nature and cost of the action needed under this part;

(2) The overall financial resources of the site or sites involved in the action; the number of persons employed at the site; the effect on expenses and resources; legitimate safety requirements that are necessary for safe operation, including crime prevention measures; or the impact otherwise of the action upon the operation of the site;

(3) The geographic separateness, and the administrative or fiscal relationship of the site or sites in question to any parent corporation or entity;

(4) If applicable, the overall financial resources of any parent corporation or entity; the overall size of the parent corporation or entity with respect to the number of its employees; the number, type, and location of its facilities; and

(5) If applicable, the type of operation or operations of any parent corporation or entity, including the composition, structure, and functions of the workforce of the parent corporation or entity.

Religious entity means a religious organization, including a place of worship.

Service animal means any dog that is individually trained to do work or perform tasks for the benefit of an individual with a disability, including a physical, sensory, psychiatric, intellectual, or other mental disability. Other species of animals, whether wild or domestic, trained or untrained, are not service animals for the purposes of this definition. The work or tasks performed by a service animal must be directly related to the individual's disability. Examples of work or tasks include, but are not limited to, assisting individuals who are blind or have low vision with navigation and other tasks, alerting individuals who are deaf or hard of hearing to the presence of people or sounds, providing non-violent protection or rescue work, pulling a wheelchair, assisting an individual during a seizure, alerting individuals to the presence of allergens, retrieving items such as medicine or the telephone, providing physical support and assistance with balance and stability to individuals with mobility disabilities, and helping persons with psychiatric and neurological disabilities by preventing or interrupting impulsive or destructive behaviors. The crime deterrent effects of an animal's presence and the provision of emotional support, well-being, comfort, or companionship do not constitute work or tasks for the purposes of this definition.

Specified public transportation means transportation by bus, rail, or any other conveyance (other than by aircraft) that provides the general public with general or special service (including charter service) on a regular and continuing basis.

State means each of the several States, the District of Columbia, the Commonwealth of Puerto Rico, Guam, American Samoa, the Virgin Islands, the Trust Territory of the Pacific Islands, and the Commonwealth of the Northern Mariana Islands.

Undue burden means significant difficulty or expense. In determining whether an action would result in an undue burden, factors to be considered include —

(1) The nature and cost of the action needed under this part;

(2) The overall financial resources of the site or sites involved in the action; the number of persons employed at the site; the effect on expenses and resources; legitimate safety requirements that are necessary for safe operation, including crime prevention measures; or the impact otherwise of the action upon the operation of the site;

(3) The geographic separateness, and the administrative or fiscal relationship of the site or sites in question to any parent corporation or entity;

(4) If applicable, the overall financial resources of any parent corporation or entity; the overall size of the parent corporation or entity with respect to the number of its employees; the number, type, and location of its facilities; and

(5) If applicable, the type of operation or operations of any parent corporation or entity, including the composition, structure, and functions of the workforce of the parent corporation or entity.

Video remote interpreting (VRI) service means an interpreting service that uses video conference technology over dedicated lines or wireless technology offering high-speed, wide-bandwidth video connection that delivers high-quality video images as provided in § 36.303(f).

Wheelchair means a manually-operated or power-driven device designed primarily for use by an individual with a mobility disability for the main purpose of indoor or of both indoor and outdoor locomotion. This definition does not apply to Federal wilderness areas; wheelchairs in such areas are defined in section 508(c)(2) of the ADA, 42 U.S.C. 12207(c)(2).

36.105–36.199   [Reserved]

Subpart B — General Requirements

36.201   General

(a) *Prohibition of discrimination.* No individual shall be discriminated against on the basis of disability in the full and equal enjoyment of the goods, services, facilities, privileges, advantages, or accommodations of any place of public accommodation by any private entity who owns, leases (or leases to), or operates a place of public accommodation.

(b) *Landlord and tenant responsibilities.* Both the landlord who owns the building that houses a place of public accommodation and the tenant who owns or operates the place of public accommodation are public accommodations subject to the requirements of this part. As between the parties, allocation of responsibility for complying with the obligations of this part may be determined by lease or other contract.

36.202   Activities

(a) *Denial of participation.* A public accommodation shall not subject an individual or class of individuals on the basis of a disability or disabilities of such individual or class, directly, or through contractual, licensing, or other arrangements, to a denial of the opportunity of the individual or class to participate in or benefit from the goods, services, facilities, privileges, advantages, or accommodations of a place of public accommodation.

(b) *Participation in unequal benefit.* A public accommodation shall not afford an individual or class of individuals, on the basis of a disability or disabilities of such individual or class, directly, or through contractual, licensing, or other arrangements, with the opportunity to participate in or benefit from a good, service, facility, privilege, advantage, or accommodation that is not equal to that afforded to other individuals.

(c) *Separate benefit.* A public accommodation shall not provide an individual or class of individuals, on the basis of a disability or disabilities of such individual or class, directly, or through contractual, licensing, or other arrangements with a good, service, facility, privilege, advantage, or accommodation that is different or separate from that provided to other individuals, unless such action is necessary to provide the individual or class of individuals with a good, service, facility, privilege, advantage, or accommodation, or other opportunity that is as effective as that provided to others.

(d) *Individual or class of individuals.* For purposes of paragraphs (a) through (c) of this section, the term "individual or class of individuals" refers to the clients or customers of the public accommodation that enters into the contractual, licensing, or other arrangement.

36.203   Integrated settings

(a) *General.* A public accommodation shall afford goods, services, facilities, privileges, advantages, and accommodations to an individual with a disability in the most integrated setting appropriate to the needs of the individual.

(b) *Opportunity to participate.* Notwithstanding the existence of separate or different programs or activities provided in accordance with this subpart, a public accommodation shall not deny an individual with a disability an opportunity to participate in such programs or activities that are not separate or different.

(c) *Accommodations and services.*

(1) Nothing in this part shall be construed to require an individual with a disability to accept an accommodation, aid, service, opportunity, or benefit available under this part that such individual chooses not to accept.

(2) Nothing in the Act or this part authorizes the representative or guardian of an individual with a disability to decline food, water, medical treatment, or medical services for that individual.

36.204   Administrative methods

A public accommodation shall not, directly or through contractual or other arrangements, utilize standards or criteria or methods of administration that have the effect of discriminating on the basis of disability, or that perpetuate the discrimination of others who are subject to common administrative control.

36.205   Association

A public accommodation shall not exclude or otherwise deny equal goods, services, facilities, privileges, advantages, accommodations, or other opportunities to an individual or entity because of the known disability of an individual with whom the individual or entity is known to have a relationship or association.

36.206   Retaliation or coercion

(a) No private or public entity shall discriminate against any individual because that individual has opposed any act or practice made unlawful by this part, or because that individual made a charge, testified, assisted, or participated in any manner in an investigation, proceeding, or hearing under the Act or this part.

(b) No private or public entity shall coerce, intimidate, threaten, or interfere with any individual in the exercise or enjoyment of, or on account of his or her having exercised or enjoyed, or on account of his or her having aided or encouraged any other individual in the exercise or enjoyment of, any right granted or protected by the Act or this part.

(c) Illustrations of conduct prohibited by this section include, but are not limited to:

(1) Coercing an individual to deny or limit the benefits, services, or advantages to which he or she is entitled under the Act or this part;

(2) Threatening, intimidating, or interfering with an individual with a disability who is seeking to obtain or use the goods, services, facilities, privileges, advantages, or accommodations of a public accommodation;

(3) Intimidating or threatening any person because that person is assisting or encouraging an individual or group entitled to claim the rights granted or protected by the Act or this part to exercise those rights; or

(4) Retaliating against any person because that person has participated in any investigation or action to enforce the Act or this part.

36.207 Places of public accommodation located in private residences

(a) When a place of public accommodation is located in a private residence, the portion of the residence used exclusively as a residence is not covered by this part, but that portion used exclusively in the operation of the place of public accommodation or that portion used both for the place of public accommodation and for residential purposes is covered by this part.

(b) The portion of the residence covered under paragraph (a) of this section extends to those elements used to enter the place of public accommodation, including the homeowner's front sidewalk, if any, the door or entryway, and hallways; and those portions of the residence, interior or exterior, available to or used by customers or clients, including restrooms.

36.208 Direct threat

(a) This part does not require a public accommodation to permit an individual to participate in or benefit from the goods, services, facilities, privileges, advantages and accommodations of that public accommodation when that individual poses a direct threat to the health or safety of others.

(b) In determining whether an individual poses a direct threat to the health or safety of others, a public accommodation must make an individualized assessment, based on reasonable judgment that relies on current medical knowledge or on the best available objective evidence, to ascertain: The nature, duration, and severity of the risk; the probability that the potential injury will actually occur; and whether reasonable modifications of policies, practices, or procedures or the provision of auxiliary aids or services will mitigate the risk.

36.209 Illegal use of drugs

(a) *General.*

(1) Except as provided in paragraph (b) of this section, this part does not prohibit discrimination against an individual based on that individual's current illegal use of drugs.

(2) A public accommodation shall not discriminate on the basis of illegal use of drugs against an individual who is not engaging in current illegal use of drugs and who —

(i) Has successfully completed a supervised drug rehabilitation program or has otherwise been rehabilitated successfully;

(ii) Is participating in a supervised rehabilitation program; or

(iii) Is erroneously regarded as engaging in such use.

(b) *Health and drug rehabilitation services.*

(1) A public accommodation shall not deny health services, or services provided in connection with drug rehabilitation, to an individual on the basis of that

individual's current illegal use of drugs, if the individual is otherwise entitled to such services.

(2) A drug rehabilitation or treatment program may deny participation to individuals who engage in illegal use of drugs while they are in the program.

(c) *Drug testing.*

(1) This part does not prohibit a public accommodation from adopting or administering reasonable policies or procedures, including but not limited to drug testing, designed to ensure that an individual who formerly engaged in the illegal use of drugs is not now engaging in current illegal use of drugs.

(2) Nothing in this paragraph (c) shall be construed to encourage, prohibit, restrict, or authorize the conducting of testing for the illegal use of drugs.

36.210 Smoking

This part does not preclude the prohibition of, or the imposition of restrictions on, smoking in places of public accommodation.

36.211 Maintenance of accessible features

(a) A public accommodation shall maintain in operable working condition those features of facilities and equipment that are required to be readily accessible to and usable by persons with disabilities by the Act or this part.

(b) This section does not prohibit isolated or temporary interruptions in service or access due to maintenance or repairs.

(c) If the 2010 Standards reduce the technical requirements or the number of required accessible elements below the number required by the 1991 Standards, the technical requirements or the number of accessible elements in a facility subject to this part may be reduced in accordance with the requirements of the 2010 Standards.

36.212 Insurance

(a) This part shall not be construed to prohibit or restrict —

(1) An insurer, hospital or medical service company, health maintenance organization, or any agent, or entity that administers benefit plans, or similar organizations from underwriting risks, classifying risks, or administering such risks that are based on or not inconsistent with State law; or

(2) A person or organization covered by this part from establishing, sponsoring, observing or administering the terms of a bona fide benefit plan that are based on underwriting risks, classifying risks, or administering such risks that are based on or not inconsistent with State law; or

(3) A person or organization covered by this part from establishing, sponsoring, observing or administering the terms of a bona fide benefit plan that is not subject to State laws that regulate insurance.

(b) Paragraphs (a) (1), (2), and (3) of this section shall not be used as a subterfuge to evade the purposes of the Act or this part.

(c) A public accommodation shall not refuse to serve an individual with a disability because its insurance company conditions coverage or rates on the absence of individuals with disabilities.

36.213   Relationship of subpart B to subparts C and D of this part

Subpart B of this part sets forth the general principles of nondiscrimination applicable to all entities subject to this part. Subparts C and D of this part provide guidance on the application of the statute to specific situations. The specific provisions, including the limitations on those provisions, control over the general provisions in circumstances where both specific and general provisions apply.

36.214–36.299   [Reserved]

Subpart C — Specific Requirements

36.301   Eligibility criteria

(a) *General.* A public accommodation shall not impose or apply eligibility criteria that screen out or tend to screen out an individual with a disability or any class of individuals with disabilities from fully and equally enjoying any goods, services, facilities, privileges, advantages, or accommodations, unless such criteria can be shown to be necessary for the provision of the goods, services, facilities, privileges, advantages, or accommodations being offered.

(b) *Safety.* A public accommodation may impose legitimate safety requirements that are necessary for safe operation. Safety requirements must be based on actual risks and not on mere speculation, stereotypes, or generalizations about individuals with disabilities.

(c) *Charges.* A public accommodation may not impose a surcharge on a particular individual with a disability or any group of individuals with disabilities to cover the costs of measures, such as the provision of auxiliary aids, barrier removal, alternatives to barrier removal, and reasonable modifications in policies, practices, or procedures, that are required to provide that individual or group with the nondiscriminatory treatment required by the Act or this part.

36.302   Modifications in policies, practices, or procedures

(a) *General.* A public accommodation shall make reasonable modifications in policies, practices, or procedures, when the modifications are necessary to afford goods, services, facilities, privileges, advantages, or accommodations to individuals with disabilities, unless the public accommodation can demonstrate that making the modifications would fundamentally alter the nature of the goods, services, facilities, privileges, advantages, or accommodations.

(b) *Specialties* —

(1) *General.* A public accommodation may refer an individual with a disability to another public accommodation, if that individual is seeking, or requires, treatment or services outside of the referring public accommodation's area of specialization, and if, in the normal course of its operations, the referring public accommodation would make a similar referral for an individual without a disability who seeks or requires the same treatment or services.

(2) *Illustration — medical specialties.* A health care provider may refer an individual with a disability to another provider, if that individual is seeking, or requires, treatment or services outside of the referring provider's area of specialization, and if the referring provider would make a similar referral for an individual without a disability who seeks or requires the same treatment or services. A physician who specializes in treating only a particular condition cannot refuse to treat an individual with a disability for that condition, but is not required to treat the individual for a different condition.

(c) *Service animals.*

(1) *General.* Generally, a public accommodation shall modify policies, prac-

tices, or procedures to permit the use of a service animal by an individual with a disability.

(c)(2) *Exceptions.* A public accommodation may ask an individual with a disability to remove a service animal from the premises if:

(i) The animal is out of control and the animal's handler does not take effective action to control it; or

(ii) The animal is not housebroken.

(3) *If an animal is properly excluded.* If a public accommodation properly excludes a service animal under § 36.302(c)(2), it shall give the individual with a disability the opportunity to obtain goods, services, and accommodations without having the service animal on the premises.

(4) *Animal under handler's control.* A service animal shall be under the control of its handler. A service animal shall have a harness, leash, or other tether, unless either the handler is unable because of a disability to use a harness, leash, or other tether, or the use of a harness, leash, or other tether would interfere with the service animal's safe, effective performance of work or tasks, in which case the service animal must be otherwise under the handler's control (*e.g.*, voice control, signals, or other effective means).

(5) *Care or supervision.* A public accommodation is not responsible for the care or supervision of a service animal.

(6) *Inquiries.* A public accommodation shall not ask about the nature or extent of a person's disability, but may make two inquiries to determine whether an animal qualifies as a service animal. A public accommodation may ask if the animal is required because of a disability and what work or task the animal has been trained to perform. A public accommodation shall not require documentation, such as proof that the animal has been certified, trained, or licensed as a service animal. Generally, a public accommodation may not make these inquiries about a service animal when it is readily apparent that an animal is trained to do work or perform tasks for an individual with a disability (*e.g.*, the dog is observed guiding an individual who is blind or has low vision, pulling a person's wheelchair, or providing assistance with stability or balance to an individual with an observable mobility disability).

(7) *Access to areas of a public accommodation.* Individuals with disabilities shall be permitted to be accompanied by their service animals in all areas of a place of public accommodation where members of the public, program participants, clients, customers, patrons, or invitees, as relevant, are allowed to go.

(8) *Surcharges.* A public accommodation shall not ask or require an individual with a disability to pay a surcharge, even if people accompanied by pets are required to pay fees, or to comply with other requirements generally not applicable to people without pets. If a public accommodation normally charges individuals for the damage they cause, an individual with a disability may be charged for damage caused by his or her service animal.

(9) *Miniature horses.*

(i) A public accommodation shall make reasonable modifications in policies, practices, or procedures to permit the use of a miniature horse by an individual with a disability if the miniature horse has been individually trained to do work or perform tasks for the benefit of the individual with a disability.

(ii) *Assessment factors.* In determining whether reasonable modifications in policies, practices, or procedures can be made to allow a miniature horse into a specific facility, a public accommodation shall consider —

(A) The type, size, and weight of the miniature horse and whether the facility can accommodate these features;

(B) Whether the handler has sufficient control of the miniature horse;

(C) Whether the miniature horse is housebroken; and

(D) Whether the miniature horse's presence in a specific facility compromises legitimate safety requirements that are necessary for safe operation.

(iii) *Other requirements.* Sections 36.302(c)(3) through (c)(8), which apply to service animals, shall also apply to miniature horses.

(d) *Check-out aisles.* A store with check-out aisles shall ensure that an adequate number of accessible check-out aisles are kept open during store hours, or shall otherwise modify its policies and practices, in order to ensure that an equivalent level of convenient service is provided to individuals with disabilities as is provided to others. If only one check-out aisle is accessible, and it is generally used for express service, one way of providing equivalent service is to allow persons with mobility impairments to make all their purchases at that aisle.

(e)

(1) *Reservations made by places of lodging.* A public accommodation that owns, leases (or leases to), or operates a place of lodging shall, with respect to reservations made by any means, including by telephone, in-person, or through a third party —

(i) Modify its policies, practices, or procedures to ensure that individuals with disabilities can make reservations for accessible guest rooms during the same hours and in the same manner as individuals who do not need accessible rooms;

(ii) Identify and describe accessible features in the hotels and guest rooms offered through its reservations service in enough detail to reasonably permit individuals with disabilities to assess independently whether a given hotel or guest room meets his or her accessibility needs;

(iii) Ensure that accessible guest rooms are held for use by individuals with disabilities until all other guest rooms of that type have been rented and the accessible room requested is the only remaining room of that type;

(iv) Reserve, upon request, accessible guest rooms or specific types of guest rooms and ensure that the guest rooms requested are blocked and removed from all reservations systems; and

(v) Guarantee that the specific accessible guest room reserved through its reservations service is held for the reserving customer, regardless of whether a specific room is held in response to reservations made by others.

(2) *Exception.* The requirements in paragraphs (iii), (iv), and (v) of this section do not apply to reservations for individual guest rooms or other units not owned or substantially controlled by the entity that owns, leases, or operates the overall facility.

(3) *Compliance date.* The requirements in this section will apply to reservations made on or after March 15, 2012.

(f) *Ticketing.*

(1)

(i) For the purposes of this section, "accessible seating" is defined as wheelchair spaces and companion seats that comply with sections 221 and 802 of the 2010 Standards along with any other seats required to be offered for sale to the individual with a disability pursuant to paragraph (4) of this section.

(ii) *Ticket sales.* A public accommodation that sells tickets for a single event or series of events shall modify its policies, practices, or procedures to ensure that individuals with disabilities have an equal opportunity to purchase tickets for accessible seating —

(A) During the same hours;

(B) During the same stages of ticket sales, including, but not limited to, pre-sales, promotions, lotteries, wait-lists, and general sales;

(C) Through the same methods of distribution;

(D) In the same types and numbers of ticketing sales outlets, including telephone service, in-person ticket sales at the facility, or third-party ticketing services, as other patrons; and

(E) Under the same terms and conditions as other tickets sold for the same event or series of events.

(2) *Identification of available accessible seating.* A public accommodation that sells or distributes tickets for a single event or series of events shall, upon inquiry —

(i) Inform individuals with disabilities, their companions, and third parties purchasing tickets for accessible seating on behalf of individuals with disabilities of the locations of all unsold or otherwise available accessible seating for any ticketed event or events at the facility;

(ii) Identify and describe the features of available accessible seating in enough detail to reasonably permit an individual with a disability to assess independently whether a given accessible seating location meets his or her accessibility needs; and

(iii) Provide materials, such as seating maps, plans, brochures, pricing charts, or other information, that identify accessible seating and information relevant thereto with the same text or visual representations as other seats, if such materials are provided to the general public.

(3) *Ticket prices.* The price of tickets for accessible seating for a single event or series of events shall not be set higher than the price for other tickets in the same seating section for the same event or series of events. Tickets for accessible seating must be made available at all price levels for every event or series of events. If tickets for accessible seating at a particular price level cannot be provided because barrier removal in an existing facility is not readily achievable, then the percentage of tickets for accessible seating that should have been available at that price level but for the barriers (determined by the ratio of the total number of tickets at that price level to the total number of tickets in the assembly area) shall be offered for purchase, at that price level, in a nearby or similar accessible location.

(4) *Purchasing multiple tickets.*

(i) *General.* For each ticket for a wheelchair space purchased by an individual with a disability or a third-party purchasing such a ticket at his or her request, a public accommodation shall make available for purchase three additional tickets for seats in the same row that are contiguous with the wheelchair space, provided that at the time of purchase there are three such seats available. A public accommodation is not required to provide more than three contiguous seats for each wheelchair space. Such seats may include wheelchair spaces.

(ii) *Insufficient additional contiguous seats available.* If patrons are allowed to purchase at least four tickets, and there are fewer than three additional contiguous seat tickets available for purchase, a public accommodation shall offer the next highest number of such seat tickets available for purchase and shall make up the difference by offering tickets for sale for seats that are as close as possible to the accessible seats.

(iii) *Sales limited to fewer than four tickets.* If a public accommodation limits sales of tickets to fewer than four seats per patron, then the public accommodation is only obligated to offer as many seats to patrons with disabilities, including the ticket for the wheelchair space, as it would offer to patrons without disabilities.

(iv) *Maximum number of tickets patrons may purchase exceeds four.* If patrons are allowed to purchase more than four tickets, a public accommodation shall allow patrons with disabilities to purchase up to the same number of tickets, including the ticket for the wheelchair space.

(v) *Group sales.* If a group includes one or more individuals who need to use accessible seating because of a mobility disability or because their disability requires the use of the accessible features that are provided in accessible seating, the group shall be placed in a seating area with accessible seating so that, if possible, the group can sit together. If it is necessary to divide the group, it should be divided so that the individuals in the group who use wheelchairs are not isolated from their group.

(5) *Hold and release of tickets for accessible seating.*

(i) *Tickets for accessible seating may be released for sale in certain limited circumstances.* A public accommodation may release unsold tickets for accessible seating for sale to individuals without disabilities for their own use for a single event or series of events only under the following circumstances —

(A) When all non-accessible tickets (excluding luxury boxes, club boxes, or suites) have been sold;

(B) When all non-accessible tickets in a designated seating area have been sold and the tickets for accessible seating are being released in the same designated area; or

(C) When all non-accessible tickets in a designated price category have been sold and the tickets for accessible seating are being released within the same designated price category.

(ii) *No requirement to release accessible tickets.* Nothing in this paragraph requires a facility to release tickets for accessible seating to individuals without disabilities for their own use.

(iii) *Release of series-of-events tickets on a series-of-events basis.*

(A) *Series-of-events tickets sell-out when no ownership rights are attached.* When series-of-events tickets are sold out and a public accommodation releases and sells accessible seating to individuals without disabilities for a series of events, the public accommodation shall establish a process that prevents the automatic reassignment of the accessible seating to such ticket holders for future seasons, future years, or future series, so that individuals with disabilities who require the features of accessible seating and who become newly eligible to purchase tickets when these series-of-events tickets are available for purchase have an opportunity to do so.

(B) *Series-of-events tickets when ownership rights are attached.* When series-of-events tickets with an ownership right in accessible seating areas are forfeited or otherwise returned to a public accommodation, the public accommodation shall make reasonable modifications in its policies, practices, or procedures to afford individuals with mobility disabilities or individuals with disabilities that require the features of accessible seating an opportunity to purchase such tickets in accessible seating areas.

(6) *Ticket transfer.* Individuals with disabilities who hold tickets for accessible seating shall be permitted to transfer tickets to third parties under the same terms and conditions and to the same extent as other spectators holding the same type of tickets, whether they are for a single event or series of events.

(7) *Secondary ticket market.*

A public accommodation shall modify its policies, practices, or procedures to ensure that an individual with a disability may use a ticket acquired in the secondary ticket market under the same terms and conditions as other individuals who hold a ticket acquired in the secondary ticket market for the same event or series of events.

If an individual with a disability acquires a ticket or series of tickets to an inaccessible seat through the secondary market, a public accommodation shall make reasonable modifications to its policies, practices, or procedures to allow the individual to exchange his ticket for one to an accessible seat in a comparable location if accessible seating is vacant at the time the individual presents the ticket to the public accommodation.

(8) *Prevention of fraud in purchase of tickets for accessible seating.* A public accommodation may not require proof of disability, including, for example, a doctor's note, before selling tickets for accessible seating.

Single-event tickets. For the sale of single-event tickets, it is permissible to inquire whether the individual purchasing the tickets for accessible seating has a mobility disability or a disability that requires the use of the accessible features that are provided in accessible seating, or is purchasing the tickets for an individual who has a mobility disability or a disability that requires the use of the accessible features that are provided in the accessible seating.

Series-of-events tickets. For series-of-events tickets, it is permissible to ask the individual purchasing the tickets for accessible seating to attest in writing that the accessible seating is for a person who has a mobility disability or a disability that requires the use of the accessible features that are provided in the accessible seating.

Investigation of fraud. A public accommodation may investigate the potential misuse of accessible seating where there is good cause to believe that such seating has been purchased fraudulently.

36.303 Auxiliary aids and services

(a) *General.* A public accommodation shall take those steps that may be necessary to ensure that no individual with a disability is excluded, denied services, segregated or otherwise treated differently than other individuals because of the absence of auxiliary aids and services, unless the public accommodation can demonstrate that taking those steps would fundamentally alter the nature of the goods, services, facilities, privileges, advantages, or accommodations being offered or would result in an undue burden, *i.e.*, significant difficulty or expense.

(b) *Examples.* The term "auxiliary aids and services" includes —

(1) Qualified interpreters on-site or through video remote interpreting (VRI) services; notetakers; real-time computer-aided transcription services; written materials; exchange of written notes; telephone handset amplifiers; assistive listening devices; assistive listening systems; telephones compatible with hearing aids; closed caption decoders; open and closed captioning, including real-time captioning; voice, text, and video-based telecommunications products and systems, including text telephones (TTYs), videophones, and captioned telephones, or equally effective telecommunications devices; videotext displays; accessible electronic and information technology; or other effective methods of making aurally delivered information available to individuals who are deaf or hard of hearing;

(2) Qualified readers; taped texts; audio recordings; Brailled materials and

displays; screen reader software; magnification software; optical readers; secondary auditory programs (SAP); large print materials; accessible electronic and information technology; or other effective methods of making visually delivered materials available to individuals who are blind or have low vision;

(3) Acquisition or modification of equipment or devices; and

(4) Other similar services and actions.

(c) *Effective communication.*

(1) A public accommodation shall furnish appropriate auxiliary aids and services where necessary to ensure effective communication with individuals with disabilities. This includes an obligation to provide effective communication to companions who are individuals with disabilities.

(i) For purposes of this section, "companion" means a family member, friend, or associate of an individual seeking access to, or participating in, the goods, services, facilities, privileges, advantages, or accommodations of a public accommodation, who, along with such individual, is an appropriate person with whom the public accommodation should communicate.

(ii) The type of auxiliary aid or service necessary to ensure effective communication will vary in accordance with the method of communication used by the individual; the nature, length, and complexity of the communication involved; and the context in which the communication is taking place. A public accommodation should consult with individuals with disabilities whenever possible to determine what type of auxiliary aid is needed to ensure effective communication, but the ultimate decision as to what measures to take rests with the public accommodation, provided that the method chosen results in effective communication. In order to be effective, auxiliary aids and services must be provided in accessible formats, in a timely manner, and in such a way as to protect the privacy and independence of the individual with a disability.

(2) A public accommodation shall not require an individual with a disability to bring another individual to interpret for him or her.

(3) A public accommodation shall not rely on an adult accompanying an individual with a disability to interpret or facilitate communication, except —

(i) In an emergency involving an imminent threat to the safety or welfare of an individual or the public where there is no interpreter available; or

(ii) Where the individual with a disability specifically requests that the accompanying adult interpret or facilitate communication, the accompanying adult agrees to provide such assistance, and reliance on that adult for such assistance is appropriate under the circumstances.

(4) A public accommodation shall not rely on a minor child to interpret or facilitate communication, except in an emergency involving an imminent threat to the safety or welfare of an individual or the public where there is no interpreter available.

(d) *Telecommunications.*

(1) When a public accommodation uses an automated-attendant system, including, but not limited to, voicemail and messaging, or an interactive voice response system, for receiving and directing incoming telephone calls, that system must provide effective real-time communication with individuals using auxiliary aids and services, including text telephones (TTYs) and all forms of FCC-approved telecommunications relay systems, including Internet-based relay systems.

(2) A public accommodation that offers a customer, client, patient, or participant the opportunity to make outgoing telephone calls using the public accommodation's equipment on more than an incidental convenience basis shall make available public telephones, TTYs, or other telecommunications products and systems for use by an individual who is deaf or hard of hearing, or has a speech impairment.

(3) A public accommodation may use relay services in place of direct telephone communication for receiving or making telephone calls incident to its operations.

(4) A public accommodation shall respond to telephone calls from a telecommunications relay service established under title IV of the ADA in the same manner that it responds to other telephone calls.

(5) This part does not require a public accommodation to use a TTY for receiving or making telephone calls incident to its operations.

(e) *Closed caption decoders.* Places of lodging that provide televisions in five or more guest rooms and hospitals that provide televisions for patient use shall provide, upon request, a means for decoding captions for use by an individual with impaired hearing.

(f) *Video remote interpreting (VRI) services.* A public accommodation that chooses to provide qualified interpreters via VRI service shall ensure that it provides —

(1) Real-time, full-motion video and audio over a dedicated high-speed, wide-bandwidth video connection or wireless connection that delivers high-quality video images that do not produce lags, choppy, blurry, or grainy images, or irregular pauses in communication;

(2) A sharply delineated image that is large enough to display the interpreter's face, arms, hands, and fingers, and the participating individual's face, arms, hands, and fingers, regardless of his or her body position;

(3) A clear, audible transmission of voices; and

(4) Adequate training to users of the technology and other involved individuals so that they may quickly and efficiently set up and operate the VRI.

(g) *Alternatives.* If provision of a particular auxiliary aid or service by a public accommodation would result in a fundamental alteration in the nature of the goods, services, facilities, privileges, advantages, or accommodations being offered or in an undue burden, *i.e.*, significant difficulty or expense, the public accommodation shall provide an alternative auxiliary aid or service, if one exists, that would not result in an alteration or such burden but would nevertheless ensure that, to the maximum extent possible, individuals with disabilities receive the goods, services, facilities, privileges, advantages, or accommodations offered by the public accommodation.

36.304   Removal of barriers

(a) *General.* A public accommodation shall remove architectural barriers in existing facilities, including communication barriers that are structural in nature, where such removal is readily achievable, *i.e.,* easily accomplishable and able to be carried out without much difficulty or expense.

(b) *Examples.* Examples of steps to remove barriers include, but are not limited to, the following actions —

(1) Installing ramps;

(2) Making curb cuts in sidewalks and entrances;

(3) Repositioning shelves;

(4) Rearranging tables, chairs, vending machines, display racks, and other furniture;

(5) Repositioning telephones;

(6) Adding raised markings on elevator control buttons;

(7) Installing flashing alarm lights;

(8) Widening doors;

(9) Installing offset hinges to widen doorways;

(10) Eliminating a turnstile or providing an alternative accessible path;

(11) Installing accessible door hardware;

(12) Installing grab bars in toilet stalls;

(13) Rearranging toilet partitions to increase maneuvering space;

(14) Insulating lavatory pipes under sinks to prevent burns;

(15) Installing a raised toilet seat;

(16) Installing a full-length bathroom mirror;

(17) Repositioning the paper towel dispenser in a bathroom;

(18) Creating designated accessible parking spaces;

(19) Installing an accessible paper cup dispenser at an existing inaccessible water fountain;

(20) Removing high pile, low density carpeting; or

(21) Installing vehicle hand controls.

(c) *Priorities.* A public accommodation is urged to take measures to comply with the barrier removal requirements of this section in accordance with the following order of priorities.

(1) First, a public accommodation should take measures to provide access to a place of public accommodation from public sidewalks, parking, or public transportation. These measures include, for example, installing an entrance ramp, widening entrances, and providing accessible parking spaces.

(2) Second, a public accommodation should take measures to provide access to those areas of a place of public accommodation where goods and services are made available to the public. These measures include, for example, adjusting the layout of display racks, rearranging tables, providing Brailled and raised character signage, widening doors, providing visual alarms, and installing ramps.

(3) Third, a public accommodation should take measures to provide access to restroom facilities. These measures include, for example, removal of obstructing furniture or vending machines, widening of doors, installation of ramps, providing accessible signage, widening of toilet stalls, and installation of grab bars.

(4) Fourth, a public accommodation should take any other measures necessary to provide access to the goods, services, facilities, privileges, advantages, or accommodations of a place of public accommodation.

(d) *Relationship to alterations requirements of subpart D of this part.*

(1) Except as provided in paragraph (d)(3) of this section, measures taken to comply with the barrier removal requirements of this section shall comply with the applicable requirements for alterations in § 36.402 and §§ 36.404 through 36.406 of this part for the element being altered. The path of travel requirements of § 36.403 shall not apply to measures taken solely to comply with the barrier removal requirements of this section.

(2)

(i) *Safe harbor.* Elements that have not been altered in existing facilities on or after March 15, 2012, and that comply with the corresponding technical and scoping specifications for those elements in the 1991 Standards are not required to be modified in order to comply with the requirements set forth in the 2010 Standards.

(ii)

(A) Before March 15, 2012, elements in existing facilities that do not comply with the corresponding technical and scoping specifications for those elements in the 1991 Standards must be modified to the extent readily achievable to comply with either the 1991 Standards or the 2010 Standards. Noncomplying newly constructed and altered elements may also be subject to the requirements of § 36.406(a)(5).

(B) On or after March 15, 2012, elements in existing facilities that do not comply with the corresponding technical and scoping specifications for those elements in the 1991 Standards must be modified to the extent readily achievable to comply with the requirements set forth in the 2010 Standards. Noncomplying newly constructed and altered elements may also be subject to the requirements of § 36.406(a)(5).

(iii) The safe harbor provided in § 36.304(d)(2)(i) does not apply to those elements in existing facilities that are subject to supplemental requirements (*i.e.*, elements for which there are neither technical nor scoping specifications in the 1991 Standards), and therefore those elements must be modified to the extent readily achievable to comply with the 2010 Standards. Noncomplying newly constructed and altered elements may also be subject to the requirements of § 36.406(a)(5). Elements in the 2010 Standards not eligible for the element-by-element safe harbor are identified as follows —

(A) *Residential facilities and dwelling units*, sections 233 and 809.

(B) *Amusement rides*, sections 234 and 1002; 206.2.9; 216.12.

(C) *Recreational boating facilities*, sections 235 and 1003; 206.2.10.

(D) *Exercise machines and equipment*, sections 236 and 1004; 206.2.13.

(E) *Fishing piers and platforms*, sections 237 and 1005; 206.2.14.

(F) *Golf facilities*, sections 238 and 1006; 206.2.15.

(G) *Miniature golf facilities*, sections 239 and 1007; 206.2.16.

(H) *Play areas*, sections 240 and 1008; 206.2.17.

(I) *Saunas and steam rooms*, sections 241 and 612.

(J) *Swimming pools, wading pools, and spas*, sections 242 and 1009.

(K) *Shooting facilities with firing positions*, sections 243 and 1010.

(L) *Miscellaneous.*

(1) Team or player seating, section 221.2.1.4.

(2) Accessible route to bowling lanes, section 206.2.11.

(3) Accessible route in court sports facilities, section 206.2.12.

(3) If, as a result of compliance with the alterations requirements specified in paragraph (d)(1) and (d)(2) of this section, the measures required to remove a barrier would not be readily achievable, a public accommodation may take other readily achievable measures to remove the barrier that do not fully comply with the specified requirements. Such measures include, for example, providing a ramp with a steeper slope or widening a doorway to a narrower width than that mandated by the alterations requirements. No measure shall be taken, however, that poses a significant risk to the health or safety of individuals with disabilities or others.

Appendix to § 36.304(d)

Compliance Dates and Applicable Standards for Barrier Removal and Safe Harbor		
Date	Requirement	Applicable Standards
Before March 15, 2012	Elements that do not comply with the requirements for those elements in the 1991 Standards must be modified to the extent readily achievable.	1991 Standards or 2010 Standards
	Note: Noncomplying newly constructed and altered elements may also be subject to the requirements of § 36.406(a)(5).	
On or after March 15, 2012	Elements that do not comply with the requirements for those elements in the 1991 Standards or that do not comply with the supplemental requirements (*i.e.*, elements for which there are neither technical nor scoping specifications in the 1991 Standards) must be modified to the extent readily achievable.	2010 Standards
	Note: Noncomplying newly constructed and altered elements may also be subject to the requirements of § 36.406(a)(5).	
Elements not altered after March 15, 2012	Elements that comply with the requirements for those elements in the 1991 Standards do not need to be modified.	Safe Harbor

(e) *Portable ramps.* Portable ramps should be used to comply with this section only when installation of a permanent ramp is not readily achievable. In order to avoid any significant risk to the health or safety of individuals with disabilities or others in using portable ramps, due consideration shall be given to safety features such as nonslip surfaces, railings, anchoring, and strength of materials.

(f) *Selling or serving space.* The rearrangement of temporary or movable structures, such as furniture, equipment, and display racks is not readily achievable to the extent that it results in a significant loss of selling or serving space.

(g) *Limitation on barrier removal obligations.*

(1) The requirements for barrier removal under § 36.304 shall not be interpreted to exceed the standards for alterations in subpart D of this part.

(2) To the extent that relevant standards for alterations are not provided in

subpart D of this part, then the requirements of § 36.304 shall not be interpreted to exceed the standards for new construction in subpart D of this part.

(3) This section does not apply to rolling stock and other conveyances to the extent that § 36.310 applies to rolling stock and other conveyances.

(4) This requirement does not apply to guest rooms in existing facilities that are places of lodging where the guest rooms are not owned by the entity that owns, leases, or operates the overall facility and the physical features of the guest room interiors are controlled by their individual owners.

36.305   Alternatives to barrier removal

(a) *General.* Where a public accommodation can demonstrate that barrier removal is not readily achievable, the public accommodation shall not fail to make its goods, services, facilities, privileges, advantages, or accommodations available through alternative methods, if those methods are readily achievable.

(b) *Examples.* Examples of alternatives to barrier removal include, but are not limited to, the following actions —

(1) Providing curb service or home delivery;

(2) Retrieving merchandise from inaccessible shelves or racks;

(3) Relocating activities to accessible locations;

(c) *Multiscreen cinemas.* If it is not readily achievable to remove barriers to provide access by persons with mobility impairments to all of the theaters of a multiscreen cinema, the cinema shall establish a film rotation schedule that provides reasonable access for individuals who use wheelchairs to all films. Reasonable notice shall be provided to the public as to the location and time of accessible showings.

36.306   Personal devices and services

This part does not require a public accommodation to provide its customers, clients, or participants with personal devices, such as wheelchairs; individually prescribed devices, such as prescription eyeglasses or hearing aids; or services of a personal nature including assistance in eating, toileting, or dressing.

36.307   Accessible or special goods

(a) This part does not require a public accommodation to alter its inventory to include accessible or special goods that are designed for, or facilitate use by, individuals with disabilities.

(b) A public accommodation shall order accessible or special goods at the request of an individual with disabilities, if, in the normal course of its operation, it makes special orders on request for unstocked goods, and if the accessible or special goods can be obtained from a supplier with whom the public accommodation customarily does business.

(c) Examples of accessible or special goods include items such as Brailled versions of books, books on audio cassettes, closed-captioned video tapes, special sizes or lines of clothing, and special foods to meet particular dietary needs.

36.308   Seating in assembly areas

A public accommodation shall ensure that wheelchair spaces and companion seats are provided in each specialty seating area that provides spectators with distinct services or amenities that generally are not available to other spectators. If it is not readily achievable for a public accommodation to place wheelchair spaces and companion seats in each such specialty seating area, it shall provide those services or amenities to individuals with disabilities and their companions at other designated accessible locations at no additional cost. The number of wheelchair spaces and companion seats provided in specialty seating areas shall be included in, rather than in addition to, wheelchair space requirements set forth in table 221.2.1.1 in the 2010 Standards.

36.309   Examinations and courses

(a)   *General.* Any private entity that offers examinations or courses related to applications, licensing, certification, or credentialing for secondary or postsecondary education, professional, or trade purposes shall offer such examinations or courses in a place and manner accessible to persons with disabilities or offer alternative accessible arrangements for such individuals.

(b)   *Examinations.*

(1) Any private entity offering an examination covered by this section must assure that —

(i) The examination is selected and administered so as to best ensure that, when the examination is administered to an individual with a disability that impairs sensory, manual, or speaking skills, the examination results accurately reflect the individual's aptitude or achievement level or whatever other factor the examination purports to measure, rather than reflecting the individual's impaired sensory, manual, or speaking skills (except where those skills are the factors that the examination purports to measure);

(ii) An examination that is designed for individuals with impaired sensory, manual, or speaking skills is offered at equally convenient locations, as often, and in as timely a manner as are other examinations; and

(iii) The examination is administered in facilities that are accessible to individuals with disabilities or alternative accessible arrangements are made.

(iv) Any request for documentation, if such documentation is required, is reasonable and limited to the need for the modification, accommodation, or auxiliary aid or service requested.

(v) When considering requests for modifications, accommodations, or auxiliary aids or services, the entity gives considerable weight to documentation of past modifications, accommodations, or auxiliary aids or services received in similar testing situations, as well as such modifications, accommodations, or related aids and services provided in response to an Individualized Education Program (IEP) provided under the Individuals with Disabilities Education Act or a plan describing services provided pursuant to section 504 of the Rehabilitation Act of 1973, as amended (often referred as a Section 504 Plan).

(vi) The entity responds in a timely manner to requests for modifications, accommodations, or aids to ensure equal opportunity for individuals with disabilities.

(2) Required modifications to an examination may include changes in the length of time permitted for completion of the examination and adaptation of the manner in which the examination is given.

(3) A private entity offering an examination covered by this section shall provide appropriate auxiliary aids for persons with impaired sensory, manual, or speaking skills, unless that private entity can demonstrate that offering a particular auxiliary aid would fundamentally alter the measurement of the skills or knowledge the examination is intended to test or would result in an undue burden. Auxiliary aids and services required by this section may include taped examinations, interpreters or other effective methods of making orally delivered materials available to individuals with hearing impairments, Brailled or large print examinations and answer sheets or qualified readers for individuals with visual impairments or learning disabilities, transcribers for individuals with manual impairments, and other similar services and actions.

(4) Alternative accessible arrangements may include, for example, provision of an examination at an individual's home with a proctor if accessible facilities or equipment are unavailable. Alternative arrangements must provide comparable conditions to those provided for nondisabled individuals.

(c) *Courses.*

(1) Any private entity that offers a course covered by this section must make such modifications to that course as are necessary to ensure that the place and manner in which the course is given are accessible to individuals with disabilities.

(2) Required modifications may include changes in the length of time permitted for the completion of the course, substitution of specific requirements, or adaptation of the manner in which the course is conducted or course materials are distributed.

(3) A private entity that offers a course covered by this section shall provide appropriate auxiliary aids and services for persons with impaired sensory, manual, or speaking skills, unless the private entity can demonstrate that offering a particular auxiliary aid or service would fundamentally alter the course or would result in an undue burden. Auxiliary aids and services required by this section may include taped texts, interpreters or other effective methods of making orally delivered materials available to individuals with hearing impairments, Brailled or large print texts or qualified readers for individuals with visual impairments and learning disabilities, classroom equipment adapted for use by individuals with manual impairments, and other similar services and actions.

(4) Courses must be administered in facilities that are accessible to individuals with disabilities or alternative accessible arrangements must be made.

(5) Alternative accessible arrangements may include, for example, provision of the course through videotape, cassettes, or prepared notes. Alternative arrange-

ments must provide comparable conditions to those provided for nondisabled individuals.

36.310   Transportation provided by public accommodations

(a)   *General.*

(1) A public accommodation that provides transportation services, but that is not primarily engaged in the business of transporting people, is subject to the general and specific provisions in subparts B, C, and D of this part for its transportation operations, except as provided in this section.

(2)   *Examples.* Transportation services subject to this section include, but are not limited to, shuttle services operated between transportation terminals and places of public accommodation, customer shuttle bus services operated by private companies and shopping centers, student transportation systems, and transportation provided within recreational facilities such as stadiums, zoos, amusement parks, and ski resorts.

(b)   *Barrier removal.* A public accommodation subject to this section shall remove transportation barriers in existing vehicles and rail passenger cars used for transporting individuals (not including barriers that can only be removed through the retrofitting of vehicles or rail passenger cars by the installation of a hydraulic or other lift) where such removal is readily achievable.

(c)   *Requirements for vehicles and systems.* A public accommodation subject to this section shall comply with the requirements pertaining to vehicles and transportation systems in the regulations issued by the Secretary of Transportation pursuant to section 306 of the Act.

36.311   Mobility devices

(a)   *Use of wheelchairs and manually-powered mobility aids.* A public accommodation shall permit individuals with mobility disabilities to use wheelchairs and manually-powered mobility aids, such as walkers, crutches, canes, braces, or other similar devices designed for use by individuals with mobility disabilities in any areas open to pedestrian use.

(b)

(1)   *Use of other power-driven mobility devices.* A public accommodation shall make reasonable modifications in its policies, practices, or procedures to permit the use of other power-driven mobility devices by individuals with mobility disabilities, unless the public accommodation can demonstrate that the class of other power-driven mobility devices cannot be operated in accordance with legitimate safety requirements that the public accommodation has adopted pursuant to § 36.301(b).

(2)   *Assessment factors.* In determining whether a particular other power-driven mobility device can be allowed in a specific facility as a reasonable modification under paragraph (b)(1) of this section, a public accommodation shall consider —

(i) The type, size, weight, dimensions, and speed of the device;

(ii) The facility's volume of pedestrian traffic (which may vary at different times of the day, week, month, or year);

(iii) The facility's design and operational characteristics (*e.g.*, whether its business is conducted indoors, its square footage, the density and placement of stationary devices, and the availability of storage for the device, if requested by the user);

(iv) Whether legitimate safety requirements can be established to permit the safe operation of the other power-driven mobility device in the specific facility; and

(v) Whether the use of the other power-driven mobility device creates a substantial risk of serious harm to the immediate environment or natural or cultural resources, or poses a conflict with Federal land management laws and regulations.

(c)

(1) *Inquiry about disability.* A public accommodation shall not ask an individual using a wheelchair or other power-driven mobility device questions about the nature and extent of the individual's disability.

(2) *Inquiry into use of other power-driven mobility device.* A public accommodation may ask a person using an other power-driven mobility device to provide a credible assurance that the mobility device is required because of the person's disability. A public accommodation that permits the use of an other power-driven mobility device by an individual with a mobility disability shall accept the presentation of a valid, State-issued disability parking placard or card, or State-issued proof of disability, as a credible assurance that the use of the other power-driven mobility device is for the individual's mobility disability. In lieu of a valid, State-issued disability parking placard or card, or State-issued proof of disability, a public accommodation shall accept as a credible assurance a verbal representation, not contradicted by observable fact, that the other power-driven mobility device is being used for a mobility disability. A "valid" disability placard or card is one that is presented by the individual to whom it was issued and is otherwise in compliance with the State of issuance's requirements for disability placards or cards.

36.312–36.399   [Reserved]

Subpart D — New Construction and Alterations

36.401   New construction

(a) *General.*

(1) Except as provided in paragraphs (b) and (c) of this section, discrimination for purposes of this part includes a failure to design and construct facilities for first occupancy after January 26, 1993, that are readily accessible to and usable by individuals with disabilities.

(2) For purposes of this section, a facility is designed and constructed for first occupancy after January 26, 1993, only —

(i) If the last application for a building permit or permit extension for the facility is certified to be complete, by a State, County, or local government after January 26, 1992 (or, in those jurisdictions where the government does not certify completion of applications, if the last application for a building permit or permit extension for the facility is received by the State, County, or local government after January 26, 1992); and

(ii) If the first certificate of occupancy for the facility is issued after January 26, 1993.

(b) *Commercial facilities located in private residences.*

(1) When a commercial facility is located in a private residence, the portion of the residence used exclusively as a residence is not covered by this subpart, but that portion used exclusively in the operation of the commercial facility or that portion used both for the commercial facility and for residential purposes is covered by the new construction and alterations requirements of this subpart.

(2) The portion of the residence covered under paragraph (b)(1) of this section extends to those elements used to enter the commercial facility, including the homeowner's front sidewalk, if any, the door or entryway, and hallways; and those portions of the residence, interior or exterior, available to or used by employees or visitors of the commercial facility, including restrooms.

(c) *Exception for structural impracticability.*

(1) Full compliance with the requirements of this section is not required where an entity can demonstrate that it is structurally impracticable to meet the requirements. Full compliance will be considered structurally impracticable only in those rare circumstances when the unique characteristics of terrain prevent the incorporation of accessibility features.

(2) If full compliance with this section would be structurally impracticable, compliance with this section is required to the extent that it is not structurally impracticable. In that case, any portion of the facility that can be made accessible shall be made accessible to the extent that it is not structurally impracticable.

(3) If providing accessibility in conformance with this section to individuals with certain disabilities (*e.g.*, those who use wheelchairs) would be structurally impracticable, accessibility shall nonetheless be ensured to persons with other types of disabilities (*e.g.*, those who use crutches or who have sight, hearing, or

mental impairments) in accordance with this section.

(d) *Elevator exemption.*

(1) For purposes of this paragraph (d) —

(i) Professional office of a health care provider means a location where a person or entity regulated by a State to provide professional services related to the physical or mental health of an individual makes such services available to the public. The facility housing the "professional office of a health care provider" only includes floor levels housing at least one health care provider, or any floor level designed or intended for use by at least one health care provider.

(ii) Shopping center or shopping mall means —

(A) A building housing five or more sales or rental establishments; or

(B) A series of buildings on a common site, either under common ownership or common control or developed either as one project or as a series of related projects, housing five or more sales or rental establishments. For purposes of this section, places of public accommodation of the types listed in paragraph (5) of the definition of "place of public accommodation" in section § 36.104 are considered sales or rental establishments. The facility housing a "shopping center or shopping mall" only includes floor levels housing at least one sales or rental establishment, or any floor level designed or intended for use by at least one sales or rental establishment.

(2) This section does not require the installation of an elevator in a facility that is less than three stories or has less than 3000 square feet per story, except with respect to any facility that houses one or more of the following:

(i) A shopping center or shopping mall, or a professional office of a health care provider.

(ii) A terminal, depot, or other station used for specified public transportation, or an airport passenger terminal. In such a facility, any area housing passenger services, including boarding and debarking, loading and unloading, baggage claim, dining facilities, and other common areas open to the public, must be on an accessible route from an accessible entrance.

(3) The elevator exemption set forth in this paragraph (d) does not obviate or limit, in any way the obligation to comply with the other accessibility requirements established in paragraph (a) of this section. For example, in a facility that houses a shopping center or shopping mall, or a professional office of a health care provider, the floors that are above or below an accessible ground floor and that do not house sales or rental establishments or a professional office of a health care provider, must meet the requirements of this section but for the elevator.

36.402   Alterations

(a) *General.*

(1) Any alteration to a place of public accommodation or a commercial facility,

after January 26, 1992, shall be made so as to ensure that, to the maximum extent feasible, the altered portions of the facility are readily accessible to and usable by individuals with disabilities, including individuals who use wheelchairs.

(2) An alteration is deemed to be undertaken after January 26, 1992, if the physical alteration of the property begins after that date.

(b) *Alteration.* For the purposes of this part, an alteration is a change to a place of public accommodation or a commercial facility that affects or could affect the usability of the building or facility or any part thereof.

(1) Alterations include, but are not limited to, remodeling, renovation, rehabilitation, reconstruction, historic restoration, changes or rearrangement in structural parts or elements, and changes or rearrangement in the plan configuration of walls and full-height partitions. Normal maintenance, reroofing, painting or wallpapering, asbestos removal, or changes to mechanical and electrical systems are not alterations unless they affect the usability of the building or facility.

(2) If existing elements, spaces, or common areas are altered, then each such altered element, space, or area shall comply with the applicable provisions of appendix A to this part.

(c) *To the maximum extent feasible.* The phrase "to the maximum extent feasible," as used in this section, applies to the occasional case where the nature of an existing facility makes it virtually impossible to comply fully with applicable accessibility standards through a planned alteration. In these circumstances, the alteration shall provide the maximum physical accessibility feasible. Any altered features of the facility that can be made accessible shall be made accessible. If providing accessibility in conformance with this section to individuals with certain disabilities (*e.g.*, those who use wheelchairs) would not be feasible, the facility shall be made accessible to persons with other types of disabilities (*e.g.*, those who use crutches, those who have impaired vision or hearing, or those who have other impairments).

36.403   Alterations: Path of travel

(a) *General.*

(1) An alteration that affects or could affect the usability of or access to an area of a facility that contains a primary function shall be made so as to ensure that, to the maximum extent feasible, the path of travel to the altered area and the restrooms, telephones, and drinking fountains serving the altered area, are readily accessible to and usable by individuals with disabilities, including individuals who use wheelchairs, unless the cost and scope of such alterations is disproportionate to the cost of the overall alteration.

(2) If a private entity has constructed or altered required elements of a path of travel at a place of public accommodation or commercial facility in accordance with the specifications in the 1991 Standards, the private entity is not required to retrofit such elements to reflect the incremental changes in the 2010 Standards solely because of an alteration to a primary function area served by that path of travel.

(b) *Primary function.* A "primary function" is a major activity for which the facility is intended. Areas that contain a primary function include, but are not limited to, the customer services lobby of a bank, the dining area of a cafeteria, the meeting rooms in a conference center, as well as offices and other work areas in which the activities of the public accommodation or other private entity using the facility are carried out. Mechanical rooms, boiler rooms, supply storage rooms, employee lounges or locker rooms, janitorial closets, entrances, corridors, and restrooms are not areas containing a primary function.

(c) *Alterations to an area containing a primary function.*

(1) Alterations that affect the usability of or access to an area containing a primary function include, but are not limited to —

(i) Remodeling merchandise display areas or employee work areas in a department store;

(ii) Replacing an inaccessible floor surface in the customer service or employee work areas of a bank;

(iii) Redesigning the assembly line area of a factory; or

(iv) Installing a computer center in an accounting firm.

(2) For the purposes of this section, alterations to windows, hardware, controls, electrical outlets, and signage shall not be deemed to be alterations that affect the usability of or access to an area containing a primary function.

(d) *Landlord/tenant*: If a tenant is making alterations as defined in § 36.402 that would trigger the requirements of this section, those alterations by the tenant in areas that only the tenant occupies do not trigger a path of travel obligation upon the landlord with respect to areas of the facility under the landlord's authority, if those areas are not otherwise being altered.

(e) *Path of travel.*

(1) A "path of travel" includes a continuous, unobstructed way of pedestrian passage by means of which the altered area may be approached, entered, and exited, and which connects the altered area with an exterior approach (including sidewalks, streets, and parking areas), an entrance to the facility, and other parts of the facility.

(2) An accessible path of travel may consist of walks and sidewalks, curb ramps and other interior or exterior pedestrian ramps; clear floor paths through lobbies, corridors, rooms, and other improved areas; parking access aisles; elevators and lifts; or a combination of these elements.

(3) For the purposes of this part, the term "path of travel" also includes the restrooms, telephones, and drinking fountains serving the altered area.

(f) *Disproportionality.*

(1) Alterations made to provide an accessible path of travel to the altered area will be deemed disproportionate to the overall alteration when the cost exceeds 20% of the cost of the alteration to the primary function area.

(2) Costs that may be counted as expenditures required to provide an accessible path of travel may include:

(i) Costs associated with providing an accessible entrance and an accessible route to the altered area, for example, the cost of widening doorways or installing ramps;

(ii) Costs associated with making restrooms accessible, such as installing grab bars, enlarging toilet stalls, insulating pipes, or installing accessible faucet controls;

(iii) Costs associated with providing accessible telephones, such as relocating the telephone to an accessible height, installing amplification devices, or installing a text telephone (TTY);

(iv) Costs associated with relocating an inaccessible drinking fountain.

(g) *Duty to provide accessible features in the event of disproportionality.*

(1) When the cost of alterations necessary to make the path of travel to the altered area fully accessible is disproportionate to the cost of the overall alteration, the path of travel shall be made accessible to the extent that it can be made accessible without incurring disproportionate costs.

(2) In choosing which accessible elements to provide, priority should be given to those elements that will provide the greatest access, in the following order:

(i) An accessible entrance;

(ii) An accessible route to the altered area;

(iii) At least one accessible restroom for each sex or a single unisex restroom;

(iv) Accessible telephones;

(v) Accessible drinking fountains; and

(vi) When possible, additional accessible elements such as parking, storage, and alarms.

(h) *Series of smaller alterations.*

(1) The obligation to provide an accessible path of travel may not be evaded by performing a series of small alterations to the area served by a single path of travel if those alterations could have been performed as a single undertaking.

(2)

(i) If an area containing a primary function has been altered without providing an accessible path of travel to that area, and subsequent alterations of that area, or a different area on the same path of travel, are undertaken within three years of the original alteration, the total cost of alterations to the primary function areas on that path of travel during the preceding three year period shall be considered in determining whether the cost of making that path of travel accessible is disproportionate.

(ii) Only alterations undertaken after January 26, 1992, shall be considered in determining if the cost of providing an accessible path of travel is disproportionate to the overall cost of the alterations.

36.404   Alterations: Elevator exemption

(a) This section does not require the installation of an elevator in an altered facility that is less than three stories or has less than 3,000 square feet per story, except with respect to any facility that houses a shopping center, a shopping mall, the professional office of a health care provider, a terminal, depot, or other station used for specified public transportation, or an airport passenger terminal.

(1) For the purposes of this section, "professional office of a health care provider" means a location where a person or entity regulated by a State to provide professional services related to the physical or mental health of an individual makes such services available to the public. The facility that houses a "professional office of a health care provider" only includes floor levels housing by at least one health care provider, or any floor level designed or intended for use by at least one health care provider.

(2) For the purposes of this section, shopping center or shopping mall means —

(i) A building housing five or more sales or rental establishments; or

(ii) A series of buildings on a common site, connected by a common pedestrian access route above or below the ground floor, that is either under common ownership or common control or developed either as one project or as a series of related projects, housing five or more sales or rental establishments. For purposes of this section, places of public accommodation of the types listed in paragraph (5) of the definition of "place of public accommodation" in § 36.104 are considered sales or rental establishments. The facility housing a "shopping center or shopping mall" only includes floor levels housing at least one sales or rental establishment, or any floor level designed or intended for use by at least one sales or rental establishment.

(b) The exemption provided in paragraph (a) of this section does not obviate or limit in any way the obligation to comply with the other accessibility requirements established in this subpart. For example, alterations to floors above or below the accessible ground floor must be accessible regardless of whether the altered facility has an elevator.

36.405   Alterations: Historic preservation

(a) Alterations to buildings or facilities that are eligible for listing in the National Register of Historic Places under the National Historic Preservation Act (16 U.S.C. 470 *et seq*) or are designated as historic under State or local law, shall comply to the maximum extent feasible with this part.

(b) If it is determined that it is not feasible to provide physical access to an historic property that is a place of public accommodation in a manner that will not threaten or destroy the historic significance of the building or the facility, alternative methods of access shall be provided pursuant to the requirements of subpart C of this part.

36.406   Standards for new construction and alterations

(a) *Accessibility standards and compliance date.*

(1) New construction and alterations subject to §§ 36.401 or 36.402 shall comply with the 1991 Standards if the date when the last application for a building permit or permit extension is certified to be complete by a State, county, or local government (or, in those jurisdictions where the government does not certify completion of applications, if the date when the last application for a building permit or permit extension is received by the State, county, or local government) is before September 15, 2010, or if no permit is required, if the start of physical construction or alterations occurs before September 15, 2010.

(2) New construction and alterations subject to §§ 36.401 or 36.402 shall comply either with the 1991 Standards or with the 2010 Standards if the date when the last application for a building permit or permit extension is certified to be complete by a State, county, or local government (or, in those jurisdictions where the government does not certify completion of applications, if the date when the last application for a building permit or permit extension is received by the State, county, or local government) is on or after September 15, 2010, and before March 15, 2012, or if no permit is required, if the start of physical construction or alterations occurs on or after September 15, 2010, and before March 15, 2012.

(3) New construction and alterations subject to §§ 36.401 or 36.402 shall comply with the 2010 Standards if the date when the last application for a building permit or permit extension is certified to be complete by a State, county, or local government (or, in those jurisdictions where the government does not certify completion of applications, if the date when the last application for a building permit or permit extension is received by the State, county, or local government) is on or after March 15, 2012, or if no permit is required, if the start of physical construction or alterations occurs on or after March 15, 2012.

(4) For the purposes of this section, "start of physical construction or alterations" does not mean ceremonial groundbreaking or razing of structures prior to site preparation.

(5) *Noncomplying new construction and alterations.*

(i) Newly constructed or altered facilities or elements covered by §§ 36.401 or 36.402 that were constructed or altered before March 15, 2012, and that do not comply with the 1991 Standards shall, before March 15, 2012, be made accessible in accordance with either the 1991 Standards or the 2010 Standards.

(ii) Newly constructed or altered facilities or elements covered by §§ 36.401 or 36.402 that were constructed or altered before March 15, 2012 and that do not comply with the 1991 Standards shall, on or after March 15, 2012, be made accessible in accordance with the 2010 Standards.

Appendix to § 36.406(a)

Compliance Dates for New Construction and Alterations	Applicable Standards
On or after January 26, 1993 and before September 15, 2010	1991 Standards
On or after September 15, 2010, and before March 15, 2012	1991 Standards or 2010 Standards
On or after March 15, 2012	2010 Standards

(b) *Scope of coverage.* The 1991 Standards and the 2010 Standards apply to fixed or built-in elements of buildings, structures, site improvements, and pedestrian routes or vehicular ways located on a site. Unless specifically stated otherwise, advisory notes, appendix notes, and figures contained in the 1991 Standards and 2010 Standards explain or illustrate the requirements of the rule; they do not establish enforceable requirements.

(c) *Places of lodging.* Places of lodging subject to this part shall comply with the provisions of the 2010 Standards applicable to transient lodging, including, but not limited to, the requirements for transient lodging guest rooms in sections 224 and 806 of the 2010 Standards.

(1) *Guest rooms.* Guest rooms with mobility features in places of lodging subject to the transient lodging requirements of 2010 Standards shall be provided as follows —

(i) Facilities that are subject to the same permit application on a common site that each have 50 or fewer guest rooms may be combined for the purposes of determining the required number of accessible rooms and type of accessible bathing facility in accordance with table 224.2 to section 224.2 of the 2010 Standards.

(ii) Facilities with more than 50 guest rooms shall be treated separately for the purposes of determining the required number of accessible rooms and type of accessible bathing facility in accordance with table 224.2 to section 224.2 of the 2010 Standards.

(2) *Exception.* Alterations to guest rooms in places of lodging where the guest rooms are not owned or substantially controlled by the entity that owns, leases, or operates the overall facility and the physical features of the guest room interiors are controlled by their individual owners are not required to comply with § 36.402 or the alterations requirements in section 224.1.1 of the 2010 Standards.

(3) *Facilities with residential units and transient lodging units.* Residential dwelling units that are designed and constructed for residential use exclusively are not subject to the transient lodging standards.

(d) *Social service center establishments.* Group homes, halfway houses, shelters, or similar social service center establishments that provide either temporary sleeping accommodations or residential dwelling units that are subject to this part shall comply with the provisions of the 2010 Standards applicable to residential facilities, including, but not limited to, the provisions in sections 233 and 809.

(1) In sleeping rooms with more than 25 beds covered by this part, a minimum of 5% of the beds shall have clear floor space complying with section 806.2.3 of the 2010 Standards.

(2) Facilities with more than 50 beds covered by this part that provide common use bathing facilities shall provide at least one roll-in shower with a seat that complies with the relevant provisions of section 608 of the 2010 Standards. Transfer-type showers are not permitted in lieu of a roll-in shower with a seat, and the exceptions in sections 608.3 and 608.4 for residential dwelling units are not permitted. When separate shower facilities are provided for men and for women, at least one roll-in shower shall be provided for each group.

(e) *Housing at a place of education.* Housing at a place of education that is subject to this part shall comply with the provisions of the 2010 Standards applicable to transient lodging, including, but not limited to, the requirements for transient lodging guest rooms in sections 224 and 806, subject to the following exceptions. For the purposes of the application of this section, the term "sleeping room" is intended to be used interchangeably with the term "guest room" as it is used in the transient lodging standards.

(1) Kitchens within housing units containing accessible sleeping rooms with mobility features (including suites and clustered sleeping rooms) or on floors containing accessible sleeping rooms with mobility features shall provide turning spaces that comply with section 809.2.2 of the 2010 Standards and kitchen work surfaces that comply with section 804.3 of the 2010 Standards.

(2) Multi-bedroom housing units containing accessible sleeping rooms with mobility features shall have an accessible route throughout the unit in accordance with section 809.2 of the 2010 Standards.

(3) Apartments or townhouse facilities that are provided by or on behalf of a place of education, which are leased on a year-round basis exclusively to graduate students or faculty and do not contain any public use or common use areas available for educational programming, are not subject to the transient lodging standards and shall comply with the requirements for residential facilities in sections 233 and 809 of the 2010 Standards.

(f) *Assembly areas.* Assembly areas that are subject to this part shall comply with the provisions of the 2010 Standards applicable to assembly areas, including, but not limited to, sections 221 and 802. In addition, assembly areas shall ensure that —

(1) In stadiums, arenas, and grandstands, wheelchair spaces and companion seats are dispersed to all levels that include seating served by an accessible route;

(2) In assembly areas that are required to horizontally disperse wheelchair spaces and companion seats by section 221.2.3.1 of the 2010 Standards and that have seating encircling, in whole or in part, a field of play or performance, wheelchair spaces and companion seats are dispersed around that field of play or performance area;

(3) Wheelchair spaces and companion seats are not located on (or obstructed by) temporary platforms or other movable structures, except that when an entire seating section is placed on temporary platforms or other movable structures in an area where fixed seating is not provided, in order to increase seating for an event, wheelchair spaces and companion seats may be placed in that section. When wheelchair spaces and companion seats are not required to accommodate persons eligible for those spaces and seats, individual, removable seats may be placed in those spaces and seats;

(4) In stadium-style movie theaters, wheelchair spaces and companion seats are located on a riser or cross-aisle in the stadium section that satisfies at least one of the following criteria —

(i) It is located within the rear 60% of the seats provided in an auditorium; or

(ii) It is located within the area of an auditorium in which the vertical viewing angles (as measured to the top of the screen) are from the 40th to the 100th percentile of vertical viewing angles for all seats as ranked from the seats in the first row (1st percentile) to seats in the back row (100th percentile).

(g) *Medical care facilities.* Medical care facilities that are subject to this part shall comply with the provisions of the 2010 Standards applicable to medical care facilities, including, but not limited to, sections 223 and 805. In addition, medical care facilities that do not specialize in the treatment of conditions that affect mobility shall disperse the accessible patient bedrooms required by section 223.2.1 of the 2010 Standards in a manner that is proportionate by type of medical specialty.

36.407–36.499   [Reserved]

Subpart E — Enforcement

36.501   Private suits

(a)   *General.* Any person who is being subjected to discrimination on the basis of disability in violation of the Act or this part or who has reasonable grounds for believing that such person is about to be subjected to discrimination in violation of section 303 of the Act or subpart D of this part may institute a civil action for preventive relief, including an application for a permanent or temporary injunction, restraining order, or other order. Upon timely application, the court may, in its discretion, permit the Attorney General to intervene in the civil action if the Attorney General or his or her designee certifies that the case is of general public importance. Upon application by the complainant and in such circumstances as the court may deem just, the court may appoint an attorney for such complainant and may authorize the commencement of the civil action without the payment of fees, costs, or security. Nothing in this section shall require a person with a disability to engage in a futile gesture if the person has actual notice that a person or organization covered by title III of the Act or this part does not intend to comply with its provisions.

(b)   *Injunctive relief.* In the case of violations of § 36.304, §§ 36.308, 36.310(b), 36.401, 36.402, 36.403, and 36.405 of this part, injunctive relief shall include an order to alter facilities to make such facilities readily accessible to and usable by individuals with disabilities to the extent required by the Act or this part. Where appropriate, injunctive relief shall also include requiring the provision of an auxiliary aid or service, modification of a policy, or provision of alternative methods, to the extent required by the Act or this part.

36.502   Investigations and compliance reviews

(a) The Attorney General shall investigate alleged violations of the Act or this part.

(b) Any individual who believes that he or she or a specific class of persons has been subjected to discrimination prohibited by the Act or this part may request the Department to institute an investigation.

(c) Where the Attorney General has reason to believe that there may be a violation of this part, he or she may initiate a compliance review.

36.503   Suit by the Attorney General

Following a compliance review or investigation under § 36.502, or at any other time in his or her discretion, the Attorney General may commence a civil action in any appropriate United States district court if the Attorney General has reasonable cause to believe that —

(a) Any person or group of persons is engaged in a pattern or practice of discrimination in violation of the Act or this part; or

(b) Any person or group of persons has been discriminated against in violation of the Act or this part and the discrimination raises an issue of general public importance.

36.504   Relief

(a) Authority of court. In a civil action under § 36.503, the court —

(1) May grant any equitable relief that such court considers to be appropriate, including, to the extent required by the Act or this part —

(i) Granting temporary, preliminary, or permanent relief;

(ii) Providing an auxiliary aid or service, modification of policy, practice, or procedure, or alternative method; and

(iii) Making facilities readily accessible to and usable by individuals with disabilities;

(2) May award other relief as the court considers to be appropriate, including monetary damages to persons aggrieved when requested by the Attorney General; and

(3) May, to vindicate the public interest, assess a civil penalty against the entity in an amount

(i) Not exceeding $50,000 for a first violation occurring before September 29, 1999, and not exceeding $55,000 for a first violation occurring on or after September 29, 1999; and

(ii) Not exceeding $100,000 for any subsequent violation occurring before September 29, 1999, and not exceeding $110,000 for any subsequent violation occurring on or after September 29, 1999.

(b) Single violation. For purposes of paragraph (a) (3) of this section, in determining whether a first or subsequent violation has occurred, a determination in a single action, by judgment or settlement, that the covered entity has engaged in more than one discriminatory act shall be counted as a single violation.

(c) Punitive damages. For purposes of paragraph (a)(2) of this section, the terms "monetary damages" and "such other relief" do not include punitive damages.

(d) Judicial consideration. In a civil action under § 36.503, the court, when considering what amount of civil penalty, if any, is appropriate, shall give consideration to any good faith effort or attempt to comply with this part by the entity. In evaluating good faith, the court shall consider, among other factors it deems relevant, whether the entity could have reasonably anticipated the need for an appropriate type of auxiliary aid needed to accommodate the unique needs of a particular individual with a disability.

36.505   Attorneys fees

In any action or administrative proceeding commenced pursuant to the Act or this part, the court or agency, in its discretion, may allow the prevailing party, other than the United States, a reasonable attorney's fee, including litigation expenses, and costs, and the United States shall be liable for the foregoing the same as a private individual.

36.506   Alternative means of dispute resolution

Where appropriate and to the extent authorized by law, the use of alternative means of dispute resolution, including settlement negotiations, conciliation, facilitation, mediation, factfinding, minitrials, and arbitration, is encouraged to resolve disputes arising under the Act and this part.

36.507   Effect of unavailability of technical assistance

A public accommodation or other private entity shall not be excused from compliance with the requirements of this part because of any failure to receive technical assistance, including any failure in the development or dissemination of any technical assistance manual authorized by the Act.

36.508   Effective date

(a) *General.* Except as otherwise provided in this section and in this part, this part shall become effective on January 26, 1992.

(b) *Civil actions.* Except for any civil action brought for a violation of section 303 of the Act, no civil action shall be brought for any act or omission described in section 302 of the Act that occurs —

(1) Before July 26, 1992, against businesses with 25 or fewer employees and gross receipts of $1,000,000 or less.

(2) Before January 26, 1993, against businesses with 10 or fewer employees and gross receipts of $500,000 or less.

(c) Transportation services provided by public accommodations. Newly purchased or leased vehicles required to be accessible by § 36.310 must be readily accessible to and usable by individuals with disabilities, including individuals who use wheelchairs, if the solicitation for the vehicle is made after August 25, 1990.

36.509–36.599   [Reserved]

Subpart F   — Certification of State Laws or Local Building Codes

[Omitted in Statutory Supplement]

Chapter 5
CIVIL RIGHTS ACT OF 1964, TITLE VII

Civil Rights Act of 1964, Title VII,
42 U.S.C.

§ 1981a.   Damages in cases of intentional discrimination in employment

(a)   Right of recovery

(1)   Civil rights

In an action brought by a complaining party under section 706 or 717 of the Civil Rights Act of 1964 (42 U.S.C. 2000e-5) [42 U.S.C.A. § 2000e-5 or 42 U.S.C.A. § 2000e-16] against a respondent who engaged in unlawful intentional discrimination (not an employment practice that is unlawful because of its disparate impact) prohibited under section 703, 704, or 717 of the Act (42 U.S.C. 2000e-2 or 2000e-3) [42 U.S.C.A. § 2000e-2, 42 U.S.C.A. § 2000e-3, or 42 U.S.C.A. § 2000e-16], and provided that the complaining party cannot recover under section 1981 of this title, the complaining party may recover compensatory and punitive damages as allowed in subsection (b) of this section, in addition to any relief authorized by section 706(g) of the Civil Rights Act of 1964 [42 U.S.C.A. § 2000e-5(g)], from the respondent.

(2)   Disability

In an action brought by a complaining party under the powers, remedies, and procedures set forth in section 706 or 717 of the Civil Rights Act of 1964 [42 U.S.C.A. § 2000e-5 or 42 U.S.C.A. § 2000e-16] (as provided in section 107(a) of the Americans with Disabilities Act of 1990 (42 U.S.C. 12117(a)), and section 794a(a)(1) of Title 29, respectively) against a respondent who engaged in unlawful intentional discrimination (not an employment practice that is unlawful because of its disparate impact) under section 791 of Title 29 and the regulations implementing section 791 of Title 29, or who violated the requirements of section 791 of Title 29 or the regulations implementing section 791 of Title 29 concerning the provision of a reasonable accommodation, or section 102 of the Americans with Disabilities Act of 1990 (42 U.S.C. 12112), or committed a violation of section 102(b)(5) of the Act [42 U.S.C.A. § 12112(b)(5)], against an individual, the complaining party may recover compensatory and punitive damages as allowed in subsection (b) of this section, in addition to any relief authorized by section 706(g) of the Civil Rights Act of 1964 [42 U.S.C.A. § 2000e-5(g)], from the respondent.

(3)   Reasonable accommodation and good faith effort

In cases where a discriminatory practice involves the provision of a reasonable accommodation pursuant to section 102(b)(5) of the Americans with Disabilities Act of 1990 [42 U.S.C.A. § 12112(b)(5)] or regulations implementing section 791 of Title 29, damages may not be awarded under this section where the covered entity demonstrates good faith efforts, in consultation with the person with the disability who has informed the covered entity that accommodation is needed, to identify and make a reasonable accommodation that would provide such individual with an equally effective opportunity and would not cause an undue hardship on the operation of the business.

(b)   Compensatory and punitive damages

(1)   Determination of punitive damages

A complaining party may recover punitive damages under this section against a respondent (other than a government, government agency or political subdivision) if the complaining party demonstrates that the respondent engaged in a discriminatory practice or discriminatory practices with malice or with reckless indifference to the federally protected rights of an aggrieved individual.

(2)   Exclusions from compensatory damages

Compensatory damages awarded under this section shall not include backpay, interest on backpay, or any other type of relief authorized under section 706(g) of the Civil Rights Act of 1964 [42 U.S.C.A. § 2000e-5(g)].

(3)   Limitations

The sum of the amount of compensatory damages awarded under this section for future pecuniary losses, emotional pain, suffering, inconvenience, mental anguish, loss of enjoyment of life, and other nonpecuniary losses, and the amount of punitive damages awarded under this section, shall not exceed, for each complaining party —

(A) in the case of a respondent who has more than 14 and fewer than 101 employees in each of 20 or more calendar weeks in the current or preceding calendar year, $50,000;

(B) in the case of a respondent who has more than 100 and fewer than 201 employees in each of 20 or more calendar weeks in the current or preceding calendar year, $100,000; and

(C) in the case of a respondent who has more than 200 and fewer than 501 employees in each of 20 or more calendar weeks in the current or preceding calendar year, $200,000; and

(D) in the case of a respondent who has more than 500 employees in each of 20 or more calendar weeks in the current or preceding calendar year, $300,000.

(4)   Construction

Nothing in this section shall be construed to limit the scope of, or the relief available under, section 1981 of this title.

(c)   Jury trial

If a complaining party seeks compensatory or punitive damages under this section —

(1) any party may demand a trial by jury; and

(2) the court shall not inform the jury of the limitations described in subsection (b)(3) of this section.

(d)   Definitions

As used in this section:

(1)   Complaining party

The term "complaining party" means —

(A) in the case of a person seeking to bring an action under subsection (a)(1) of this section, the Equal Employment Opportunity Commission, the Attorney General, or a person who may bring an action or proceeding under title VII of the Civil Rights Act of 1964 (42 U.S.C. 2000e et seq.); or

(B) in the case of a person seeking to bring an action under subsection (a)(2) of this section, the Equal Employment Opportunity Commission, the Attorney General, a person who may bring an action or proceeding under section 794a(a)(1) of Title 29, or a person who may bring an action or proceeding under title I of the Americans with Disabilities Act of 1990 (42 U.S.C. 12101 et seq.).

(2)   Discriminatory practice

The term "discriminatory practice" means the discrimination described in paragraph (1), or the discrimination or the violation described in paragraph (2), of subsection (a) of this section.

2000e-5.   Enforcement provisions

(a) Power of Commission to prevent unlawful employment practices. The Commission is empowered, as hereinafter provided, to prevent any person from engaging in any unlawful employment practice as set forth in section 703 or 704 of this title [42 USCS §§ 2000e-2 or 2000e-3].

(b) Charges by persons aggrieved or member of Commission of unlawful employment practices by employers, etc.; filing; allegations; notice to respondent; contents of notice; investigation by Commission; contents of charges; prohibition on disclosure of charges; determination of reasonable cause; conference, conciliation, and persuasion for elimination of unlawful practices; prohibition on disclosure of informal endeavors to end unlawful practices; use of evidence in subsequent proceedings; penalties for disclosure of information; time for determination of reasonable cause. Whenever a charge is filed by or on behalf of a person claiming to be aggrieved, or by a member of the Commission, alleging that an employer, employment agency, labor organization, or joint labor-management committee controlling apprenticeship or other training or retraining, including on-the-job training programs, has engaged in an unlawful employment practice, the Commission shall serve a notice of the charge (including the date, place and circumstances of the alleged unlawful employment practice) on such employer, employment agency, labor organization, or joint labor-management committee (hereinafter referred to as the "respondent") within ten days, and shall make an investigation thereof. Charges shall be in writing under oath or affirmation and shall contain such information and be in such form as the Commission requires. Charges shall not be made public by the Commission. If the Commission determines after such investigation that there is not reasonable cause to believe that the charge is true, it shall dismiss the charge and promptly notify the person claiming to be aggrieved and the respondent of its action. In determining whether reasonable cause exists, the Commission shall accord substantial weight to final findings and orders made by State or local authorities in proceedings commenced under State or local law pursuant to the requirements of subsections (c) and (d). If the Commission determines after such investigation that there is reasonable cause to believe that the charge is true, the Commission shall endeavor to eliminate any such alleged unlawful employment practice by informal methods of conference, conciliation, and persuasion. Nothing said or done during and as a part of such informal endeavors may be made public by the Commission, its officers or employees, or used as evidence in a subsequent proceeding without the written consent of the persons concerned. Any person who makes public information in violation of this subsection shall be fined not more than $1,000 or imprisoned for not more than one year, or both. The Commission shall make its determination on reasonable cause as promptly as possible and, so far as practicable, not later than one hundred and twenty days from the filing of the charge or, where applicable under subsection (c) or (d), from the date upon which the Commission is authorized to take action with respect to the charge.

(c) State or local enforcement proceedings; notification of State or local authority; time for filing charges with Commission; commencement of proceedings. In the case of an alleged unlawful employment practice occurring in a State, or political subdivision of a State, which has a State or local law prohibiting the unlawful employment practice alleged and establishing or authorizing a State or local authority to grant or seek relief from such practice or to institute criminal proceedings with respect thereto upon receiving notice thereof, no charge may be filed under subsection (a) [(b)] by the person aggrieved before the expiration of sixty days after proceedings have been commenced under the State or local law, unless such proceedings have been earlier terminated, provided that such sixty-day period shall be extended to one hundred and twenty days during the first year after the effective date of such State or local law. If any requirement for the commencement of such proceedings is imposed by a State or local authority other than a requirement of the filing of a written and signed statement of the facts upon which the proceeding is based, the proceeding shall be deemed to have been commenced for the purposes of this subsection at the time such statement is sent by registered mail to the appropriate State or local authority.

(d) State or local enforcement proceedings; notification of State or local authority; time for action on charges by Commission. In the case of any charge filed by a member of the Commission alleging an unlawful employment practice occurring in a State or political subdivision of a State which has a State or local law prohibiting the practice alleged and establishing or authorizing a State or local authority to grant or seek relief from such practice or to institute criminal proceedings with respect thereto upon receiving notice thereof, the Commission shall, before taking any action with respect to such charge, notify the appropriate State or local officials and, upon request, afford them a reasonable time, but not less than sixty days (provided that such sixty-day period shall be extended to one hundred and twenty days during the first year after the effective day of such State or local law), unless a shorter period is requested, to act under such State or local law to remedy the practice alleged.

(e) Time for filing charges; time for service of notice of charge on respondent; filing of charge by Commission with State or local agency.

(1) A charge under this section shall be filed within one hundred and eighty

days after the alleged unlawful employment practice occurred and notice of the charge (including the date, place and circumstances of the alleged unlawful employment practice) shall be served upon the person against whom such charge is made within ten days thereafter, except that in a case of an unlawful employment practice with respect to which the person aggrieved has initially instituted proceedings with a State or local agency with authority to grant or seek relief from such practice or to institute criminal proceedings with respect thereto upon receiving notice thereof, such charge shall be filed by or on behalf of the person aggrieved within three hundred days after the alleged unlawful employment practice occurred, or within thirty days after receiving notice that the State or local agency has terminated the proceedings under the State or local law, whichever is earlier, and a copy of such charge shall be filed by the Commission with the State or local agency.

(2) For purposes of this section, an unlawful employment practice occurs, with respect to a seniority system that has been adopted for an intentionally discriminatory purpose in violation of this title [42 USCS §§ 2000e et seq.] (whether or not that discriminatory purpose is apparent on the face of the seniority provision), when the seniority system is adopted, when an individual becomes subject to the seniority system, or when a person aggrieved is injured by the application of the seniority system or provision of the system.

(3)

(A) For purposes of this section, an unlawful employment practice occurs, with respect to discrimination in compensation in violation of this title [42 USCS §§ 2000e et seq.], when a discriminatory compensation decision or other practice is adopted, when an individual becomes subject to a discriminatory compensation decision or other practice, or when an individual is affected by application of a discriminatory compensation decision or other practice, including each time wages, benefits, or other compensation is paid, resulting in whole or in part from such a decision or other practice.

(B) In addition to any relief authorized by section 1977A of the Revised Statutes (42 U.S.C. 1981a), liability may accrue and an aggrieved person may obtain relief as provided in subsection (g)(1), including recovery of back pay for up to two years preceding the filing of the charge, where the unlawful employment practices that have occurred during the charge filing period are similar or related to unlawful employment practices with regard to discrimination in compensation that occurred outside the time for filing a charge.

(f) Civil action by Commission, Attorney General, or person aggrieved; preconditions; procedure; appointment of attorney; payment of fees, costs, or security; intervention; stay of Federal proceedings; action for appropriate temporary or preliminary relief pending final disposition of charge; jurisdiction and venue of United States courts; designation of judge to hear and determine case; assignment of case for hearing; expedition of case; appointment of master.

(1) If within thirty days after a charge is filed with the Commission or within thirty days after expiration of any period of reference under subsection (c) or (d), the Commission has been unable to secure from the respondent a conciliation

agreement acceptable to the Commission, the Commission may bring a civil action against any respondent not a government, governmental agency, or political subdivision named in the charge. In the case of a respondent which is a government, governmental agency, or political subdivision, if the Commission has been unable to secure from the respondent a conciliation agreement acceptable to the Commission, the Commission shall take no further action and shall refer the case to the Attorney General who may bring a civil action against such respondent in the appropriate United States district court. The person or persons aggrieved shall have the right to intervene in a civil action brought by the Commission or the Attorney General in a case involving a government, governmental agency, or political subdivision. If a charge filed with the Commission pursuant to subsection (b) is dismissed by the Commission, or if within one hundred and eighty days from the filing of such charge or the expiration of any period of reference under subsection (c) or (d), whichever is later, the Commission has not filed a civil action under this section or the Attorney General has not filed a civil action in a case involving a government, governmental agency, or political subdivision, or the Commission has not entered into a conciliation agreement to which the person aggrieved is a party, the Commission, or the Attorney General in a case involving a government, governmental agency, or political subdivision, shall so notify the person aggrieved and within ninety days after the giving of such notice a civil action may be brought against the respondent named in the charge (A) by the person claiming to be aggrieved or (B) if such charge was filed by a member of the Commission, by any person whom the charge alleges was aggrieved by the alleged unlawful employment practice. Upon application by the complainant and in such circumstances as the court may deem just, the court may appoint an attorney for such complainant and may authorize the commencement of the action without the payment of fees, costs, or security. Upon timely application, the court may, in its discretion, permit the Commission, or the Attorney General in a case involving a government, governmental agency, or political subdivision, to intervene in such civil action upon certification that the case is of general public importance. Upon request, the court may, in its discretion, stay further proceedings for not more than sixty days pending the termination of State or local proceedings described in subsections (c) or (d) of this section or further efforts of the Commission to obtain voluntary compliance.

(2) Whenever a charge is filed with the Commission and the Commission concludes on the basis of a preliminary investigation, that prompt judicial action is necessary to carry out the purposes of this Act [title], the Commission, or the Attorney General in a case involving a government, governmental agency, or political subdivision, may bring an action for appropriate temporary or preliminary relief pending final disposition of such charge. Any temporary restraining order or other order granting preliminary or temporary relief shall be issued in accordance with rule 65 of the Federal Rules of Civil Procedure. It shall be the duty of a court having jurisdiction over proceedings under this section to assign cases for hearing at the earliest practicable date and to cause such cases to be in every way expedited.

(3) Each United States district court and each United States court of a place

subject to the jurisdiction of the United States shall have jurisdiction of actions brought under this title [42 USCS §§ 2000e et seq.]. Such an action may be brought in any judicial district in the State in which the unlawful employment practice is alleged to have been committed, in the judicial district in which the employment records relevant to such practice are maintained and administered, or in the judicial district in which the aggrieved person would have worked but for the alleged unlawful employment practice, but if the respondent is not found within any such district, such an action may be brought within the judicial district in which the respondent has his principal office. For purposes of sections 1404 and 1406 of title 28 of the United States Code, the judicial district in which the respondent has his principal office shall in all cases be considered a district in which the action might have been brought.

(4) It shall be the duty of the chief judge of the district (or in his absence, the acting chief judge) in which the case is pending immediately to designate a judge in such district to hear and determine the case. In the event that no judge in the district is available to hear and determine the case, the chief judge of the district, or the acting chief judge, as the case may be, shall certify this fact to the chief judge of the circuit (or in his absence, the acting chief judge) who shall then designate a district or circuit judge of the circuit to hear and determine the case.

(5) It shall be the duty of the judge designated pursuant to this subsection to assign the case for hearing at the earliest practicable date and to cause the case to be in every way expedited. If such judge has not scheduled the case for trial within one hundred and twenty days after issue has been joined, that judge may appoint a master pursuant to rule 53 of the Federal Rules of Civil Procedure.

(g) Injunctions; affirmative action; equitable relief; accrual of back pay; reduction of back pay; limitations on judicial orders.

(1) If the court finds that the respondent has intentionally engaged in or is intentionally engaging in an unlawful employment practice charged in the complaint, the court may enjoin the respondent from engaging in such unlawful employment practice, and order such affirmative action as may be appropriate, which may include, but is not limited to, reinstatement or hiring of employees, with or without back pay (payable by the employer, employment agency, or labor organization, as the case may be, responsible for the unlawful employment practice), or any other equitable relief as the court deems appropriate. Back pay liability shall not accrue from a date more than two years prior to the filing of a charge with the Commission. Interim earnings or amounts earnable with reasonable diligence by the person or persons discriminated against shall operate to reduce the back pay otherwise allowable.

(2)

(A) No order of the court shall require the admission or reinstatement of an individual as a member of a union, or the hiring, reinstatement, or promotion of an individual as an employee, or the payment to him of any back pay, if such individual was refused admission, suspended, or expelled, or was refused employment or advancement or was suspended or discharged for any reason other than discrimination on account of race, color, religion, sex, or national origin or in violation of section 704(a) [42 USCS § 2000e-3(a)].

(B) On a claim in which an individual proves a violation under section 703(m) [42 USCS § 2000e-2(m)] and a respondent demonstrates that the respondent would have taken the same action in the absence of the impermissible motivating factor, the court —

(i) may grant declaratory relief, injunctive relief (except as provided in clause (ii)), and attorney's fees and costs demonstrated to be directly attributable only to the pursuit of a claim under section 703(m) § 42 USCS § 2000e-2(m)]; and

(ii) shall not award damages or issue an order requiring any admission, reinstatement, hiring, promotion, or payment, described in subparagraph (A).

(h) Provisions of 29 USCS §§ 101 et seq. not applicable to civil actions for prevention of unlawful practices. The provisions of the Act entitled "An Act to amend the Judicial Code and to define and limit the jurisdiction of courts sitting in equity, and for other purposes," approved March 23, 1932 (29 U. S. C. 101-115), shall not apply with respect to civil actions brought under this section.

(i) Proceedings by Commission to compel compliance with judicial orders. In any case in which an employer, employment agency, or labor organization fails to comply with an order of a court issued in a civil action brought under this section, the Commission may commence proceedings to compel compliance with such order.

(j) Appeals. Any civil action brought under this section and any proceedings brought under subsection (i) shall be subject to appeal as provided in sections 1291 and 1292, title 28, United States Code.

(k) Attorney's fee, liability of Commission and United States for costs. In any action or proceeding under this title [42 USCS §§ 2000e et seq.] the court, in its discretion, may allow the prevailing party, other than the Commission or the United States, a reasonable attorney's fee (including expert fees) as part of the costs, and the Commission and the United States shall be liable for costs the same as a private person.

Chapter 6
FAIR HOUSING ACT

<hr>

Fair Housing Act
42 U.S.C. § 3601 et seq.
(sections relating to disability discrimination)

Editor's Note: The term "handicap" is used instead of the preferred term of "disability" in most federal statutes and regulations.

3601 Declaration of policy

It is the policy of the United States to provide, within constitutional limitations, for fair housing throughout the United States.

3602 Definitions

As used in this title —

(a) "Secretary" means the Secretary of Housing and Urban Development.

(b) "Dwelling" means any building, structure, or portion thereof which is occupied as, or designed or intended for occupancy as, a residence by one or more families, and any vacant land which is offered for sale or lease for the construction or location thereon of any such building, structure, or portion thereof.

(c) "Family" includes a single individual.

(d) "Person" includes one or more individuals, corporations, partnerships, associations, labor organizations, legal representatives, mutual companies, joint-stock companies, trusts, unincorporated organizations, trustees, trustees in cases under title 11 of the United States Code [11 USCS §§ 101 et seq.], receivers, and fiduciaries.

(e) "To rent" includes to lease, to sublease, to let and otherwise to grant for a consideration the right to occupy premises not owned by the occupant.

(f) "Discriminatory housing practice" means an act that is unlawful under section 804, 805, 806, or 818 [42 USCS §§ 3604, 3605, 3606, or 3617].

(g) "State" means any of the several States, the District of Columbia, the Commonwealth of Puerto Rico, or any of the territories and possessions of the United States.

(h) "Handicap" means, with respect to a person —

(1) a physical or mental impairment which substantially limits one or more of such person's major life activities,

(2) a record of having such an impairment, or

(3) being regarded as having such an impairment,

but such term does not include current, illegal use of or addiction to a controlled substance (as defined in section 102 of the Controlled Substances Act (21 U.S.C. 802)).

(i) "Aggrieved person" includes any person who —

(1) claims to have been injured by a discriminatory housing practice; or

(2) believes that such person will be injured by a discriminatory housing practice that is about to occur.

(j) "Complainant" means the person (including the Secretary) who files a complaint under section 810 [42 USCS § 3610].

(k) "Familial status" means one or more individuals (who have not attained the age of 18 years) being domiciled with —

(1) a parent or another person having legal custody of such individual or individuals; or

(2)   the designee of such parent or other person having such custody, with the written permission of such parent or other person.

The protections afforded against discrimination on the basis of familial status shall apply to any person who is pregnant or is in the process of securing legal custody of any individual who has not attained the age of 18 years.

(l) "Conciliation" means the attempted resolution of issues raised by a complaint, or by the investigation of such complaint, through informal negotiations involving the aggrieved person, the respondent, and the Secretary.

(m) "Conciliation agreement" means a written agreement setting forth the resolution of the issues in conciliation.

(n) "Respondent" means —

(1) the person or other entity accused in a complaint of an unfair housing practice; and

(2) any other person or entity identified in the course of investigation and notified as required with respect to respondents so identified under section 810(a) [42 USCS § 3610(a)].

(o) "Prevailing party" has the same meaning as such term has in section 722 of the Revised Statutes of the United States (42 U.S.C. 1988).

3603   Effective dates of certain prohibitions [Omitted from Statutory Supplement]

3604   Discrimination in sale or rental of housing and other prohibited practices

As made applicable by section 803 of this title and except as exempted by sections 803(b) and 807 of this title, it shall be unlawful —

(a) To refuse to sell or rent after the making of a bona fide offer, or to refuse to negotiate for the sale or rental of, or otherwise make unavailable or deny, a dwelling to any person because of race, color, religion, sex, familial status, or national origin.

(b) To discriminate against any person in the terms, conditions, or privileges of sale or rental of a dwelling, or in the provision of services or facilities in connection therewith, because of race, color, religion, sex, familial status, or national origin.

(c) To make, print, or publish, or cause to be made, printed, or published any notice, statement, or advertisement, with respect to the sale or rental of a dwelling that indicates any preference, limitation, or discrimination based on race, color, religion, sex, handicap, familial status, or national origin, or an intention to make any such preference, limitation, or discrimination.

(d) To represent to any person because of race, color, religion, sex, handicap, familial status, or national origin that any dwelling is not available for inspection, sale, or rental when such dwelling is in fact so available.

(e) For profit, to induce or attempt to induce any person to sell or rent any dwelling by representations regarding the entry or prospective entry into the neighborhood of a person or persons of a particular race, color, religion, sex, handicap, familial status, or national origin.

(f)

(1) To discriminate in the sale or rental, or to otherwise make unavailable or deny, a dwelling to any buyer or renter because of a handicap of —

    (A) that buyer or renter,

    (B) a person residing in or intending to reside in that dwelling after it is so sold, rented, or made available; or

    (C) any person associated with that buyer or renter.

(2) To discriminate against any person in the terms, conditions, or privileges of sale or rental of a dwelling, or in the provision of services or facilities in connection with such dwelling, because of a handicap of —

    (A) that person; or

    (B) a person residing in or intending to reside in that dwelling after it is so sold, rented, or made available; or

    (C) any person associated with that person.

(3) For purposes of this subsection, discrimination includes —

    (A) a refusal to permit, at the expense of the handicapped person, reasonable modifications of existing premises occupied or to be occupied by such person if such modifications may be necessary to afford such person full enjoyment of the premises, except that, in the case of a rental, the landlord may where it is reasonable to do so condition permission for a modification on the renter agreeing to restore the interior of the premises to the condition that existed before the modification, reasonable wear and tear excepted.

    (B) a refusal to make reasonable accommodations in rules, policies, practices, or services, when such accommodations may be necessary to afford such person equal opportunity to use and enjoy a dwelling; or

(C) in connection with the design and construction of covered multifamily dwellings for first occupancy after the date that is 30 months after the date of enactment of the Fair Housing Amendments Act of 1988, a failure to design and construct those dwelling in such a manner that —

(i) the public use and common use portions of such dwellings are readily accessible to and usable by handicapped persons;

(ii) all the doors designed to allow passage into and within all premises within such dwellings are sufficiently wide to allow passage by handicapped persons in wheelchairs; and

(iii) all premises within such dwellings contain the following features of adaptive design:

(I) an accessible route into and through the dwelling;

(II) light switches, electrical outlets, thermostats, and other environmental controls in accessible locations;

(III) reinforcements in bathroom walls to allow later installation of grab bars; and

(IV) usable kitchens and bathrooms such that an individual in a wheelchair can maneuver about the space.

(4) Compliance with the appropriate requirements of the American National Standard for buildings and facilities providing accessibility and usability for physically handicapped people (commonly cited as "ANSI A117.1") suffices to satisfy the requirements of paragraph (3)(C)(iii).

(5)

(A) If a State or unit of general local government has incorporated into its laws the requirements set forth in paragraph (3)(C), compliance with such laws shall be deemed to satisfy the requirements of that paragraph.

(B) A State or unit of general local government may review and approve newly constructed covered multifamily dwellings for the purpose of making determinations as to whether the design and construction requirements of paragraph (3)(C) are met.

(C) The Secretary shall encourage, but may not require, States and units of local government to include in their existing procedures for the review and approval of newly constructed covered multifamily dwellings, determinations as to whether the design and construction of such dwellings are consistent with paragraph (3)(C), and shall provide technical assistance to States and units of local government and other persons to implement the requirements of paragraph (3)(C).

(D) Nothing in this title shall be construed to require the Secretary to review or approve the plans, designs or construction of all covered multifamily dwellings, to determine whether the design and construction of such dwellings are consistent with the requirements of paragraph 3(C).

(6)

(A) Nothing in paragraph (5) shall be construed to affect the authority and responsibility of the Secretary or a State or local public agency certified pursuant to section 810(f)(3) of this Act to receive and process complaints or otherwise engage in enforcement activities under this title.

(B) Determinations by a State or a unit of general local government under paragraphs (5)(A) and (B) shall not be conclusive in enforcement proceedings under this title.

(7) As used in this subsection, the term "covered multifamily dwellings" means —

(A) buildings consisting of 4 or more units if such buildings have one or more elevators; and

(B) ground floor units in other buildings consisting of 4 or more units.

(8) Nothing in this title shall be construed to invalidate or limit any law of a State or political subdivision of a State, or other jurisdiction in which this title shall be effective, that requires dwellings to be designed and constructed in a manner that affords handicapped persons greater access than is required by this title.

(9) Nothing in this subsection requires that a dwelling be made available to an individual whose tenancy would constitute a direct threat to the health or safety of other individuals or whose tenancy would result in substantial physical damage to the property of others.

3605 Discrimination in Residential Real Estate-Related Transactions

(a) In General. — It shall be unlawful for any person or other entity whose business includes engaging in residential real estate-related transactions to discriminate against any person in making available such a transaction, or in the terms or conditions of such a transaction, because of race, color, religion, sex, handicap, familial status, or national origin.

(b) Definition. — As used in this section, the term "residential real estate-related transaction" means any of the following:

(1) The making or purchasing of loans or providing other financial assistance —

(A) for purchasing, constructing, improving, repairing, or maintaining a dwelling; or

(B) secured by residential real estate.

(2) The selling, brokering, or appraising of residential real property.

(c) Appraisal Exemption. — Nothing in this title prohibits a person engaged in the business of furnishing appraisals of real property to take into consideration factors other than race, color, religion, national origin, sex, handicap, or familial status.

3606   Discrimination in provision of brokerage services

After December 31, 1968, it shall be unlawful to deny any person access to or membership or participation in any multiple-listing service, real estate brokers' organization or other service, organization, or facility relating to the business of selling or renting dwellings, or to discriminate against him in the terms or conditions of such access, membership, or participation, on account of race, color, religion, sex, handicap, familial status, or national origin.

3607   Religious organization or private club exemption

(a) Nothing in this subchapter shall prohibit a religious organization, association, or society, or any nonprofit institution or organization operated, supervised or controlled by or in conjunction with a religious organization, association, or society, from limiting the sale, rental or occupancy of dwellings which it owns or operates for other than a commercial purpose to persons of the same religion, or from giving preference to such persons, unless membership in such religion is restricted on account of race, color, or national origin. Nor shall anything in this subchapter prohibit a private club not in fact open to the public, which as an incident to its primary purpose or purposes provides lodgings which it owns or operates for other than a commercial purpose, from limiting the rental or occupancy of such lodgings to its members or from giving preference to its members.

(b)

(1) Nothing in this title limits the applicability of any reasonable local, State, or Federal restrictions regarding the maximum number of occupants permitted to occupy a dwelling. Nor does any provision in this title regarding familial status apply with respect to housing for older persons.

(2) As used in this section "housing for older persons" means housing —

(A) provided under any State or Federal program that the Secretary determines is specifically designed and operated to assist elderly persons (as defined in the State or Federal program); or

(B) intended for, and solely occupied by, persons 62 years of age or older; or

(C) intended and operated for occupancy by persons 55 years of age or older, and —

(i) at least 80 percent of the occupied units are occupied by at least one person who is 55 years of age or older;

(ii) the housing facility or community publishes and adheres to policies and procedures that demonstrate the intent required under this subparagraph; and

(iii) the housing facility or community complies with rules issued by the Secretary for verification of occupancy, which shall —

(I) provide for verification by reliable surveys and affidavits; and

(II) include examples of the types of policies and procedures relevant to a determination of compliance with the requirement of clause (ii). Such surveys and affidavits shall be admissible in administrative and judicial proceedings for the purposes of such verification.

(3) Housing shall not fail to meet the requirements for housing for older persons by reason of:

(A) persons residing in such housing as of the date of enactment of this Act who do not meet the age requirements of subsections (2)(B) or (C): **Provided,** That new occupants of such housing meet the age requirements of sections (2)(B) or (C); or

(B) unoccupied units: **Provided,** That such units are reserved for occupancy by persons who meet the age requirements of subsections (2)(B) or (C).

(4) Nothing in this title prohibits conduct against a person because such person has been convicted by any court of competent jurisdiction of the illegal manufacture or distribution of a controlled substance as defined in section 102 of the Controlled Substances Act (21 U.S.C. 802).

(5)

(A) A person shall not be held personally liable for monetary damages for a violation of this title if such person reasonably relied, in good faith, on the application of the exemption under this subsection relating to housing for older persons.

(B) For the purposes of this paragraph, a person may only show good faith reliance on the application of the exemption by showing that —

(i) such person has no actual knowledge that the facility or community is not, or will not be, eligible for such exemption; and

(ii) the facility or community has stated formally, in writing, that the facility or community complies with the requirements for such exemption.

3608 Administration [Omitted from the Statutory Supplement]

3610 Administrative Enforcement; Preliminary Matters

(a) Complaints and Answers. —

(1)

(A)

(i) An aggrieved person may, not later than one year after an alleged discriminatory housing practice has occurred or terminated, file a complaint with the Secretary alleging such discriminatory housing practice. The Secretary, on the Secretary's own initiative, may also file such a complaint.

(ii) Such complaints shall be in writing and shall contain such information and be in such form as the Secretary requires.

(iii) The Secretary may also investigate housing practices to determine whether a complaint should be brought under this section.

(B) Upon the filing of such a complaint —

(i) the Secretary shall serve notice upon the aggrieved person acknowledging such filing and advising the aggrieved person of the time limits and choice of forums provided under this title;

(ii) the Secretary shall, not later than 10 days after such filing or the identification of an additional respondent under paragraph (2), serve on the respondent a notice identifying the alleged discriminatory housing practice and advising such respondent of the procedural rights and obligations of respondents under this title, together with a copy of the original complaint;

(iii) each respondent may file, not later than 10 days after receipt of notice from the Secretary, an answer to such complaint; and

(iv) the Secretary shall make an investigation of the alleged discriminatory housing practice and complete such investigation within 100 days after the filing of the complaint (or, when the Secretary takes further action under subsection (f)(2) with respect to a complaint, within 100 days after the commencement of such further action), unless it is impracticable to do so.

(C) If the Secretary is unable to complete the investigation within 100 days after the filing of the complaint (or, when the Secretary takes further action under subsection (f)(2) with respect to a complaint, within 100 days after the commencement of such further action), the Secretary shall notify the complainant and respondent in writing of the reasons for not doing so.

(D) Complaints and answers shall be under oath or affirmation, and may be reasonably and fairly amended at any time.

(2)

(A) A person who is not named as a respondent in a complaint, but who is identified as a respondent in the course of investigation, may be joined as an additional or substitute respondent upon written notice, under paragraph (1), to such person, from the Secretary.

(B) Such notice, in addition to meeting the requirements of paragraph (1), shall explain the basis for the Secretary's belief that the person to whom the notice is addressed is properly joined as a respondent.

(b) Investigative Report and Conciliation. —

(1) During the period beginning with the filing of such complaint and ending with the filing of a charge or a dismissal by the Secretary, the Secretary shall, to the extent feasible, engage in conciliation with respect to such complaint.

(2) A conciliation agreement arising out of such conciliation shall be an agreement between the respondent and the complainant, and shall be subject to approval by the Secretary.

(3) A conciliation agreement may provide for binding arbitration of the dispute arising from the complaint. Any such arbitration that results from a conciliation agreement may award appropriate relief, including monetary relief.

(4) Each conciliation agreement shall be made public unless the complainant and respondent otherwise agree and the Secretary determines that disclosure is

not required to further the purposes of this title.

(5)

(A) At the end of each investigation under this section, the Secretary shall prepare a final investigative report containing —

(i) the names and dates of contacts with witnesses;

(ii) a summary and the dates of correspondence and other contacts with the aggrieved person and the respondent;

(iii) a summary description of other pertinent records;

(iv) a summary of witness statements; and

(v) answers to interrogatories.

(B) A final report under this paragraph may be amended if additional evidence is later discovered.

(c) Failure to Comply With Conciliation Agreement. — Whenever the Secretary has reasonable cause to believe that a respondent has breached a conciliation agreement, the Secretary shall refer the matter to the Attorney General with a recommendation that a civil action be filed under section 814 for the enforcement of such agreement.

(d) Prohibitions and Requirements With Respect to Disclosure of Information. —

(1) Nothing said or done in the course of conciliation under this title may be made public or used as evidence in a subsequent proceeding under this title without the written consent of the persons concerned.

(2) Notwithstanding paragraph (1), the Secretary shall make available to the aggrieved person and the respondent, at any time, upon request following completion of the Secretary's investigation, information derived from an investigation and any final investigative report relating to that investigation.

(e) Prompt Judicial Action. —

(1) If the Secretary concludes at any time following the filing of a complaint that prompt judicial action is necessary to carry out the purposes of this title, the Secretary may authorize a civil action for appropriate temporary or preliminary relief pending final disposition of the complaint under this section. Upon receipt of such authorization, the Attorney General shall promptly commence and maintain such an action. Any temporary restraining order or other order granting preliminary or temporary relief shall be issued in accordance with the Federal Rules of Civil Procedure. The commencement of a civil action under this subsection does not affect the initiation or continuation of administrative proceedings under this section and section 812 of this title.

(2) Whenever the Secretary has reason to believe that a basis may exist for the commencement of proceedings against any respondent under section 814(a) and 814(c) or for proceedings by any governmental licensing or supervisory authorities, the Secretary shall transmit the information upon which such belief is based to the Attorney General, or to such authorities, as the case may be.

(f) Referral for State or Local Proceedings. —

(1) Whenever a complaint alleges a discriminatory housing practice —

(A) within the jurisdiction of a State or local public agency; and

(B) as to which such agency has been certified by the Secretary under this subsection; the Secretary shall refer such complaint to that certified agency before taking any action with respect to such complaint.

(2) Except with the consent of such certified agency, the Secretary, after that referral is made, shall take no further action with respect to such complaint unless —

(A) the certified agency has failed to commence proceedings with respect to the complaint before the end of the 30th day after the date of such referral;

(B) the certified agency, having so commenced such proceedings, fails to carry forward such proceedings with reasonable promptness; or

(C) the Secretary determines that the certified agency no longer qualifies for certification under this subsection with respect to the relevant jurisdiction.

(3)

(A) The Secretary may certify an agency under this subsection only if the Secretary determines that —

(i) the substantive rights protected by such agency in the jurisdiction with respect to which certification is to be made;

(ii) the procedures followed by such agency;

(iii) the remedies available to such agency; and

(iv)   the availability of judicial review of such agency's action;

are substantially equivalent to those created by and under this title.

(B) Before making such certification, the Secretary shall take into account the current practices and past performance, if any, of such agency.

(4) During the period which begins on the date of the enactment of the Fair Housing Amendments Act of 1988 and ends 40 months after such date, each agency certified (including an agency certified for interim referrals pursuant to 24 CFR 115.11, unless such agency is subsequently denied recognition under 24 CFR 115.7) for the purposes of this title on the day before such date shall for the purposes of this subsection be considered certified under this subsection with respect to those matters for which such agency was certified on that date. If the Secretary determines in an individual case that an agency has not been able to meet the certification requirements within this 40-month period due to exceptional circumstances, such as the infrequency of legislative sessions in that jurisdiction, the Secretary may extend such period by not more than 8 months.

(5) Not less frequently than every 5 years, the Secretary shall determine whether each agency certified under this subsection continues to qualify for certification. The Secretary shall take appropriate action with respect to any

agency not so qualifying.

(g) Reasonable Cause Determination and Effect. —

(1) The Secretary shall, within 100 days after the filing of the complaint (or, when the Secretary takes further action under subsection (f)(2) with respect to a complaint, within 100 days after the commencement of such further action), determine based on the facts whether reasonable cause exists to believe that a discriminatory housing practice has occurred or is about to occur, unless it is impracticable to do so, or unless the Secretary has approved a conciliation agreement with respect to the complaint. If the Secretary is unable to make the determination within 100 days after the filing of the complaint (or, when the Secretary takes further action under subsection (f)(2) with respect to a complaint, within 100 days after the commencement of such further action), the Secretary shall notify the complainant and respondent in writing of the reasons for not doing so.

(2)

(A) If the Secretary determines that reasonable cause exists to believe that a discriminatory housing practice has occurred or is about to occur, the Secretary shall, except as provided in subparagraph (C), immediately issue a charge on behalf of the aggrieved person, for further proceedings under section 812.

(B) Such charge —

(i) shall consist of a short and plain statement of the facts upon which the Secretary has found reasonable cause to believe that a discriminatory housing practice has occurred or is about to occur;

(ii) shall be based on the final investigative report; and

(iii) need not be limited to the facts or grounds alleged in the complaint filed under section 810(a).

(C) If the Secretary determines that the matter involves the legality of any State or local zoning or other land use law or ordinance, the Secretary shall immediately refer the matter to the Attorney General for appropriate action under section 814, instead of issuing such charge.

(3) If the Secretary determines that no reasonable cause exists to believe that a discriminatory housing practice has occurred or is about to occur, the Secretary shall promptly dismiss the complaint. The Secretary shall make public disclosure of each such dismissal.

(4) The Secretary may not issue a charge under this section regarding an alleged discriminatory housing practice after the beginning of the trial of a civil action commenced by the aggrieved party under an Act of Congress or a State law, seeking relief with respect to that discriminatory housing practice.

(h) Service of Copies of Charge. — After the Secretary issues a charge under this section, the Secretary shall cause a copy thereof, together with information as to how to make an election under section 812(a) and the effect of such an election, to be served —

(1) on each respondent named in such charge, together with a notice of opportunity for a hearing at a time and place specified in the notice, unless that election is made; and

(2) on each aggrieved person on whose behalf the complaint was filed.

3611 Subpoenas; Giving of Evidence [Omitted from the Statutory Supplement.]

3612 Enforcement by Secretary [Omitted from the Statutory Supplement]

3613 Enforcement by Private Persons

(a) Civil Action. —

(1)

(A) An aggrieved person may commence a civil action in an appropriate United States district court or State court not later than 2 years after the occurrence or the termination of an alleged discriminatory housing practice, or the breach of a conciliation agreement entered into under this title, whichever occurs last, to obtain appropriate relief with respect to such discriminatory housing practice or breach.

(B) The computation of such 2-year period shall not include any time during which an administrative proceeding under this title was pending with respect to a complaint or charge under this title based upon such discriminatory housing practice. This subparagraph does not apply to actions arising from a breach of a conciliation agreement.

(2) An aggrieved person may commence a civil action under this subsection whether or not a complaint has been filed under section 810(a) and without regard to the status of any such complaint, but if the Secretary or a State or local agency has obtained a conciliation agreement with the consent of an aggrieved person, no action may be filed under this subsection by such aggrieved person with respect to the alleged discriminatory housing practice which forms the basis for such complaint except for the purpose of enforcing the terms of such an agreement.

(3) An aggrieved person may not commence a civil action under this subsection with respect to an alleged discriminatory housing practice which forms the basis of a charge issued by the Secretary if an administrative law judge has commenced a hearing on the record under this title with respect to such charge.

(b) Appointment of Attorney by Court. — Upon application by a person alleging a discriminatory housing practice or a person against whom such a practice is alleged, the court may —

(1) appoint an attorney for such person; or

(2) authorize the commencement or continuation of a civil action under subsection (a) without the payment of fees, costs, or security, if in the opinion of the court such person is financially unable to bear the costs of such action.

(c) Relief Which May Be Granted. —

(1) In a civil action under subsection (a), if the court finds that a discriminatory housing practice has occurred or is about to occur, the court may award to the plaintiff actual and punitive damages, and subject to subsection (d), may grant as relief, as the court deems appropriate, any permanent or temporary injunction, temporary restraining order, or other order (including an order enjoining the defendant from engaging in such practice or ordering such affirmative action as may be appropriate).

(2) In a civil action under subsection (a), the court, in its discretion, may allow the prevailing party, other than the United States, a reasonable attorney's fee and costs. The United States shall be liable for such fees and costs to the same extent as a private person.

(d) Effect on Certain Sales, Encumbrances, and Rentals. — Relief granted under this section shall not affect any contract, sale, encumbrance, or lease consummated before the granting of such relief and involving a bona fide purchaser, encumbrancer, or tenant, without actual notice of the filing of a complaint with the Secretary or civil action under this title.

(e) Intervention by Attorney General. — Upon timely application, the Attorney General may intervene in such civil action, if the Attorney General certifies that the case is of general public importance. Upon such intervention the Attorney General may obtain such relief as would be available to the Attorney General under section 814(e) in a civil action to which such section applies.

3614 Enforcement by the Attorney General [Omitted from Statutory Supplement]

3614-1 Incentives for Self-Testing and Self-Correction [Omitted from Statutory Supplement]

3614a Rules to Implement Title [Omitted from Statutory Supplement]

3615 Effect on State laws

Nothing in this subchapter shall be constructed to invalidate or limit any law of a State or political subdivision of a State, or of any other jurisdiction in which this subchapter shall be effective, that grants, guarantees, or protects the same rights as are granted by this subchapter; but any law of a State, a political subdivision, or other such jurisdiction that purports to require or permit any action that would be a discriminatory housing practice under this subchapter shall to that extent be invalid.

3616 Cooperation with State and local agencies administering fair housing laws; utilization of services and personnel; reimbursement; written agreements; publication in Federal Register [Omitted from Statutory Supplement]

3617 Interference, coercion, or intimidation; enforcement by civil action [Omitted from Statutory Supplement]

Chapter 7
FAIR HOUSING ACT REGULATIONS

Fair Housing Act Regulations
24 C.F.R. § 100.200 et seq.
(sections relating to disability discrimination)

Editor's Note: The term "handicap" is used instead of the preferred term of "disability" in most federal statutes and regulations.

100.200 Purpose

The purpose of this subpart is to effectuate sections 6 (a) and (b) and 15 of the Fair Housing Amendments Act of 1988.

100.201 Definitions

As used in this subpart:

Accessible, when used with respect to the public and common use areas of a building containing covered multifamily dwellings, means that the public or common use areas of the building can be approached, entered, and used by individuals with physical disabilities. The phrase "readily accessible to and usable by" is synonymous with accessible. A public or common use area that complies with the appropriate requirements of ICC/ANSI A117.1-2003 (incorporated by reference at § 100.201a), ICC/ANSI A117.1-1998 (incorporated by reference at § 100.201a), CABO/ANSI A117.1-1992 (incorporated by reference at § 100.201a), ANSI A117.1-1986 (incorporated by reference at § 100.201a), or a comparable standard is deemed "accessible" within the meaning of this paragraph.

Accessible route means a continuous unobstructed path connecting accessible elements and spaces in a building or within a site that can be negotiated by a person with a severe disability using a wheelchair and that is also safe for and usable by people with other disabilities. Interior accessible routes may include corridors, floors, ramps, elevators, and lifts. Exterior accessible routes may include parking access aisles, curb ramps, walks, ramps, and lifts. A route that complies with the appropriate requirements of ICC/ANSI A117.1-2003 (incorporated by reference at § 100.201a), ICC/ANSI A117.1-1998 (incorporated by reference at § 100.201a), CABO/ANSI A117.1-1992, ANSI A117.1-1986 (incorporated by reference at § 100.201a), or a comparable standard is an "accessible route."

Building means a structure, facility or portion thereof that contains or serves one or more dwelling units.

Building entrance on an accessible route means an accessible entrance to a building that is connected by an accessible route to public transportation stops, to accessible parking and passenger loading zones, or to public streets or sidewalks, if available. A building entrance that complies with ICC/ANSI A117.1-2003 (incorporated by reference at § 100.201a), ICC/ANSI A117.1-1998 (incorporated by reference at § 100.201a), CABO/ANSI A117.1-1992 (incorporated by reference at § 100.201a), ANSI A117.1-1986 (incorporated by reference at § 100.201a), or a comparable standard complies with the requirements of this paragraph.

Common use areas means rooms, spaces or elements inside or outside of a building that are made available for the use of residents of a building or the guests thereof. These areas include hallways, lounges, lobbies, laundry rooms, refuse rooms, mail rooms, recreational areas and passageways among and between buildings.

Controlled substance means any drug or other substance, or immediate precursor included in the definition in section 102 of the Controlled Substances Act (21 U.S.C. 802).

Covered multifamily dwellings means buildings consisting of 4 or more dwelling units if such buildings have one or more elevators; and ground floor dwelling units in other buildings consisting of 4 or more dwelling units.

Dwelling unit means a single unit of residence for a family or one or more persons. Examples of dwelling units include: a single family home; an apartment unit within an apartment building; and in other types of dwellings in which sleeping accommodations are provided but toileting or cooking facilities are shared by occupants of more than one room or portion of the dwelling, rooms in which people sleep. Examples of the latter include dormitory rooms and sleeping accommodations in shelters intended for occupancy as a residence for homeless persons.

Entrance means any access point to a building or portion of a building used by residents for the purpose of entering.

Exterior means all areas of the premises outside of an individual dwelling unit.

First occupancy means a building that has never before been used for any purpose.

Ground floor means a floor of a building with a building entrance on an accessible route. A building may have more than one ground floor.

Handicap means, with respect to a person, a physical or mental impairment which substantially limits one or more major life activities; a record of such an impairment; or being regarded as having such an impairment. This term does not include current, illegal use of or addiction to a controlled substance. For purposes of this part, an individual shall not be considered to have a handicap solely because that individual is a transvestite. As used in this definition:

(a) Physical or mental impairment includes:

(1) Any physiological disorder or condition, cosmetic disfigurement, or anatomical loss affecting one or more of the following body systems: Neurological; musculoskeletal; special sense organs; respiratory, including speech organs; cardiovascular; reproductive; disgestive; genito-urinary; hemic and lymphatic; skin; and endocrine; or

(2) Any mental or psychological disorder, such as mental retardation, organic brain syndrome, emotional or mental illness, and specific learning disabilities. The term physical or mental impairment includes, but is not limited to, such diseases and conditions as orthopedic, visual, speech and hearing impairments, cerebral palsy, autism, epilepsy, muscular dystrophy, multiple sclerosis, cancer, heart disease, diabetes, Human Immunodeficiency Virus infection, mental retardation, emotional illness, drug addiction (other

than addiction caused by current, illegal use of a controlled substance) and alcoholism.

(b) Major life activities means functions such as caring for one's self, performing manual tasks, walking, seeing, hearing, speaking, breathing, learning and working.

(c) Has a record of such an impairment means has a history of, or has been misclassified as having, a mental or physical impairment that substantially limits one or more major life activities.

(d) Is regarded as having an impairment means:

(1) Has a physical or mental impairment that does not substantially limit one or more major life activities but that is treated by another person as constituting such a limitation;

(2) Has a physical or mental impairment that substantially limits one or more major life activities only as a result of the attitudes of other toward such impairment; or

(3)

Has none of the impairments defined in paragraph (a) of this definition but is treated by another person as having such an impairment.

Interior means the spaces, parts, components or elements of an individual dwelling unit.

Modification means any change to the public or common use areas of a building or any change to a dwelling unit.

Premises means the interior or exterior spaces, parts, components or elements of a building, including individual dwelling units and the public and common use areas of a building.

Public use areas means interior or exterior rooms or spaces of a building that are made available to the general public. Public use may be provided at a building that is privately or publicly owned.

Site means a parcel of land bounded by a property line or a designated portion of a public right of way.

100.201a   Incorporation by reference [Omitted]

100.202   General prohibitions against discrimination because of handicap

(a) It shall be unlawful to discriminate in the sale or rental, or to otherwise make unavailable or deny, a dwelling to any buyer or renter because of a handicap of —

(1) That buyer or renter;

(2) A person residing in or intending to reside in that dwelling after it is so sold, rented, or made available; or

(3) Any person associated with that person.

(b) It shall be unlawful to discriminate against any person in the terms, conditions, or privileges of the sale or rental of a dwelling, or in the provision of services or facilities in connection with such dwelling, because of a handicap of —

(1) That buyer or renter;

(2) A person residing in or intending to reside in that dwelling after it is so sold, rented, or made available; or

(3) Any person associated with that person.

(c) It shall be unlawful to make an inquiry to determine whether an applicant for a dwelling, a person intending to reside in that dwelling after it is so sold, rented or made available, or any person associated with that person, has a handicap or to make inquiry as to the nature or severity of a handicap of such a person. However, this paragraph does not prohibit the following inquiries, provided these inquiries are made of all applicants, whether or not they have handicaps:

(1) Inquiry into an applicant's ability to meet the requirements of ownership or tenancy;

(2) Inquiry to determine whether an applicant is qualified for a dwelling available only to persons with handicaps or to persons with a particular type of handicap;

(3) Inquiry to determine whether an applicant for a dwelling is qualified for a priority available to persons with handicaps or to persons with a particular type of handicap;

(4) Inquiring whether an applicant for a dwelling is a current illegal abuser or addict of a controlled substance;

(5) Inquiring whether an applicant has been convicted of the illegal manufacture or distribution of a controlled substance.

(d) Nothing in this subpart requires that a dwelling be made available to an individual whose tenancy would constitute a direct threat to the health or safety of other individuals or whose tenancy would result in substantial physical damage to the property of others.

100.203　Reasonable modifications of existing premises

(a) It shall be unlawful for any person to refuse to permit, at the expense of a handicapped person, reasonable modifications of existing premises, occupied or to be occupied by a handicapped person, if the proposed modifications may be necessary to afford the handicapped person full enjoyment of the premises of a dwelling. In the case of a rental, the landlord may, where it is reasonable to do so, condition permission for a modification on the renter agreeing to restore the interior of the premises to the condition that existed before the modification, reasonable wear and tear excepted. The landlord may not increase for handicapped persons any customarily required security deposit. However, where it is necessary in order to ensure with reasonable certainty that funds will be available to pay for the restorations at the end of the tenancy, the landlord may negotiate as part of such a restoration agreement a provision requiring that the tenant pay into an interest bearing escrow account, over a reasonable period, a reasonable amount of money not to exceed the cost of the restorations. The interest in any such account shall accrue to the benefit of the tenant.

(b) A landlord may condition permission for a modification on the renter providing a reasonable description of the proposed modifications as well as reasonable assurances that the work will be done in a workmanlike manner and that any required building permits will be obtained.

(c) The application of paragraph (a) of this section may be illustrated by the following examples:

Example (1):

A tenant with a handicap asks his or her landlord for permission to install grab bars in the bathroom at his or her own expense. It is necessary to reinforce the walls with blocking between studs in order to affix the grab bars. It is unlawful for the landlord to refuse to permit the tenant, at the tenant's own expense, from making the modifications necessary to add the grab bars. However, the landlord may condition permission for the modification on the tenant agreeing to restore the bathroom to the condition that existed before the modification, reasonable wear and tear excepted. It would be reasonable for the landlord to require the tenant to remove the grab bars at the end of the tenancy. The landlord may also reasonably require that the wall to which the grab bars are to be attached be repaired and restored to its original condition, reasonable wear and tear excepted. However, it would be unreasonable for the landlord to require the tenant to remove the blocking, since the reinforced walls will not interfere in any way with the landlord's or the next tenant's use and enjoyment of the premises and may be needed by some future tenant.

Example (2):

An applicant for rental housing has a child who uses a wheelchair. The bathroom door in the dwelling unit is too narrow to permit the wheelchair to pass. The applicant asks the landlord for permission to widen the doorway at the applicant's own expense. It is unlawful for the landlord to refuse to permit the applicant to make the modification. Further, the landlord may not, in usual circumstances, condition permission for the modification on the applicant paying for the doorway to be narrowed at the end of the lease because a wider doorway will not interfere with the landlord's or the next tenant's use and enjoyment of the premises.

100.204 Reasonable accommodations

(a) It shall be unlawful for any person to refuse to make reasonable accommodations in rules, policies, practices, or services, when such accommodations may be necessary to afford a handicapped person equal opportunity to use and enjoy a dwelling unit, including public and common use areas.

(b) The application of this section may be illustrated by the following examples:

Example (1):

A blind applicant for rental housing wants live in a dwelling unit with a seeing eye dog. The building has a no pets policy. It is a violation of § 100.204 for the owner or manager of the apartment complex to refuse to permit the applicant to live in the apartment with a seeing eye dog because, without the seeing eye dog, the blind person will not have an equal opportunity to use and enjoy a dwelling.

Example (2):

Progress Gardens is a 300 unit apartment complex with 450 parking spaces which are available to tenants and guests of Progress Gardens on a first come first served basis. John applies for housing in Progress Gardens. John is mobility impaired and is unable to walk more than a short distance and therefore requests that a parking space near his unit be reserved for him so he will not have to walk very far to get to his apartment. It is a violation of § 100.204 for the owner or manager of Progress Gardens to refuse to make this accommodation. Without a reserved space, John might be unable to live in Progress Gardens at all or, when he has to park in a space far from his unit, might have great difficulty getting from his car to his apartment unit. The accommodation therefore is necessary to afford John an equal opportunity to use and enjoy a dwelling. The accommodation is reasonable because it is feasible and practical under the circumstances.

100.205   Design and construction requirements

(a) Covered multifamily dwellings for first occupancy after March 13, 1991 shall be designed and constructed to have at least one building entrance on an accessible route unless it is impractical to do so because of the terrain or unusual characteristics of the site. For purposes of this section, a covered multifamily dwelling shall be deemed to be designed and constructed for first occupancy on or before March 13, 1991, if the dwelling is occupied by that date, or if the last building permit or renewal thereof for the dwelling is issued by a State, County or local government on or before June 15, 1990. The burden of establishing impracticality because of terrain or unusual site characteristics is on the person or persons who designed or constructed the housing facility.

(b)   The application of paragraph (a) of this section may be illustrated by the following examples:

Example (1):

A real estate developer plans to construct six covered multifamily dwelling units on a site with a hilly terrain. Because of the terrain, it will be necessary to climb a long and steep stairway in order to enter the dwellings. Since there is no practical way to provide an accessible route to any of the dwellings, one need not be provided.

Example (2):

A real estate developer plans to construct a building consisting of 10 units of multifamily housing on a waterfront site that floods frequently. Because of this unusual characteristic of the site, the builder plans to construct the building on stilts. It is customary for housing in the geographic area where the site is located to be built on stilts. The housing may lawfully be constructed on the proposed site on stilts even though this means that there will be no practical way to provide an accessible route to the building entrance.

Example (3):

A real estate developer plans to construct a multifamily housing facility on a particular site. The developer would like the facility to be built on the site to contain as many units as possible. Because of the configuration and terrain of the site, it is possible to construct a building with 105 units on the site provided the site does not have an accessible route leading to the building entrance. It is also possible to construct a building on the site with an accessible route leading to the building entrance. However, such a building would have no more than 100 dwelling units. The building to be constructed on the site must have a building entrance on an accessible route because it is not impractical to provide such an entrance because of the terrain or unusual characteristics of the site.

(c) All covered multifamily dwellings for first occupancy after March 13, 1991 with a building entrance on an accessible route shall be designed and constructed in such a manner that —

(1) The public and common use areas are readily accessible to and usable by handicapped persons;

(2) All the doors designed to allow passage into and within all premises are sufficiently wide to allow passage by handicapped persons in wheelchairs; and

(3) All premises within covered multifamily dwelling units contain the following features of adaptable design:

(i) An accessible route into and through the covered dwelling unit;

(ii) Light switches, electrical outlets, thermostats, and other environmental controls in accessible locations;

(iii) Reinforcements in bathroom walls to allow later installation of grab bars around the toilet, tub, shower, stall and shower seat, where such facilities are provided; and

(iv) Usable kitchens and bathrooms such that an individual in a wheelchair can maneuver about the space.

(d)   The application of paragraph (c) of this section may be illustrated by the following examples:

Example (1):

A developer plans to construct a 100 unit condominium apartment building with one elevator. In accordance with paragraph (a), the building has at least one accessible route leading to an accessible entrance. All 100 units are covered multifamily dwelling units and they all must be designed and constructed so that they comply with the accessibility requirements of paragraph (c) of this section.

Example (2):

A developer plans to construct 30 garden apartments in a three story building. The building will not have an elevator. The building will have one accessible entrance which will be on the first floor. Since the building does not have an elevator, only the ground floor units are covered multifamily units. The ground floor is the first floor because that is the floor that has an accessible entrance. All of the dwelling units on the first floor must meet the accessibility requirements of paragraph (c) of this section and must have access to at least one of each type of public or common use area available for residents in the building.

(e)

(1) Compliance with the appropriate requirements of ICC/ANSI A117.1-2003 (incorporated by reference at § 100.201a), ICC/ANSI A117.1-1998 (incorporated by reference at § 100.201a), CABO/ANSI A117.1-1992 (incorporated by reference at § 100.201a), or ANSI A117.1-1986 (incorporated by reference at § 100.201a) suffices to satisfy the requirements of paragraph (c)(3) of this section.

(2) The following also qualify as HUD-recognized safe harbors for compliance with the Fair Housing Act design and construction requirements:

(i) Fair Housing Accessibility Guidelines, March 6, 1991, in conjunction with the Supplement to Notice of Fair Housing Accessibility Guidelines: Questions and Answers About the Guidelines, June 28, 1994;

(ii) Fair Housing Act Design Manual, published by HUD in 1996, updated in 1998;

(iii) 2000 ICC Code Requirements for Housing Accessibility (CRHA), published by the International Code Council (ICC), October 2000 (with corrections contained in ICC-issued errata sheet), if adopted without modification and without waiver of any of the provisions;

(iv) 2000 International Building Code (IBC), as amended by the 2001 Supplement to the International Building Code (2001 IBC Supplement), if adopted without modification and without waiver of any of the provisions intended to address the Fair Housing Act's design and construction requirements;

(v) 2003 International Building Code (IBC), if adopted without modification and without waiver of any of the provisions intended to address the Fair Housing Act's design and construction requirements, and conditioned upon the ICC publishing and distributing a statement to jurisdictions and past and future purchasers of the 2003 IBC stating, "ICC interprets Section 1104.1, and specifically, the Exception to Section 1104.1, to be read together with Section 1107.4, and that the Code requires an accessible pedestrian route from site arrival points to accessible building entrances, unless site impracticality applies. Exception 1 to Section 1107.4 is not applicable to site arrival points for any Type B dwelling units because site impracticality is addressed under Section 1107.7."

(vi) 2006 International Building Code; published by ICC, January 2006, with the January 31, 2007, erratum to correct the text missing from Section 1107.7.5, if adopted without modification and without waiver of any of the provisions intended to address the Fair Housing Act's design and construction requirements, and interpreted in accordance with the relevant 2006 IBC Commentary;

(3) Compliance with any other safe harbor recognized by HUD in the future and announced in the Federal Register will also suffice to satisfy the requirements of paragraph (c)(3) of this section.

(f) Compliance with a duly enacted law of a State or unit of general local government that includes the requirements of paragraphs (a) and (c) of this section satisfies the requirements of paragraphs (a) and (c) of this section.

(g)

(1) It is the policy of HUD to encourage States and units of general local government to include, in their existing procedures for the review and approval of newly constructed covered multifamily dwellings, determinations as to whether the design and construction of such dwellings are consistent with paragraphs (a) and (c) of this section.

(2) A State or unit of general local government may review and approve newly constructed multifamily dwellings for the purpose of making determinations as to whether the requirements of paragraphs (a) and (c) of this section are met.

(h) Determinations of compliance or noncompliance by a State or a unit of general local government under paragraph (f) or (g) of this section are not conclusive in enforcement proceedings under the Fair Housing Amendments Act.

(i) This subpart does not invalidate or limit any law of a State or political subdivision of a State that requires dwellings to be designed and constructed in a manner that affords handicapped persons greater access than is required by this subpart.

Chapter 8
FAMILY AND MEDICAL LEAVE ACT

Family and Medical Leave Act
29 U.S.C. § 2601 et seq

§ 2601.   Findings and purposes

(a)   Findings. Congress finds that —

(1) the number of single-parent households and two-parent households in which the single parent or both parents work is increasing significantly;

(2) it is important for the development of children and the family unit that fathers and mothers be able to participate in early childrearing and the care of family members who have serious health conditions;

(3) the lack of employment policies to accommodate working parents can force individuals to choose between job security and parenting;

(4) there is inadequate job security for employees who have serious health conditions that prevent them from working for temporary periods;

(5) due to the nature of the roles of men and women in our society, the primary responsibility for family caretaking often falls on women, and such responsibility affects the working lives of women more than it affects the working lives of men; and

(6) employment standards that apply to one gender only have serious potential for encouraging employers to discriminate against employees and applicants for employment who are of that gender.

(b)   Purposes. It is the purpose of this Act —

(1) to balance the demands of the workplace with the needs of families, to promote the stability and economic security of families, and to promote national interests in preserving family integrity;

(2) to entitle employees to take reasonable leave for medical reasons, for the birth or adoption of a child, and for the care of a child, spouse, or parent who has a serious health condition;

(3) to accomplish the purposes described in paragraphs (1) and (2) in a manner that accommodates the legitimate interests of employers;

(4) to accomplish the purposes described in paragraphs (1) and (2) in a manner that, consistent with the Equal Protection Clause of the Fourteenth Amendment [U.S.C., Constitution, Amendment 14, § 1], minimizes the potential for employment discrimination on the basis of sex by ensuring generally that leave is available for eligible medical reasons (including maternity-related disability) and for compelling family reasons, on a gender-neutral basis; and

(5) to promote the goal of equal employment opportunity for women and men, pursuant to such clause.

GENERAL REQUIREMENTS FOR LEAVE

2611. Definitions

As used in this title [29 U.S.C. §§ 2611 et seq.]:

(1) Commerce. The terms "commerce" and "industry or activity affecting commerce" mean any activity, business, or industry in commerce or in which a labor dispute would hinder or obstruct commerce or the free flow of commerce, and include "commerce" and any "industry affecting commerce", as defined in paragraphs (1) and (3) of section 501 of the Labor Management Relations Act, 1947 (29 U.S.C. 142 (1) and (3)).

(2) Eligible employee.

(A) In general. The term "eligible employee" means an employee who has been employed —

(i) for at least 12 months by the employer with respect to whom leave is requested under section 102 [29 U.S.C. § 2612]; and

(ii) for at least 1,250 hours of service with such employer during the previous 12-month period.

(B) Exclusions. The term "eligible employee" does not include —

(i) any Federal officer or employee covered under subchapter V of chapter 63 of title 5, United States Code [5 U.S.C. §§ 6381 et seq.] (as added by title II of this Act); or

(ii) any employee of an employer who is employed at a worksite at which such employer employs less than 50 employees if the total number of employees employed by that employer within 75 miles of that worksite is less than 50.

(C) Determination. For purposes of determining whether an employee meets the hours of service requirement specified in subparagraph (A)(ii), the legal standards established under section 7 of the Fair Labor Standards Act of 1938 (29 U.S.C. 207) shall apply.

(D) Airline flight crews.

(i) Determination. For purposes of determining whether an employee who is a flight attendant or flight crewmember (as such terms are defined in regulations of the Federal Aviation Administration) meets the hours of service requirement specified in subparagraph (A)(ii), the employee will be considered to meet the requirement if —

(I) the employee has worked or been paid for not less than 60 percent of the applicable total monthly guarantee, or the equivalent, for the previous 12-month period, for or by the employer with respect to whom leave is requested under section 102 [29 U.S.C. § 2612]; and

(II) the employee has worked or been paid for not less than 504 hours (not counting personal commute time or time spent on vacation leave or medical or sick leave) during the previous 12-month period, for or by that employer.

(ii) File. Each employer of an employee described in clause (i) shall maintain on file with the Secretary (in accordance with such regulations as the Secretary may prescribe) containing information specifying the applicable monthly guarantee with respect to each category of employee to which such guarantee applies.

(iii) Definition. In this subparagraph, the term "applicable monthly guarantee" means —

(I) for an employee described in clause (i) other than an employee on reserve status, the minimum number of hours for which an employer has agreed to schedule such employee for any given month; and

(II) for an employee described in clause (i) who is on reserve status, the number of hours for which an employer has agreed to pay such employee on reserve status for any given month, as established in the applicable collective bargaining agreement or, if none exists, in the employer's policies.

(3) Employ; employee; State. The terms "employ", "employee", and "State" have the same meanings given such terms in subsections (c), (e), and (g) of section 3 of the Fair Labor Standards Act of 1938 (29 U.S.C. 203(c), (e), and (g)).

(4) Employer.

(A) In general. The term "employer" —

(i) means any person engaged in commerce or in any industry or activity affecting commerce who employs 50 or more employees for each working day during each of 20 or more calendar workweeks in the current or preceding calendar year;

(ii) includes —

(I) any person who acts, directly or indirectly, in the interest of an employer to any of the employees of such employer; and

(II) any successor in interest of an employer;

(iii) includes any "public agency", as defined in section 3(x) of the Fair Labor Standards Act of 1938 (29 U.S.C. 203(x)); and

(iv) includes the General Accounting Office [Government Accountability Office] and the Library of Congress.

(B) Public agency. For purposes of subparagraph (A)(iii), a public agency shall be considered to be a person engaged in commerce or in an industry or activity affecting commerce.

(5) Employment benefits. The term "employment benefits" means all benefits provided or made available to employees by an employer, including group life insurance, health insurance, disability insurance, sick leave, annual leave, educational benefits, and pensions, regardless of whether such benefits are provided by a practice or written policy of an employer or through an "employee benefit

plan", as defined in section 3(3) of the Employee Retirement Income Security Act of 1974 (29 U.S.C. 1002(3)).

(6) Health care provider. The term "health care provider" means —

(A) a doctor of medicine or osteopathy who is authorized to practice medicine or surgery (as appropriate) by the State in which the doctor practices; or

(B) any other person determined by the Secretary to be capable of providing health care services.

(7) Parent. The term "parent" means the biological parent of an employee or an individual who stood in loco parentis to an employee when the employee was a son or daughter.

(8) Person. The term "person" has the same meaning given such term in section 3(a) of the Fair Labor Standards Act of 1938 (29 U.S.C. 203(a)).

(9) Reduced leave schedule. The term "reduced leave schedule" means a leave schedule that reduces the usual number of hours per workweek, or hours per workday, of an employee.

(10) Secretary. The term "Secretary" means the Secretary of Labor.

(11) Serious health condition. The term "serious health condition" means an illness, injury, impairment, or physical or mental condition that involves —

(A) inpatient care in a hospital, hospice, or residential medical care facility; or

(B) continuing treatment by a health care provider.

(12) Son or daughter. The term "son or daughter" means a biological, adopted, or foster child, a stepchild, a legal ward, or a child of a person standing in loco parentis, who is —

(A) under 18 years of age; or

(B) 18 years of age or older and incapable of self-care because of a mental or physical disability.

(13) Spouse. The term "spouse" means a husband or wife, as the case may be.

(14) Covered active duty. The term "covered active duty" means —

(A) in the case of a member of a regular component of the Armed Forces, duty during the deployment of the member with the Armed Forces to a foreign country; and

(B) in the case of a member of a reserve component of the Armed Forces, duty during the deployment of the member with the Armed Forces to a foreign country under a call or order to active duty under a provision of law referred to in section 101(a)(13)(B) of title 10, United States Code.

(15) Covered servicemember. The term "covered servicemember" means —

(A) a member of the Armed Forces (including a member of the National

Guard or Reserves) who is undergoing medical treatment, recuperation, or therapy, is otherwise in outpatient status, or is otherwise on the temporary disability retired list, for a serious injury or illness; or

(B) a veteran who is undergoing medical treatment, recuperation, or therapy, for a serious injury or illness and who was a member of the Armed Forces (including a member of the National Guard or Reserves) at any time during the period of 5 years preceding the date on which the veteran undergoes that medical treatment, recuperation, or therapy.

(16) Outpatient status. The term "outpatient status", with respect to a covered servicemember, means the status of a member of the Armed Forces assigned to —

(A) a military medical treatment facility as an outpatient; or

(B) a unit established for the purpose of providing command and control of members of the Armed Forces receiving medical care as outpatients.

(17) Next of kin. The term "next of kin", used with respect to an individual, means the nearest blood relative of that individual.

(18) Serious injury or illness. The term "serious injury or illness" —

(A) in the case of a member of the Armed Forces (including a member of the National Guard or Reserves), means an injury or illness that was incurred by the member in line of duty on active duty in the Armed Forces (or existed before the beginning of the member's active duty and was aggravated by service in line of duty on active duty in the Armed Forces) and that may render the member medically unfit to perform the duties of the member's office, grade, rank, or rating; and

(B) in the case of a veteran who was a member of the Armed Forces (including a member of the National Guard or Reserves) at any time during a period described in paragraph (15)(B), means a qualifying (as defined by the Secretary of Labor) injury or illness that was incurred by the member in line of duty on active duty in the Armed Forces (or existed before the beginning of the member's active duty and was aggravated by service in line of duty on active duty in the Armed Forces) and that manifested itself before or after the member became a veteran.

(19) Veteran. The term "veteran" has the meaning given the term in section 101 of title 38, United States Code.

2612.   Leave requirement

(a)   In general.

(1) Entitlement to leave. Subject to section 103 [29 U.S.C. § 2613], an eligible employee shall be entitled to a total of 12 workweeks of leave during any 12-month period for one or more of the following:

(A) Because of the birth of a son or daughter of the employee and in order to care for such son or daughter.

(B) Because of the placement of a son or daughter with the employee for adoption or foster care.

(C) In order to care for the spouse, or a son, daughter, or parent, of the employee, if such spouse, son, daughter, or parent has a serious health condition.

(D) Because of a serious health condition that makes the employee unable to perform the functions of the position of such employee.

(E) Because of any qualifying exigency (as the Secretary shall, by regulation, determine) arising out of the fact that the spouse, or a son, daughter, or parent of the employee is on covered active duty (or has been notified of an impending call or order to covered active duty) in the Armed Forces.

(2) Expiration of entitlement. The entitlement to leave under subparagraphs (A) and (B) of paragraph (1) for a birth or placement of a son or daughter shall expire at the end of the 12-month period beginning on the date of such birth or placement.

(3) Servicemember family leave. Subject to section 103 [29 U.S.C. § 2613], an eligible employee who is the spouse, son, daughter, parent, or next of kin of a covered servicemember shall be entitled to a total of 26 workweeks of leave during a 12-month period to care for the servicemember. The leave described in this paragraph shall only be available during a single 12-month period.

(4) Combined leave total. During the single 12-month period described in paragraph (3), an eligible employee shall be entitled to a combined total of 26 workweeks of leave under paragraphs (1) and (3). Nothing in this paragraph shall be construed to limit the availability of leave under paragraph (1) during any other 12-month period.

(5) Calculation of leave for airline flight crews. The Secretary may provide, by regulation, a method for calculating the leave described in paragraph (1) with respect to employees described in section 101(2)(D) [29 U.S.C. § 2611(2)(D)].

(b) Leave taken intermittently or on a reduced leave schedule.

(1) In general. Leave under subparagraph (A) or (B) of subsection (a)(1) shall not be taken by an employee intermittently or on a reduced leave schedule unless the employee and the employer of the employee agree otherwise. Subject to paragraph (2), subsection (e)(2), and subsection (b)(5) or (f) (as appropriate) of section 103 [29 U.S.C. § 2613], leave under subparagraph (C) or (D) of subsection (a)(1) or under subsection (a)(3) may be taken intermittently or on a reduced leave schedule when medically necessary. Subject to subsection (e)(3) and section 103(f) [29 U.S.C. § 2613(f)], leave under subsection (a)(1)(E) may be taken intermittently or on a reduced leave schedule. The taking of leave intermittently or on a reduced leave schedule pursuant to this paragraph shall not result in a reduction in the total amount of leave to which the employee is entitled under subsection (a) beyond the amount of leave actually taken.

(2) Alternative position. If an employee requests intermittent leave, or leave on a reduced leave schedule, under subparagraph (C) or (D) of subsection (a)(1) or

under subsection (a)(3), that is foreseeable based on planned medical treatment, the employer may require such employee to transfer temporarily to an available alternative position offered by the employer for which the employee is qualified and that —

(A) has equivalent pay and benefits; and

(B) better accommodates recurring periods of leave than the regular employment position of the employee.

(c) Unpaid leave permitted. Except as provided in subsection (d), leave granted under subsection (a) may consist of unpaid leave. Where an employee is otherwise exempt under regulations issued by the Secretary pursuant to section 13(a)(1) of the Fair Labor Standards Act of 1938 (29 U.S.C. 213(a)(1)), the compliance of an employer with this title [29 U.S.C. §§ 2611 et seq.] by providing unpaid leave shall not affect the exempt status of the employee under such section.

(d) Relationship to paid leave.

(1) Unpaid leave. If an employer provides paid leave for fewer than 12 workweeks (or 26 workweeks in the case of leave provided under subsection (a)(3)), the additional weeks of leave necessary to attain the 12 workweeks (or 26 workweeks, as appropriate) of leave required under this title [29 U.S.C. §§ 2611 et seq.] may be provided without compensation.

(2) Substitution of paid leave.

(A) In general. An eligible employee may elect, or an employer may require the employee, to substitute any of the accrued paid vacation leave, personal leave, or family leave of the employee for leave provided under subparagraph (A), (B), (C), or (E) of subsection (a)(1) for any part of the 12-week period of such leave under such subsection.

(B) Serious health condition. An eligible employee may elect, or an employer may require the employee, to substitute any of the accrued paid vacation leave, personal leave, or medical or sick leave of the employee for leave provided under subparagraph (C) or (D) of subsection (a)(1) for any part of the 12-week period of such leave under such subsection, except that nothing in this title [29 U.S.C. §§ 2611 et seq.] shall require an employer to provide paid sick leave or paid medical leave in any situation in which such employer would not normally provide any such paid leave. An eligible employee may elect, or an employer may require the employee, to substitute any of the accrued paid vacation leave, personal leave, family leave, or medical or sick leave of the employee for leave provided under subsection (a)(3) for any part of the 26-week period of such leave under such subsection, except that nothing in this title requires an employer to provide paid sick leave or paid medical leave in any situation in which the employer would not normally provide any such paid leave.

(e) Foreseeable leave.

(1) Requirement of notice. In any case in which the necessity for leave under subparagraph (A) or (B) of subsection (a)(1) is foreseeable based on an expected birth or placement, the employee shall provide the employer with not less than

30 days' notice, before the date the leave is to begin, of the employee's intention to take leave under such subparagraph, except that if the date of the birth or placement requires leave to begin in less than 30 days, the employee shall provide such notice as is practicable.

(2) Duties of employee. In any case in which the necessity for leave under subparagraph (C) or (D) of subsection (a)(1) or under subsection (a)(3) is foreseeable based on planned medical treatment, the employee —

(A) shall make a reasonable effort to schedule the treatment so as not to disrupt unduly the operations of the employer, subject to the approval of the health care provider of the employee or the health care provider of the son, daughter, spouse, parent, or covered servicemember of the employee, as appropriate; and

(B) shall provide the employer with not less than 30 days' notice, before the date the leave is to begin, of the employee's intention to take leave under such subparagraph, except that if the date of the treatment requires leave to begin in less than 30 days, the employee shall provide such notice as is practicable.

(3) Notice for leave due to covered active duty of family member. In any case in which the necessity for leave under subsection (a)(1)(E) is foreseeable, whether because the spouse, or a son, daughter, or parent, of the employee is on covered active duty, or because of notification of an impending call or order to covered active duty, the employee shall provide such notice to the employer as is reasonable and practicable.

(f) Spouses employed by the same employer.

(1) In general. In any case in which a husband and wife entitled to leave under subsection (a) are employed by the same employer, the aggregate number of workweeks of leave to which both may be entitled may be limited to 12 workweeks during any 12-month period, if such leave is taken —

(A) under subparagraph (A) or (B) of subsection (a)(1); or

(B) to care for a sick parent under subparagraph (C) of such subsection.

(2) Servicemember family leave.

(A) In general. The aggregate number of workweeks of leave to which both that husband and wife may be entitled under subsection (a) may be limited to 26 workweeks during the single 12-month period described in subsection (a)(3) if the leave is —

(i) leave under subsection (a)(3); or

(ii) a combination of leave under subsection (a)(3) and leave described in paragraph (1).

(B) Both limitations applicable. If the leave taken by the husband and wife includes leave described in paragraph (1), the limitation in paragraph (1) shall apply to the leave described in paragraph (1).

2613. Certification

(a) In general. An employer may require that a request for leave under subparagraph (C) or (D) of paragraph (1) or paragraph (3) of section 102(a) [29 U.S.C. § 2612(a)] be supported by a certification issued by the health care provider of the eligible employee or of the son, daughter, spouse, or parent of the employee, or of the next of kin of an individual in the case of leave taken under such paragraph (3), as appropriate. The employee shall provide, in a timely manner, a copy of such certification to the employer.

(b) Sufficient certification. Certification provided under subsection (a) shall be sufficient if it states —

(1) the date on which the serious health condition commenced;

(2) the probable duration of the condition;

(3) the appropriate medical facts within the knowledge of the health care provider regarding the condition;

(4)

(A) for purposes of leave under section 102(a)(1)(C) [29 U.S.C. § 2612(a)(1)(C)], a statement that the eligible employee is needed to care for the son, daughter, spouse, or parent and an estimate of the amount of time that such employee is needed to care for the son, daughter, spouse, or parent; and

(B) for purposes of leave under section 102(a)(1)(D) [29 U.S.C. § 2612(a)(1)(D)], a statement that the employee is unable to perform the functions of the position of the employee;

(5) in the case of certification for intermittent leave, or leave on a reduced leave schedule, for planned medical treatment, the dates on which such treatment is expected to be given and the duration of such treatment;

(6) in the case of certification for intermittent leave, or leave on a reduced leave schedule, under section 102(a)(1)(D) [29 U.S.C. § 2612(a)(1)(D)], a statement of the medical necessity for the intermittent leave or leave on a reduced leave schedule, and the expected duration of the intermittent leave or reduced leave schedule; and

(7) in the case of certification for intermittent leave, or leave on a reduced leave schedule, under section 102(a)(1)(C) [29 U.S.C. § 2612(a)(1)(C)], a statement that the employee's intermittent leave or leave on a reduced leave schedule is necessary for the care of the son, daughter, parent, or spouse who has a serious health condition, or will assist in their recovery, and the expected duration and schedule of the intermittent leave or reduced leave schedule.

(c) Second opinion.

(1) In general. In any case in which the employer has reason to doubt the validity of the certification provided under subsection (a) for leave under subparagraph (C) or (D) of section 102(a)(1) [29 U.S.C. § 2612(a)(1)(C) or (D)], the employer may require, at the expense of the employer, that the eligible employee obtain the opinion of a second health care provider designated or approved by the employer concerning any information certified under subsection

(b) for such leave.

(2) Limitation. A health care provider designated or approved under paragraph (1) shall not be employed on a regular basis by the employer.

(d) Resolution of conflicting opinions.

(1) In general. In any case in which the second opinion described in subsection (c) differs from the opinion in the original certification provided under subsection (a), the employer may require, at the expense of the employer, that the employee obtain the opinion of a third health care provider designated or approved jointly by the employer and the employee concerning the information certified under subsection (b).

(2) Finality. The opinion of the third health care provider concerning the information certified under subsection (b) shall be considered to be final and shall be binding on the employer and the employee.

(e) Subsequent recertification. The employer may require that the eligible employee obtain subsequent recertifications on a reasonable basis.

(f) Certification related to covered active duty or call to covered active duty. An employer may require that a request for leave under section 102(a)(1)(E) [29 U.S.C. § 2612(a)(1)(E)] be supported by a certification issued at such time and in such manner as the Secretary may by regulation prescribe. If the Secretary issues a regulation requiring such certification, the employee shall provide, in a timely manner, a copy of such certification to the employer.

2614. Employment and benefits protection

(a) Restoration to position.

(1) In general. Except as provided in subsection (b), any eligible employee who takes leave under section 102 [29 U.S.C. § 2612] for the intended purpose of the leave shall be entitled, on return from such leave —

(A) to be restored by the employer to the position of employment held by the employee when the leave commenced; or

(B) to be restored to an equivalent position with equivalent employment benefits, pay, and other terms and conditions of employment.

(2) Loss of benefits. The taking of leave under section 102 [29 U.S.C. § 2612] shall not result in the loss of any employment benefit accrued prior to the date on which the leave commenced.

(3) Limitations. Nothing in this section shall be construed to entitle any restored employee to —

(A) the accrual of any seniority or employment benefits during any period of leave; or

(B) any right, benefit, or position of employment other than any right, benefit, or position to which the employee would have been entitled had the employee not taken the leave.

(4) Certification. As a condition of restoration under paragraph (1) for an employee who has taken leave under section 102(a)(1)(D) [29 U.S.C. § 2612(a)(1)(D)], the employer may have a uniformly applied practice or policy that requires each such employee to receive certification from the health care provider of the employee that the employee is able to resume work, except that nothing in this paragraph shall supersede a valid State or local law or a collective bargaining agreement that governs the return to work of such employees.

(5) Construction. Nothing in this subsection shall be construed to prohibit an employer from requiring an employee on leave under section 102 [29 U.S.C. § 2612] to report periodically to the employer on the status and intention of the employee to return to work.

(b) Exemption concerning certain highly compensated employees.

(1) Denial of restoration. An employer may deny restoration under subsection (a) to any eligible employee described in paragraph (2) if —

(A) such denial is necessary to prevent substantial and grievous economic injury to the operations of the employer;

(B) the employer notifies the employee of the intent of the employer to deny restoration on such basis at the time the employer determines that such injury would occur; and

(C) in any case in which the leave has commenced, the employee elects not to return to employment after receiving such notice.

(2) Affected employees. An eligible employee described in paragraph (1) is a salaried eligible employee who is among the highest paid 10 percent of the employees employed by the employer within 75 miles of the facility at which the employee is employed.

(c) Maintenance of health benefits.

(1) Coverage. Except as provided in paragraph (2), during any period that an eligible employee takes leave under section 102 [29 U.S.C. § 2612], the employer shall maintain coverage under any "group health plan" (as defined in section 5000(b)(1) of the Internal Revenue Code of 1986 [26 U.S.C. § 5000(b)(1)]) for the duration of such leave at the level and under the conditions coverage would have been provided if the employee had continued in employment continuously for the duration of such leave.

(2) Failure to return from leave. The employer may recover the premium that the employer paid for maintaining coverage for the employee under such group health plan during any period of unpaid leave under section 102 [29 U.S.C. § 2612] if —

(A) the employee fails to return from leave under section 102 [29 U.S.C. § 2612] after the period of leave to which the employee is entitled has expired; and

(B) the employee fails to return to work for a reason other than —

(i) the continuation, recurrence, or onset of a serious health condition that entitles the employee to leave under subparagraph (C) or (D) of section 102(a)(1) [29 U.S.C. § 2612(a)(1)] or under section 102(a)(3) [29 U.S.C. § 2612(a)(3)]; or

(ii) other circumstances beyond the control of the employee.

(3) Certification.

(A) Issuance. An employer may require that a claim that an employee is unable to return to work because of the continuation, recurrence, or onset of the serious health condition described in paragraph (2)(B)(i) be supported by

—

(i) a certification issued by the health care provider of the son, daughter, spouse, or parent of the employee, as appropriate, in the case of an employee unable to return to work because of a condition specified in section 102(a)(1)(C) [29 U.S.C. § 2612(a)(1)(C)];

(ii) a certification issued by the health care provider of the eligible employee, in the case of an employee unable to return to work because of a condition specified in section 102(a)(1)(D) [29 U.S.C. § 2612(a)(1)(D)]; or

(iii) a certification issued by the health care provider of the servicemember being cared for by the employee, in the case of an employee unable to return to work because of a condition specified in section 102(a)(3) [29 U.S.C. § 2612(a)(3)].

(B) Copy. The employee shall provide, in a timely manner, a copy of such certification to the employer.

(C) Sufficiency of certification.

(i) Leave due to serious health condition of employee. The certification described in subparagraph (A)(ii) shall be sufficient if the certification states that a serious health condition prevented the employee from being able to perform the functions of the position of the employee on the date that the leave of the employee expired.

(ii) Leave due to serious health condition of family member. The certification described in subparagraph (A)(i) shall be sufficient if the certification states that the employee is needed to care for the son, daughter, spouse, or parent who has a serious health condition on the date that the leave of the employee expired.

2615. Prohibited acts

(a) Interference with rights.

(1) Exercise of rights. It shall be unlawful for any employer to interfere with, restrain, or deny the exercise of or the attempt to exercise, any right provided under this title [29 U.S.C. §§ 2611 et seq.].

(2) Discrimination. It shall be unlawful for any employer to discharge or in any other manner discriminate against any individual for opposing any practice made unlawful by this title [29 U.S.C. §§ 2611 et seq.].

(b) Interference with proceedings or inquiries. It shall be unlawful for any person to discharge or in any other manner discriminate against any individual because such individual —

(1) has filed any charge, or has instituted or caused to be instituted any proceeding, under or related to this title [29 U.S.C. §§ 2611 et seq.];

(2) has given, or is about to give, any information in connection with any inquiry or proceeding relating to any right provided under this title [29 U.S.C. §§ 2611 et seq.]; or

(3) has testified, or is about to testify, in any inquiry or proceeding relating to any right provided under this title [29 U.S.C. §§ 2611 et seq.].

2616.   Investigative authority

(a) In general. To ensure compliance with the provisions of this title [29 U.S.C. §§ 2611 et seq.], or any regulation or order issued under this title [29 U.S.C. §§ 2611 et seq.], the Secretary shall have, subject to subsection (c), the investigative authority provided under section 11(a) of the Fair Labor Standards Act of 1938 (29 U.S.C. 211(a)).

(b) Obligation to keep and preserve records. Any employer shall make, keep, and preserve records pertaining to compliance with this title [29 U.S.C. §§ 2611 et seq.] in accordance with section 11(c) of the Fair Labor Standards Act of 1938 (29 U.S.C. 211(c)) and in accordance with regulations issued by the Secretary.

(c) Required submissions generally limited to an annual basis. The Secretary shall not under the authority of this section require any employer or any plan, fund, or program to submit to the Secretary any books or records more than once during any 12-month period, unless the Secretary has reasonable cause to believe there may exist a violation of this title [29 U.S.C. §§ 2611 et seq.] or any regulation or order issued pursuant to this title [29 U.S.C. §§ 2611 et seq.], or is investigating a charge pursuant to section 107(b) [29 U.S.C. § 2617(b)].

(d) Subpoena powers. For the purposes of any investigation provided for in this section, the Secretary shall have the subpoena authority provided for under section 9 of the Fair Labor Standards Act of 1938 (29 U.S.C. 209).

2617.   Enforcement

(a) Civil action by employees.

(1) Liability. Any employer who violates section 105 [29 U.S.C. § 2615] shall be liable to any eligible employee affected —

(A) for damages equal to —

(i) the amount of —

(I) any wages, salary, employment benefits, or other compensation denied or lost to such employee by reason of the violation; or

(II) in a case in which wages, salary, employment benefits, or other compensation have not been denied or lost to the employee, any actual monetary losses sustained by the employee as a direct result of the violation, such as the cost of providing care, up to a sum equal to 12 weeks (or 26 weeks, in a case involving leave under section 102(a)(3) [29 U.S.C. § 2612(a)(3)]) of wages or salary for the employee;

(ii) the interest on the amount described in clause (i) calculated at the prevailing rate; and

(iii) an additional amount as liquidated damages equal to the sum of the amount described in clause (i) and the interest described in clause (ii), except that if an employer who has violated section 105 [29 U.S.C. § 2615] proves to the satisfaction of the court that the act or omission which violated section 105 [29 U.S.C. § 2615] was in good faith and that the employer had reasonable grounds for believing that the act or omission was not a violation of section 105 [29 U.S.C. § 2615], such court may, in the discretion of the court, reduce the amount of the liability to the amount and interest determined under clauses (i) and (ii), respectively; and

(B) for such equitable relief as may be appropriate, including employment, reinstatement, and promotion.

(2) Right of action. An action to recover the damages or equitable relief prescribed in paragraph (1) may be maintained against any employer (including a public agency) in any Federal or State court of competent jurisdiction by any one or more employees for and in behalf of —

(A) the employees; or

(B) the employees and other employees similarly situated.

(3) Fees and costs. The court in such an action shall, in addition to any judgment awarded to the plaintiff, allow a reasonable attorney's fee, reasonable expert witness fees, and other costs of the action to be paid by the defendant.

(4) Limitations. The right provided by paragraph (2) to bring an action by or on behalf of any employee shall terminate —

(A) on the filing of a complaint by the Secretary in an action under subsection (d) in which restraint is sought of any further delay in the payment of the amount described in paragraph (1)(A) to such employee by an employer responsible under paragraph (1) for the payment; or

(B) on the filing of a complaint by the Secretary in an action under subsection (b) in which a recovery is sought of the damages described in paragraph (1)(A) owing to an eligible employee by an employer liable under paragraph (1), unless the action described in subparagraph (A) or (B) is dismissed without prejudice on motion of the Secretary.

(b) Action by the Secretary.

(1) Administrative action. The Secretary shall receive, investigate, and attempt to resolve complaints of violations of section 105 in the same manner that the Secretary receives, investigates, and attempts to resolve complaints of violations of sections 6 and 7 of the Fair Labor Standards Act of 1938 (29 U.S.C. 206 and

207).

(2) Civil action. The Secretary may bring an action in any court of competent jurisdiction to recover the damages described in subsection (a)(1)(A).

(3) Sums recovered. Any sums recovered by the Secretary pursuant to paragraph (2) shall be held in a special deposit account and shall be paid, on order of the Secretary, directly to each employee affected. Any such sums not paid to an employee because of inability to do so within a period of 3 years shall be deposited into the Treasury of the United States as miscellaneous receipts.

(c) Limitation.

(1) In general. Except as provided in paragraph (2), an action may be brought under this section not later than 2 years after the date of the last event constituting the alleged violation for which the action is brought.

(2) Willful violation. In the case of such action brought for a willful violation of section 105 [29 U.S.C. § 2615], such action may be brought within 3 years of the date of the last event constituting the alleged violation for which such action is brought.

(3) Commencement. In determining when an action is commenced by the Secretary under this section for the purposes of this subsection, it shall be considered to be commenced on the date when the complaint is filed.

(d) Action for injunction by Secretary. The district courts of the United States shall have jurisdiction, for cause shown, in an action brought by the Secretary —

(1) to restrain violations of section 105 [29 U.S.C. § 2615], including the restraint of any withholding of payment of wages, salary, employment benefits, or other compensation, plus interest, found by the court to be due to eligible employees; or

(2) to award such other equitable relief as may be appropriate, including employment, reinstatement, and promotion.

(e) Solicitor of Labor. [Omitted from this Statutory Supplement]

(f) General Accounting Office [Government Accountability Office] and Library of Congress. [Omitted from this Statutory Supplement]

2618. Special rules concerning employees of local educational agencies

(a) Application.

(1) In general. Except as otherwise provided in this section, the rights (including the rights under section 104 [29 U.S.C. § 2614], which shall extend throughout the period of leave of any employee under this section), remedies, and procedures under this title [29 U.S.C. §§ 2611 et seq.] shall apply to —

(A) any "local educational agency" (as defined in section 9101 of the Elementary and Secondary Education Act of 1965 [20 U.S.C. § 7801] and an eligible employee of the agency; and

(B) any private elementary or secondary school and an eligible employee of the school.

(2) Definitions. For purposes of the application described in paragraph (1):

(A) Eligible employee. The term "eligible employee" means an eligible employee of an agency or school described in paragraph (1).

(B) Employer. The term "employer" means an agency or school described in paragraph (1).

(b) Leave does not violate certain other Federal laws. A local educational agency and a private elementary or secondary school shall not be in violation of the Individuals with Disabilities Education Act (20 U.S.C. 1400 et seq.), section 504 of the Rehabilitation Act of 1973 (29 U.S.C. 794), or title VI of the Civil Rights Act of 1964 (42 U.S.C. 2000d et seq.), solely as a result of an eligible employee of such agency or school exercising the rights of such employee under this title [29 U.S.C. §§ 2611 et seq.].

(c) Intermittent leave or leave on a reduced schedule for instructional employees.

(1) In general. Subject to paragraph (2), in any case in which an eligible employee employed principally in an instructional capacity by any such educational agency or school requests leave under subparagraph (C) or (D) of section 102(a)(1) [29 U.S.C. § 2612(a)(1)(C) or (D)] or under section 102(a)(3) [29 U.S.C. § 2612(a)(3)] that is foreseeable based on planned medical treatment and the employee would be on leave for greater than 20 percent of the total number of working days in the period during which the leave would extend, the agency or school may require that such employee elect either —

(A) to take leave for periods of a particular duration, not to exceed the duration of the planned medical treatment; or

(B) to transfer temporarily to an available alternative position offered by the employer for which the employee is qualified, and that —

(i) has equivalent pay and benefits; and

(ii) better accommodates recurring periods of leave than the regular employment position of the employee.

(2) Application. The elections described in subparagraphs (A) and (B) of paragraph (1) shall apply only with respect to an eligible employee who complies with section 102(e)(2) [29 U.S.C. § 2612(e)(2)].

(d) Rules applicable to periods near the conclusion of an academic term. The following rules shall apply with respect to periods of leave near the conclusion of an academic term in the case of any eligible employee employed principally in an instructional capacity by any such educational agency or school:

(1) Leave more than 5 weeks prior to end of term. If the eligible employee begins leave under section 102 [29 U.S.C. § 2612] more than 5 weeks prior to the end of the academic term, the agency or school may require the employee to continue taking leave until the end of such term, if —

(A) the leave is of at least 3 weeks duration; and

(B) the return to employment would occur during the 3-week period before the end of such term.

(2) Leave less than 5 weeks prior to end of term. If the eligible employee begins leave under subparagraph (A), (B), or (C) of section 102(a)(1) [29 U.S.C. § 2612(a)(1)(A), (B), or (C)] or under section 102(a)(3) [29 U.S.C. § 2612(a)(3)] during the period that commences 5 weeks prior to the end of the academic term, the agency or school may require the employee to continue taking leave until the end of such term, if —

(A) the leave is of greater than 2 weeks duration; and

(B) the return to employment would occur during the 2-week period before the end of such term.

(3) Leave less than 3 weeks prior to end of term. If the eligible employee begins leave under subparagraph (A), (B), or (C) of section 102(a)(1) [29 U.S.C. § 2612(a)(1)(A), (B), or (C)] or under section 102(a)(3) [29 U.S.C. § 2612(a)(3)] during the period that commences 3 weeks prior to the end of the academic term and the duration of the leave is greater than 5 working days, the agency or school may require the employee to continue to take leave until the end of such term.

(e) Restoration to equivalent employment position. For purposes of determinations under section 104(a)(1)(B) [29 U.S.C. § 2614(a)(1)(B)] (relating to the restoration of an eligible employee to an equivalent position), in the case of a local educational agency or a private elementary or secondary school, such determination shall be made on the basis of established school board policies and practices, private school policies and practices, and collective bargaining agreements.

(f) Reduction of the amount of liability. If a local educational agency or a private elementary or secondary school that has violated this title [29 U.S.C. §§ 2611 et seq.] proves to the satisfaction of the court that the agency, school, or department had reasonable grounds for believing that the underlying act or omission was not a violation of this title [29 U.S.C. §§ 2611 et seq.], such court may, in the discretion of the court, reduce the amount of the liability provided for under section 107(a)(1)(A) [29 U.S.C. § 2617(a)(1)(A)] to the amount and interest determined under clauses (i) and (ii), respectively, of such section.

2619. Notice

(a) In general. Each employer shall post and keep posted, in conspicuous places on the premises of the employer where notices to employees and applicants for employment are customarily posted, a notice, to be prepared or approved by the Secretary, setting forth excerpts from, or summaries of, the pertinent provisions of this title [29 U.S.C. §§ 2611 et seq.] and information pertaining to the filing of a charge.

(b) Penalty. Any employer that willfully violates this section may be assessed a civil money penalty not to exceed $ 100 for each separate offense.

COMMISSION ON LEAVE

2631. Establishment

There is established a commission to be known as the Commission on Leave (referred to in this title [29 U.S.C. §§ 2631 et seq.] as the "Commission").

2632. Duties

[Omitted from this Statutory Supplement]

2633. Membership

[Omitted from this Statutory Supplement]

2634. Compensation

[Omitted from this Statutory Supplement]

2635. Powers

[Omitted from this Statutory Supplement]

2636. Termination

[Omitted from this Statutory Supplement]

MISCELLANEOUS PROVISIONS

2651. Effect on other laws

(a) Federal and State antidiscrimination laws. Nothing in this Act or any amendment made by this Act shall be construed to modify or affect any Federal or State law prohibiting discrimination on the basis of race, religion, color, national origin, sex, age, or disability.

(b) State and local laws. Nothing in this Act or any amendment made by this Act shall be construed to supersede any provision of any State or local law that provides greater family or medical leave rights than the rights established under this Act or any amendment made by this Act.

2652. Effect on existing employment benefits

(a) More protective. Nothing in this Act or any amendment made by this Act shall be construed to diminish the obligation of an employer to comply with any collective bargaining agreement or any employment benefit program or plan that provides greater family or medical leave rights to employees than the rights established under this Act or any amendment made by this Act.

(b) Less protective. The rights established for employees under this Act or any amendment made by this Act shall not be diminished by any collective bargaining agreement or any employment benefit program or plan.

2653. Encouragement of more generous leave policies

Nothing in this Act or any amendment made by this Act shall be construed to discourage employers from adopting or retaining leave policies more generous than any policies that comply with the requirements under this Act or any amendment made by this Act.

2654. Regulations

The Secretary of Labor shall prescribe such regulations as are necessary to carry out title I and this title [29 U.S.C. §§ 2611 et seq., 2651 et seq.] not later than 120 days after the date of the enactment of this Act [Feb. 5, 1993]

Chapter 9
INDIVIDUALS WITH DISABILITIES EDUCATION ACT

Individuals with Disabilities Education Act
20 U.S.C. § 1400 et seq

Editor's Note: The Implementing Regulations are found at 34 C.F.R. § 300.1 et seq.

§ 1400. Short title; table of contents; findings; purposes

(a) Short title. This title [20 U.S.C. §§ 1400 et seq.] may be cited as the "Individuals with Disabilities Education Act".

(b) [Omitted]

(c) Findings. Congress finds the following:

(1) Disability is a natural part of the human experience and in no way diminishes the right of individuals to participate in or contribute to society. Improving educational results for children with disabilities is an essential element of our national policy of ensuring equality of opportunity, full participation, independent living, and economic self-sufficiency for individuals with disabilities.

(2) Before the date of enactment of the Education for All Handicapped Children Act of 1975 (Public Law 94-142) [enacted Nov. 29, 1975], the educational needs of millions of children with disabilities were not being fully met because —

(A) the children did not receive appropriate educational services;

(B) the children were excluded entirely from the public school system and from being educated with their peers;

(C) undiagnosed disabilities prevented the children from having a successful educational experience; or

(D) a lack of adequate resources within the public school system forced families to find services outside the public school system.

(3) Since the enactment and implementation of the Education for All Handicapped Children Act of 1975 [enacted Nov. 29, 1975], this title [20 U.S.C. §§ 1400 et seq.] has been successful in ensuring children with disabilities and the families of such children access to a free appropriate public education and in improving educational results for children with disabilities.

(4) However, the implementation of this title [20 U.S.C. §§ 1400 et seq.] has been impeded by low expectations, and an insufficient focus on applying replicable research on proven methods of teaching and learning for children with disabilities.

(5) Almost 30 years of research and experience has demonstrated that the education of children with disabilities can be made more effective by —

(A) having high expectations for such children and ensuring their access to the general education curriculum in the regular classroom, to the maximum extent possible, in order to —

(i) meet developmental goals and, to the maximum extent possible, the challenging expectations that have been established for all children; and

(ii) be prepared to lead productive and independent adult lives, to the maximum extent possible;

(B) strengthening the role and responsibility of parents and ensuring that families of such children have meaningful opportunities to participate in the education of their children at school and at home;

(C) coordinating this title [20 U.S.C. §§ 1400 et seq.] with other local, educational service agency, State, and Federal school improvement efforts, including improvement efforts under the Elementary and Secondary Education Act of 1965, in order to ensure that such children benefit from such efforts and that special education can become a service for such children rather than a place where such children are sent;

(D) providing appropriate special education and related services, and aids and supports in the regular classroom, to such children, whenever appropriate;

(E) supporting high-quality, intensive preservice preparation and professional development for all personnel who work with children with disabilities in order to ensure that such personnel have the skills and knowledge necessary to improve the academic achievement and functional performance of children with disabilities, including the use of scientifically based instructional practices, to the maximum extent possible;

(F) providing incentives for whole-school approaches, scientifically based early reading programs, positive behavioral interventions and supports, and early intervening services to reduce the need to label children as disabled in order to address the learning and behavioral needs of such children;

(G) focusing resources on teaching and learning while reducing paperwork and requirements that do not assist in improving educational results; and

(H) supporting the development and use of technology, including assistive technology devices and assistive technology services, to maximize accessibility for children with disabilities.

(6-14) [Omitted from Statutory Supplement.]

§ 1401. Definitions

Except as otherwise provided, in this title [20 U.S.C. §§ 1400 et seq.]:

(1) Assistive technology device.

(A) In general. The term "assistive technology device" means any item, piece of equipment, or product system, whether acquired commercially off the shelf, modified, or customized, that is used to increase, maintain, or improve functional capabilities of a child with a disability.

(B) Exception. The term does not include a medical device that is surgically implanted, or the replacement of such device.

(2) Assistive technology service. The term "assistive technology service" means any service that directly assists a child with a disability in the selection, acquisition, or use of an assistive technology device. Such term includes —

(A) the evaluation of the needs of such child, including a functional evaluation of the child in the child's customary environment;

(B) purchasing, leasing, or otherwise providing for the acquisition of assistive technology devices by such child;

(C) selecting, designing, fitting, customizing, adapting, applying, maintaining, repairing, or replacing assistive technology devices;

(D) coordinating and using other therapies, interventions, or services with assistive technology devices, such as those associated with existing education and rehabilitation plans and programs;

(E) training or technical assistance for such child, or, where appropriate, the family of such child; and

(F) training or technical assistance for professionals (including individuals providing education and rehabilitation services), employers, or other individuals who provide services to, employ, or are otherwise substantially involved in the major life functions of such child.

(3) Child with a disability.

(A) In general. The term "child with a disability" means a child —

(i) with intellectual disabilities, hearing impairments (including deafness), speech or language impairments, visual impairments (including blindness), serious emotional disturbance (referred to in this title [20 U.S.C. §§ 1400 et seq.] as "emotional disturbance"), orthopedic impairments, autism, traumatic brain injury, other health impairments, or specific learning disabilities; and

(ii) who, by reason thereof, needs special education and related services.

(B) Child aged 3 through 9. The term "child with a disability" for a child aged 3 through 9 (or any subset of that age range, including ages 3 through 5), may, at the discretion of the State and the local educational agency, include a child —

(i) experiencing developmental delays, as defined by the State and as measured by appropriate diagnostic instruments and procedures, in 1 or more of the following areas: physical development; cognitive development; communication development; social or emotional development; or adaptive development; and

(ii) who, by reason thereof, needs special education and related services.

(4) Core academic subjects. The term "core academic subjects" has the meaning given the term in section 9101 of the Elementary and Secondary Education Act of 1965 [20 U.S.C. § 7801].

(5) Educational service agency. The term "educational service agency" —

(A) means a regional public multiservice agency —

(i) authorized by State law to develop, manage, and provide services or programs to local educational agencies; and

(ii) recognized as an administrative agency for purposes of the provision of special education and related services provided within public elementary schools and secondary schools of the State; and

(B) includes any other public institution or agency having administrative control and direction over a public elementary school or secondary school.

(6) Elementary school. The term "elementary school" means a nonprofit institutional day or residential school, including a public elementary charter school, that provides elementary education, as determined under State law.

(7) Equipment. The term "equipment" includes —

(A) machinery, utilities, and built-in equipment, and any necessary enclosures or structures to house such machinery, utilities, or equipment; and

(B) all other items necessary for the functioning of a particular facility as a facility for the provision of educational services, including items such as instructional equipment and necessary furniture; printed, published, and audio-visual instructional materials; telecommunications, sensory, and other technological aids and devices; and books, periodicals, documents, and other related materials.

(8) Excess costs. The term "excess costs" means those costs that are in excess of the average annual per-student expenditure in a local educational agency during the preceding school year for an elementary school or secondary school student, as may be appropriate, and which shall be computed after deducting —

(A) amounts received —

(i) under part B [20 U.S.C. §§ 1411 et seq.];

(ii) under part A of title I of the Elementary and Secondary Education Act of 1965 [20 U.S.C. §§ 6311 et seq.]; and

(iii) under parts A and B of title III of that Act [20 U.S.C. §§ 6811 et seq. and 6891 et seq.]; and

(B) any State or local funds expended for programs that would qualify for assistance under any of those parts.

(9) Free appropriate public education. The term "free appropriate public education" means special education and related services that — (A) have been provided at public expense, under public supervision and direction, and without charge;

(B) meet the standards of the State educational agency;

(C) include an appropriate preschool, elementary school, or secondary school education in the State involved; and

(D) are provided in conformity with the individualized education program required under section 614(d) [20 U.S.C. § 1414(d)].

(10) Highly qualified. [Specifics within this definition omitted by authors].

(11) Homeless children. The term "homeless children" has the meaning given the term "homeless children and youths" in section 725 of the McKinney-Vento Homeless Assistance Act (42 U.S.C. 11434a).

(12) Indian. The term "Indian" means an individual who is a member of an Indian tribe.

(13) Indian tribe. The term "Indian tribe" means any Federal or State Indian tribe, band, rancheria, pueblo, colony, or community, including any Alaska Native village or regional village corporation (as defined in or established under the Alaska Native Claims Settlement Act (43 U.S.C. 1601 et seq.)).

(14) Individualized education program; IEP. The term "individualized education program" or "IEP" means a written statement for each child with a disability that is developed, reviewed, and revised in accordance with section 614(d) [20 U.S.C. § 1414(d)].

(15) Individualized family service plan. The term "individualized family service plan" has the meaning given the term in section 636 [20 U.S.C. § 1436].

(16) Infant or toddler with a disability. The term "infant or toddler with a disability" has the meaning given the term in section 632 [20 U.S.C. § 1432].

(17) Institution of higher education. The term "institution of higher education" —

(A) has the meaning given the term in section 101 of the Higher Education Act of 1965 [20 U.S.C. § 1001]; and

(B) also includes any college or university receiving funding from the Secretary of the Interior under the Tribally Controlled Colleges and Universities Assistance Act of 1978.

(18) Limited English proficient. The term "limited English proficient" has the meaning given the term in section 9101 of the Elementary and Secondary Education Act of 1965 [20 U.S.C. § 7801].

(19) Local educational agency.

(A) In general. The term "local educational agency" means a public board of education or other public authority legally constituted within a State for either administrative control or direction of, or to perform a service function for, public elementary schools or secondary schools in a city, county, township, school district, or other political subdivision of a State, or for such combination of school districts or counties as are recognized in a State as an administrative agency for its public elementary schools or secondary schools.

(B) Educational service agencies and other public institutions or agencies. The term includes —

(i) an educational service agency; and

(ii) any other public institution or agency having administrative control and direction of a public elementary school or secondary school.

(C) BIA funded schools. The term includes an elementary school or secondary school funded by the Bureau of Indian Affairs, but only to the extent that such inclusion makes the school eligible for programs for which specific eligibility is not provided to the school in another provision of law and the school does not have a student population that is smaller than the student population of the local educational agency receiving assistance under this title [20 U.S.C. §§ 1400 et seq.] with the smallest student population, except that the school shall not be subject to the jurisdiction of any State educational agency other than the Bureau of Indian Affairs.

(20) Native language. The term "native language", when used with respect to an individual who is limited English proficient, means the language normally used by the individual or, in the case of a child, the language normally used by the parents of the child.

(21) Nonprofit. The term "nonprofit", as applied to a school, agency, organization, or institution, means a school, agency, organization, or institution owned and operated by 1 or more nonprofit corporations or associations no part of the net earnings of which inures, or may lawfully inure, to the benefit of any private shareholder or individual.

(22) Outlying area. The term "outlying area" means the United States Virgin Islands, Guam, American Samoa, and the Commonwealth of the Northern Mariana Islands.

(23) Parent. The term "parent" means —

(A) a natural, adoptive, or foster parent of a child (unless a foster parent is prohibited by State law from serving as a parent);

(B) a guardian (but not the State if the child is a ward of the State);

(C) an individual acting in the place of a natural or adoptive parent (including a grandparent, stepparent, or other relative) with whom the child lives, or an individual who is legally responsible for the child's welfare; or(D) except as used in sections 615(b)(2) and 639(a)(5) [20 U.S.C. §§ 1415(b)(2) and 1439(a)(5)], an individual assigned under either of those sections to be a surrogate parent.

(24) Parent organization. The term "parent organization" has the meaning given the term in section 671(g) [20 U.S.C. § 1471(g)].

(25) Parent training and information center. The term "parent training and information center" means a center assisted under section 671 or 672 [20 U.S.C. § 1471 or 1472].

(26) Related services.

(A) In general. The term "related services" means transportation, and such developmental, corrective, and other supportive services (including speech-language pathology and audiology services, interpreting services, psychological services, physical and occupational therapy, recreation, including thera-peutic recreation, social work services, school nurse services designed to enable a child with a disability to receive a free appropriate public education as described in the individualized education program of the child, counseling services, including rehabilitation counseling, orientation and mobility services, and medical services, except that such medical services shall be for diagnostic and evaluation purposes only) as may be required to assist a child with a disability to benefit from special education, and includes the early identifica-tion and assessment of disabling conditions in children.

(B) Exception. The term does not include a medical device that is surgically implanted, or the replacement of such device.

(27) Secondary school. The term "secondary school" means a nonprofit institutional day or residential school, including a public secondary charter school, that provides secondary education, as determined under State law, except that it does not include any education beyond grade 12.

(28) Secretary. The term "Secretary" means the Secretary of Education.

(29) Special education. The term "special education" means specially designed instruction, at no cost to parents, to meet the unique needs of a child with a disability, including —

(A) instruction conducted in the classroom, in the home, in hospitals and institutions, and in other settings; and

(B) instruction in physical education.

(30) Specific learning disability.

(A) In general. The term "specific learning disability" means a disorder in 1 or more of the basic psychological processes involved in understanding or in using language, spoken or written, which disorder may manifest itself in the imperfect ability to listen, think, speak, read, write, spell, or do mathematical calculations.

(B) Disorders included. Such term includes such conditions as perceptual disabilities, brain injury, minimal brain dysfunction, dyslexia, and developmen-tal aphasia.

(C) Disorders not included. Such term does not include a learning problem that is primarily the result of visual, hearing, or motor disabilities, of intellectual disabilities, of emotional disturbance, or of environmental, cultural, or economic disadvantage.

(31) State. The term "State" means each of the 50 States, the District of Columbia, the Commonwealth of Puerto Rico, and each of the outlying areas.

(32) State educational agency. The term "State educational agency" means the State board of education or other agency or officer primarily responsible for the State supervision of public elementary schools and secondary schools, or, if there is no such officer or agency, an officer or agency designated by the Governor or by State law.

(33) Supplementary aids and services. The term "supplementary aids and services" means aids, services, and other supports that are provided in regular education classes or other education-related settings to enable children with disabilities to be educated with nondisabled children to the maximum extent appropriate in accordance with section 612(a)(5) [20 U.S.C. § 1412(a)(5)].

(34) Transition services. The term "transition services" means a coordinated set of activities for a child with a disability that —

(A) is designed to be within a results-oriented process, that is focused on improving the academic and functional achievement of the child with a disability to facilitate the child's movement from school to post-school activities, including post-secondary education, vocational education, integrated employment (including supported employment), continuing and adult education, adult services, independent living, or community participation;

(B) is based on the individual child's needs, taking into account the child's strengths, preferences, and interests; and

(C) includes instruction, related services, community experiences, the development of employment and other post-school adult living objectives, and, when appropriate, acquisition of daily living skills and functional vocational evaluation.

(35) Universal design. The term "universal design" has the meaning given the term in section 3 of the Assistive Technology Act of 1998 (29 U.S.C. 3002).

(36) Ward of the State.

(A) In general. The term "ward of the State" means a child who, as determined by the State where the child resides, is a foster child, is a ward of the State, or is in the custody of a public child welfare agency.

(B) Exception. The term does not include a foster child who has a foster parent who meets the definition of a parent in paragraph (23).

§ 1402. Office of Special Education Programs [Omited from Statutory Supplement.]

§ 1403. Abrogation of State sovereign immunity

(a) In general. A State shall not be immune under the 11th amendment to the Constitution of the United States from suit in Federal court for a violation of this title [20 U.S.C. §§ 1400 et seq.].

(b) Remedies. In a suit against a State for a violation of this title [20 U.S.C. §§ 1400 et seq.], remedies (including remedies both at law and in equity) are available for such a violation to the same extent as those remedies are available for such a violation in the suit against any public entity other than a State.

(c) Effective date. Subsections (a) and (b) apply with respect to violations that occur in whole or part after the date of enactment of the Education of the Handicapped Act Amendments of 1990 [enacted Oct. 30, 1990].

1404-1411 [Omitted from Statutory Supplement.]

These sections address acquisition of equipment, construction or alteration of facilities, employment of individuals with disabilities, requirements for prescribing regulations, state administration, paperwork reduction, funding authorization, and other matters.]

1412. State eligibility

(a) In general. A State is eligible for assistance under this part [20 U.S.C. §§ 1411 et seq.] for a fiscal year if the State submits a plan that provides assurances to the Secretary that the State has in effect policies and procedures to ensure that the State meets each of the following conditions:

(1) Free appropriate public education.

(A) In general. A free appropriate public education is available to all children with disabilities residing in the State between the ages of 3 and 21, inclusive, including children with disabilities who have been suspended or expelled from school.

(B) Limitation. The obligation to make a free appropriate public education available to all children with disabilities does not apply with respect to children —

(i) aged 3 through 5 and 18 through 21 in a State to the extent that its application to those children would be inconsistent with State law or practice, or the order of any court, respecting the provision of public education to children in those age ranges; and

(ii) aged 18 through 21 to the extent that State law does not require that special education and related services under this part [20 U.S.C. §§ 1411 et seq.] be provided to children with disabilities who, in the educational placement prior to their incarceration in an adult correctional facility —

(I) were not actually identified as being a child with a disability under section 602 [20 U.S.C. § 1401]; or

(II) did not have an individualized education program under this part [20 U.S.C. §§ 1411 et seq.].

(C) State flexibility. A State that provides early intervention services in accordance with part C [20 U.S.C. §§ 1431 et seq.] to a child who is eligible for services under section 619, is not required to provide such child with a free appropriate public education.

(2) Full educational opportunity goal. The State has established a goal of providing full educational opportunity to all children with disabilities and a detailed timetable for accomplishing that goal.

(3) Child find.

(A) In general. All children with disabilities residing in the State, including children with disabilities who are homeless children or are wards of the State and children with disabilities attending private schools, regardless of the severity of their disabilities, and who are in need of special education and related services, are identified, located, and evaluated and a practical method is developed and implemented to determine which children with disabilities are currently receiving needed special education and related services.

(B) Construction. Nothing in this title [20 U.S.C. §§ 1400 et seq.] requires that children be classified by their disability so long as each child who has a disability listed in section 602 [20 U.S.C. § 1401] and who, by reason of that disability, needs special education and related services is regarded as a child with a disability under this part [20 U.S.C. §§ 1411 et seq.].

(4) Individualized education program. An individualized education program, or an individualized family service plan that meets the requirements of section 636(d) [20 U.S.C. § 1436(d)], is developed, reviewed, and revised for each child with a disability in accordance with section 614(d) [20 U.S.C. § 1414(d)].

(5) Least restrictive environment.

(A) In general. To the maximum extent appropriate, children with disabilities, including children in public or private institutions or other care facilities, are educated with children who are not disabled, and special classes, separate schooling, or other removal of children with disabilities from the regular educational environment occurs only when the nature or severity of the disability of a child is such that education in regular classes with the use of supplementary aids and services cannot be achieved satisfactorily.

(B) Additional requirement.

(i) In general. A State funding mechanism shall not result in placements that violate the requirements of subparagraph (A), and a State shall not use a funding mechanism by which the State distributes funds on the basis of the type of setting in which a child is served that will result in the failure to provide a child with a disability a free appropriate public education according to the unique needs of the child as described in the child's IEP.

(ii) Assurance. If the State does not have policies and procedures to ensure compliance with clause (i), the State shall provide the Secretary an assurance that the State will revise the funding mechanism as soon as feasible to ensure that such mechanism does not result in such placements.

(6) Procedural safeguards.

(A) In general. Children with disabilities and their parents are afforded the procedural safeguards required by section 615 [20 U.S.C. § 1415].

(B) Additional procedural safeguards. Procedures to ensure that testing and evaluation materials and procedures utilized for the purposes of evaluation and placement of children with disabilities for services under this title [20 U.S.C. §§ 1400 et seq.] will be selected and administered so as not to be racially or culturally discriminatory. Such materials or procedures shall be provided and administered in the child's native language or mode of communication, unless it clearly is not feasible to do so, and no single procedure shall be the sole criterion for determining an appropriate educational program for a child.

(7) Evaluation. Children with disabilities are evaluated in accordance with subsections (a) through (c) of section 614 [20 U.S.C. § 1414].

(8) Confidentiality. Agencies in the State comply with section 617(c) [20 U.S.C. § 1417(c)] (relating to the confidentiality of records and information).

(9) Transition from part C to preschool programs. Children participating in early intervention programs assisted under part C [20 U.S.C. §§ 1431 et seq.], and who will participate in preschool programs assisted under this part [20 U.S.C. §§ 1411 et seq.], experience a smooth and effective transition to those preschool programs in a manner consistent with section 637(a)(9) [20 U.S.C. § 1437(a)(9)]. By the third birthday of such a child, an individualized education program or, if consistent with sections 614(d)(2)(B) and 636(d) [20 U.S.C. §§ 1414(d)(2)(B) and 1436(d)], an individualized family service plan, has been developed and is being implemented for the child. The local educational agency will participate in transition planning conferences arranged by the designated lead agency under section 635(a)(10) [20 U.S.C. § 1435(a)(10)].

(10) Children in private schools.

(A) Children enrolled in private schools by their parents.

(i) In general. To the extent consistent with the number and location of children with disabilities in the State who are enrolled by their parents in private elementary schools and secondary schools in the school district served by a local educational agency, provision is made for the participation of those children in the program assisted or carried out under this part [20 U.S.C. §§ 1411 et seq.] by providing for such children special education and related services in accordance with the following requirements, unless the Secretary has arranged for services to those children under subsection (f):

(I) Amounts to be expended for the provision of those services (including direct services to parentally placed private school children) by the local educational agency shall be equal to a proportionate amount of Federal funds made available under this part [20 U.S.C. §§ 1411 et seq.].

(II) In calculating the proportionate amount of Federal funds, the local educational agency, after timely and meaningful consultation with representatives of private schools as described in clause (iii), shall conduct a thorough and complete child find process to determine the number of parentally placed children with disabilities attending private schools located in the local educational agency.

(III) Such services to parentally placed private school children with disabilities may be provided to the children on the premises of private, including religious, schools, to the extent consistent with law.

(IV) State and local funds may supplement and in no case shall supplant the proportionate amount of Federal funds required to be expended under this subparagraph.

(V) Each local educational agency shall maintain in its records and provide to the State educational agency the number of children evaluated under this subparagraph, the number of children determined to be children with disabilities under this paragraph, and the number of children served under this paragraph.

(ii) Child find requirement.

(I) In general. The requirements of paragraph (3) (relating to child find) shall apply with respect to children with disabilities in the State who are enrolled in private, including religious, elementary schools and secondary schools.

(II) Equitable participation. The child find process shall be designed to ensure the equitable participation of parentally placed private school children with disabilities and an accurate count of such children.

(III) Activities. In carrying out this clause, the local educational agency, or where applicable, the State educational agency, shall undertake activities similar to those activities undertaken for the agency's public school children.

(IV) Cost. The cost of carrying out this clause, including individual evaluations, may not be considered in determining whether a local educational agency has met its obligations under clause (i).

(V) Completion period. Such child find process shall be completed in a time period comparable to that for other students attending public schools in the local educational agency.

(iii) Consultation. To ensure timely and meaningful consultation, a local educational agency, or where appropriate, a State educational agency, shall consult with private school representatives and representatives of parents of parentally placed private school children with disabilities during the design and development of special education and related services for the children, including regarding —

(I) the child find process and how parentally placed private school children suspected of having a disability can participate equitably, including how parents, teachers, and private school officials will be informed of the process;

(II) the determination of the proportionate amount of Federal funds available to serve parentally placed private school children with disabilities under this subparagraph, including the determination of how the amount was calculated;

(III) the consultation process among the local educational agency, private school officials, and representatives of parents of parentally placed private school children with disabilities, including how such process will operate throughout the school year to ensure that parentally placed private school children with disabilities identified through the child find process can meaningfully participate in special education and related services;

(IV) how, where, and by whom special education and related services will be provided for parentally placed private school children with disabilities, including a discussion of types of services, including direct services and alternate service delivery mechanisms, how such services will be apportioned if funds are insufficient to serve all children, and how and when these decisions will be made; and

(V) how, if the local educational agency disagrees with the views of the private school officials on the provision of services or the types of services, whether provided directly or through a contract, the local educational agency shall provide to the private school officials a written explanation of the reasons why the local educational agency chose not to provide services directly or through a contract.

(iv) Written affirmation. When timely and meaningful consultation as required by clause (iii) has occurred, the local educational agency shall obtain a written affirmation signed by the representatives of participating private schools, and if such representatives do not provide such affirmation within a reasonable period of time, the local educational agency shall forward the documentation of the consultation process to the State educational agency.

(v) Compliance.

(I) In general. A private school official shall have the right to submit a complaint to the State educational agency that the local educational agency did not engage in consultation that was meaningful and timely, or did not give due consideration to the views of the private school official.

(II) Procedure. If the private school official wishes to submit a complaint, the official shall provide the basis of the noncompliance with this subparagraph by the local educational agency to the State educational agency, and the local educational agency shall forward the appropriate documentation to the State educational agency. If the private school official is dissatisfied with the decision of the State educational agency, such official may submit a complaint to the Secretary by providing the basis of the noncompliance with this subparagraph by the local educational agency to the Secretary, and the State educational agency shall forward the appropriate documentation to the Secretary.

(vi) Provision of equitable services.

(I) Directly or through contracts. The provision of services pursuant to this subparagraph shall be provided —

(aa) by employees of a public agency; or

(bb) through contract by the public agency with an individual, association, agency, organization, or other entity.

(II) Secular, neutral, nonideological. Special education and related services provided to parentally placed private school children with disabilities, including materials and equipment, shall be secular, neutral, and nonideological.

(vii) Public control of funds. The control of funds used to provide special education and related services under this subparagraph, and title to materials, equipment, and property purchased with those funds, shall be in a public agency for the uses and purposes provided in this title [20 U.S.C. §§ 1400 et seq.], and a public agency shall administer the funds and property.

(B) Children placed in, or referred to, private schools by public agencies.

(i) In general. Children with disabilities in private schools and facilities are provided special education and related services, in accordance with an individualized education program, at no cost to their parents, if such children are placed in, or referred to, such schools or facilities by the State or appropriate local educational agency as the means of carrying out the requirements of this part [20 U.S.C. §§ 1411 et seq.] or any other applicable law requiring the provision of special education and related services to all children with disabilities within such State.

(ii) Standards. In all cases described in clause (i), the State educational agency shall determine whether such schools and facilities meet standards that apply to State educational agencies and local educational agencies and that children so served have all the rights the children would have if served by such agencies.

(C) Payment for education of children enrolled in private schools without consent of or referral by the public agency.

(i) In general. Subject to subparagraph (A), this part [20 U.S.C. §§ 1411 et seq.] does not require a local educational agency to pay for the cost of education, including special education and related services, of a child with a disability at a private school or facility if that agency made a free appropriate public education available to the child and the parents elected to place the child in such private school or facility.

(ii) Reimbursement for private school placement. If the parents of a child with a disability, who previously received special education and related services under the authority of a public agency, enroll the child in a private elementary school or secondary school without the consent of or referral by the public agency, a court or a hearing officer may require the agency to reimburse the parents for the cost of that enrollment if the court or hearing officer finds that the agency had not made a free appropriate public education available to the child in a timely manner prior to that enrollment.

(iii) Limitation on reimbursement. The cost of reimbursement described in clause (ii) may be reduced or denied —

(I) if —

(aa) at the most recent IEP meeting that the parents attended prior to removal of the child from the public school, the parents did not inform the IEP Team that they were rejecting the placement proposed by the public agency to provide a free appropriate public education to their child, including stating their concerns and their intent to enroll their child in a private school at public expense; or

(bb) 10 business days (including any holidays that occur on a business day) prior to the removal of the child from the public school, the parents did not give written notice to the public agency of the information described in item (aa);

(II) if, prior to the parents' removal of the child from the public school, the public agency informed the parents, through the notice requirements described in section 615(b)(3) [20 U.S.C. § 1415(b)(3)], of its intent to evaluate the child (including a statement of the purpose of the evaluation that was appropriate and reasonable), but the parents did not make the child available for such evaluation; or

(III) upon a judicial finding of unreasonableness with respect to actions taken by the parents.

(iv) Exception. Notwithstanding the notice requirement in clause (iii)(I), the cost of reimbursement —

(I) shall not be reduced or denied for failure to provide such notice if —

(aa) the school prevented the parent from providing such notice;

(bb) the parents had not received notice, pursuant to section 615 [20 U.S.C. § 1415], of the notice requirement in clause (iii)(I); or

(cc) compliance with clause (iii)(I) would likely result in physical harm to the child; and

(II) may, in the discretion of a court or a hearing officer, not be reduced or denied for failure to provide such notice if —

(aa) the parent is illiterate or cannot write in English; or

(bb) compliance with clause (iii)(I) would likely result in serious emotional harm to the child.

(11) State educational agency responsible for general supervision.

(A) In general. The State educational agency is responsible for ensuring that —

(i) the requirements of this part [20 U.S.C. §§ 1411 et seq.] are met;

(ii) all educational programs for children with disabilities in the State, including all such programs administered by any other State agency or local agency —

(I) are under the general supervision of individuals in the State who are responsible for educational programs for children with disabilities; and

(II) meet the educational standards of the State educational agency; and

(iii) in carrying out this part [20 U.S.C. §§ 1411 et seq.] with respect to homeless children, the requirements of subtitle B of title VII of the McKinney-Vento Homeless Assistance Act (42 U.S.C. 11431 et seq.) are met.

(B) Limitation. Subparagraph (A) shall not limit the responsibility of agencies in the State other than the State educational agency to provide, or pay for some or all of the costs of, a free appropriate public education for any child with a disability in the State.

(C) Exception. Notwithstanding subparagraphs (A) and (B), the Governor (or another individual pursuant to State law), consistent with State law, may assign to any public agency in the State the responsibility of ensuring that the requirements of this part [20 U.S.C. §§ 1411 et seq.] are met with respect to children with disabilities who are convicted as adults under State law and incarcerated in adult prisons.

(12) Obligations related to and methods of ensuring services.

(A) Establishing responsibility for services. The Chief Executive Officer of a State or designee of the officer shall ensure that an interagency agreement or other mechanism for interagency coordination is in effect between each public agency described in subparagraph (B) and the State educational agency, in order to ensure that all services described in subparagraph (B)(i) that are needed to ensure a free appropriate public education are provided, including the provision of such services during the pendency of any dispute under clause (iii). Such agreement or mechanism shall include the following:

(i) Agency financial responsibility. An identification of, or a method for defining, the financial responsibility of each agency for providing services described in subparagraph (B)(i) to ensure a free appropriate public education to children with disabilities, provided that the financial responsibility of each public agency described in subparagraph (B), including the State medicaid agency and other public insurers of children with disabilities, shall precede the financial responsibility of the local educational agency (or the State agency responsible for developing the child's IEP).

(ii) Conditions and terms of reimbursement. The conditions, terms, and procedures under which a local educational agency shall be reimbursed by other agencies.

(iii) Interagency disputes. Procedures for resolving interagency disputes (including procedures under which local educational agencies may initiate proceedings) under the agreement or other mechanism to secure reimbursement from other agencies or otherwise implement the provisions of the agreement or mechanism.

(iv) Coordination of services procedures. Policies and procedures for agencies to determine and identify the interagency coordination responsibilities of each agency to promote the coordination and timely and appropriate delivery of services described in subparagraph (B)(i).

(B) Obligation of public agency.

(i) In general. If any public agency other than an educational agency is otherwise obligated under Federal or State law, or assigned responsibility under State policy pursuant to subparagraph (A), to provide or pay for any services that are also considered special education or related services (such as, but not limited to, services described in section 602(1) [20 U.S.C.

§ 1401(1)] relating to assistive technology devices, 602(2) [20 U.S.C. § 1401(2)] relating to assistive technology services, 602(26) [20 U.S.C. § 1401(26)] relating to related services, 602(33) [20 U.S.C. § 1401(33)] relating to supplementary aids and services, and 602(34) [20 U.S.C. § 1401(34)] relating to transition services) that are necessary for ensuring a free appropriate public education to children with disabilities within the State, such public agency shall fulfill that obligation or responsibility, either directly or through contract or other arrangement pursuant to subparagraph (A) or an agreement pursuant to subparagraph (C).

(ii) Reimbursement for services by public agency. If a public agency other than an educational agency fails to provide or pay for the special education and related services described in clause (i), the local educational agency (or State agency responsible for developing the child's IEP) shall provide or pay for such services to the child. Such local educational agency or State agency is authorized to claim reimbursement for the services from the public agency that failed to provide or pay for such services and such public agency shall reimburse the local educational agency or State agency pursuant to the terms of the interagency agreement or other mechanism described in subparagraph (A)(i) according to the procedures established in such agreement pursuant to subparagraph (A)(ii).

(C) Special rule. The requirements of subparagraph (A) may be met through —

(i) State statute or regulation;

(ii) signed agreements between respective agency officials that clearly identify the responsibilities of each agency relating to the provision of services; or

(iii) other appropriate written methods as determined by the Chief Executive Officer of the State or designee of the officer and approved by the Secretary.

(13) Procedural requirements relating to local educational agency eligibility. The State educational agency will not make a final determination that a local educational agency is not eligible for assistance under this part [20 U.S.C. §§ 1411 et seq.] without first affording that agency reasonable notice and an opportunity for a hearing.

(14) Personnel qualifications.

(A) In general. The State educational agency has established and maintains qualifications to ensure that personnel necessary to carry out this part [20 U.S.C. §§ 1411 et seq.] are appropriately and adequately prepared and trained, including that those personnel have the content knowledge and skills to serve children with disabilities.

(B) Related services personnel and paraprofessionals. The qualifications under subparagraph (A) include qualifications for related services personnel and paraprofessionals that —

(i) are consistent with any State-approved or State-recognized certification, licensing, registration, or other comparable requirements that apply to the professional discipline in which those personnel are providing special education or related services;

(ii) ensure that related services personnel who deliver services in their discipline or profession meet the requirements of clause (i) and have not had certification or licensure requirements waived on an emergency, temporary, or provisional basis; and

(iii) allow paraprofessionals and assistants who are appropriately trained and supervised, in accordance with State law, regulation, or written policy, in meeting the requirements of this part [20 U.S.C. §§ 1411 et seq.] to be used to assist in the provision of special education and related services under this part [20 U.S.C. §§ 1411 et seq.] to children with disabilities.

(C) Qualifications for special education teachers. The qualifications described in subparagraph (A) shall ensure that each person employed as a special education teacher in the State who teaches elementary school, middle school, or secondary school is highly qualified by the deadline established in section 1119(a)(2) of the Elementary and Secondary Education Act of 1965 [20 U.S.C. § 6319(a)(2)].

(D) Policy. In implementing this section, a State shall adopt a policy that includes a requirement that local educational agencies in the State take measurable steps to recruit, hire, train, and retain highly qualified personnel to provide special education and related services under this part [20 U.S.C. §§ 1411 et seq.] to children with disabilities.

(E) Rule of construction. Notwithstanding any other individual right of action that a parent or student may maintain under this part [20 U.S.C. §§ 1411 et seq.], nothing in this paragraph shall be construed to create a right of action on behalf of an individual student for the failure of a particular State educational agency or local educational agency staff person to be highly qualified, or to prevent a parent from filing a complaint about staff qualifications with the State educational agency as provided for under this part [20 U.S.C. §§ 1411 et seq.].

(15-25) [Omitted from Statutory Supplement.]

1413. Local educational agency eligibility

[Omitted from Statutory Supplement.]

1414. Evaluations, eligibility determinations, individualized education programs, and educational placements

(a) Evaluations, parental consent, and reevaluations.

(1) Initial evaluations.

(A) In general. A State educational agency, other State agency, or local educational agency shall conduct a full and individual initial evaluation in accordance with this paragraph and subsection (b), before the initial provision of special education and related services to a child with a disability under this part [20 U.S.C. §§ 1411 et seq.].

(B) Request for initial evaluation. Consistent with subparagraph (D), either a parent of a child, or a State educational agency, other State agency, or local educational agency may initiate a request for an initial evaluation to determine if the child is a child with a disability.

(C) Procedures.

(i) In general. Such initial evaluation shall consist of procedures —

(I) to determine whether a child is a child with a disability (as defined in section 602 [20 U.S.C. § 1401]) within 60 days of receiving parental consent for the evaluation, or, if the State establishes a timeframe within which the evaluation must be conducted, within such timeframe; and

(II) to determine the educational needs of such child.

(ii) Exception. The relevant timeframe in clause (i)(I) shall not apply to a local educational agency if —

(I) a child enrolls in a school served by the local educational agency after the relevant timeframe in clause (i)(I) has begun and prior to a determination by the child's previous local educational agency as to whether the child is a child with a disability (as defined in section 602 [20 U.S.C. § 1401]), but only if the subsequent local educational agency is making sufficient progress to ensure a prompt completion of the evaluation, and the parent and subsequent local educational agency agree to a specific time when the evaluation will be completed; or

(II) the parent of a child repeatedly fails or refuses to produce the child for the evaluation.

(D) Parental consent.

(i) In general.

(I) Consent for initial evaluation. The agency proposing to conduct an initial evaluation to determine if the child qualifies as a child with a disability as defined in section 602 [20 U.S.C. § 1401] shall obtain informed consent from the parent of such child before conducting the evaluation. Parental consent for evaluation shall not be construed as consent for placement for receipt of special education and related services.

(II) Consent for services. An agency that is responsible for making a free appropriate public education available to a child with a disability under this part [20 U.S.C. §§ 1411 et seq.] shall seek to obtain informed consent from the parent of such child before providing special education and related services to the child.

(ii) Absence of consent.

(I) For initial evaluation. If the parent of such child does not provide consent for an initial evaluation under clause (i)(I), or the parent fails to respond to a request to provide the consent, the local educational agency may pursue the initial evaluation of the child by utilizing the procedures described in section 615 [20 U.S.C. § 1415], except to the extent inconsistent with State law relating to such parental consent.

(II) For services. If the parent of such child refuses to consent to services under clause (i)(II), the local educational agency shall not provide special education and related services to the child by utilizing the procedures described in section 615 [20 U.S.C. § 1415].

(III) Effect on agency obligations. If the parent of such child refuses to consent to the receipt of special education and related services, or the parent fails to respond to a request to provide such consent —

(aa) the local educational agency shall not be considered to be in violation of the requirement to make available a free appropriate public education to the child for the failure to provide such child with the special education and related services for which the local educational agency requests such consent; and

(bb) the local educational agency shall not be required to convene an IEP meeting or develop an IEP under this section for the child for the special education and related services for which the local educational agency requests such consent.

(iii) Consent for wards of the State.

(I) In general. If the child is a ward of the State and is not residing with the child's parent, the agency shall make reasonable efforts to obtain the informed consent from the parent (as defined in section 602 [20 U.S.C. § 1401]) of the child for an initial evaluation to determine whether the child is a child with a disability.

(II) Exception. The agency shall not be required to obtain informed consent from the parent of a child for an initial evaluation to determine whether the child is a child with a disability if —

(aa) despite reasonable efforts to do so, the agency cannot discover the whereabouts of the parent of the child;

(bb) the rights of the parents of the child have been terminated in accordance with State law; or

(cc) the rights of the parent to make educational decisions have been subrogated by a judge in accordance with State law and consent for an initial evaluation has been given by an individual appointed by the judge to represent the child.

(E) Rule of construction. The screening of a student by a teacher or specialist to determine appropriate instructional strategies for curriculum implementation shall not be considered to be an evaluation for eligibility for special education and related services.

(2) Reevaluations.

(A) In general. A local educational agency shall ensure that a reevaluation of each child with a disability is conducted in accordance with subsections (b) and (c) —

(i) if the local educational agency determines that the educational or related services needs, including improved academic achievement and functional performance, of the child warrant a reevaluation; or

(ii) if the child's parents or teacher requests a reevaluation.

(B) Limitation. A reevaluation conducted under subparagraph (A) shall occur —

(i) not more frequently than once a year, unless the parent and the local educational agency agree otherwise; and

(ii) at least once every 3 years, unless the parent and the local educational agency agree that a reevaluation is unnecessary.

(b) Evaluation procedures.

(1) Notice. The local educational agency shall provide notice to the parents of a child with a disability, in accordance with subsections (b)(3), (b)(4), and (c) of section 615 [20 U.S.C. § 1415], that describes any evaluation procedures such agency proposes to conduct.

(2) Conduct of evaluation. In conducting the evaluation, the local educational agency shall —

(A) use a variety of assessment tools and strategies to gather relevant functional, developmental, and academic information, including information provided by the parent, that may assist in determining —

(i) whether the child is a child with a disability; and

(ii) the content of the child's individualized education program, including information related to enabling the child to be involved in and progress in the general education curriculum, or, for preschool children, to participate in appropriate activities;

(B) not use any single measure or assessment as the sole criterion for determining whether a child is a child with a disability or determining an appropriate educational program for the child; and

(C) use technically sound instruments that may assess the relative contribution of cognitive and behavioral factors, in addition to physical or developmental factors.

(3) Additional requirements. Each local educational agency shall ensure that —

(A) assessments and other evaluation materials used to assess a child under this section —

(i) are selected and administered so as not to be discriminatory on a racial or cultural basis;

(ii) are provided and administered in the language and form most likely to yield accurate information on what the child knows and can do academically, developmentally, and functionally, unless it is not feasible to so provide or administer;

(iii) are used for purposes for which the assessments or measures are valid and reliable;

(iv) are administered by trained and knowledgeable personnel; and

(v) are administered in accordance with any instructions provided by the producer of such assessments;

(B) the child is assessed in all areas of suspected disability;

(C) assessment tools and strategies that provide relevant information that directly assists persons in determining the educational needs of the child are provided; and

(D) assessments of children with disabilities who transfer from 1 school district to another school district in the same academic year are coordinated with such children's prior and subsequent schools, as necessary and as expeditiously as possible, to ensure prompt completion of full evaluations.

(4) Determination of eligibility and educational need. Upon completion of the administration of assessments and other evaluation measures —

(A) the determination of whether the child is a child with a disability as defined in section 602(3) [20 U.S.C. § 1401(3)] and the educational needs of the child shall be made by a team of qualified professionals and the parent of the child in accordance with paragraph (5); and

(B) a copy of the evaluation report and the documentation of determination of eligibility shall be given to the parent.

(5) Special rule for eligibility determination. In making a determination of eligibility under paragraph (4)(A), a child shall not be determined to be a child with a disability if the determinant factor for such determination is —

(A) lack of appropriate instruction in reading, including in the essential components of reading instruction (as defined in section 1208(3) of the Elementary and Secondary Education Act of 1965 [20 U.S.C. § 6368(3)]);

(B) lack of instruction in math; or

(C) limited English proficiency.

(6) Specific learning disabilities.

(A) In general. Notwithstanding section 607(b) [20 U.S.C. § 1406(b)], when determining whether a child has a specific learning disability as defined in section 602 [20 U.S.C. § 1401], a local educational agency shall not be required to take into consideration whether a child has a severe discrepancy between achievement and intellectual ability in oral expression, listening comprehension, written expression, basic reading skill, reading comprehension, mathematical calculation, or mathematical reasoning.

(B) Additional authority. In determining whether a child has a specific learning disability, a local educational agency may use a process that determines if the child responds to scientific, research-based intervention as a part of the evaluation procedures described in paragraphs (2) and (3).

(c) Additional requirements for evaluation and reevaluations.

(1) Review of existing evaluation data. As part of an initial evaluation (if appropriate) and as part of any reevaluation under this section, the IEP Team and other qualified professionals, as appropriate, shall —

(A) review existing evaluation data on the child, including —

(i) evaluations and information provided by the parents of the child;

(ii) current classroom-based, local, or State assessments, and classroom-based observations; and

(iii) observations by teachers and related services providers; and

(B) on the basis of that review, and input from the child's parents, identify what additional data, if any, are needed to determine —

(i) whether the child is a child with a disability as defined in section 602(3) [20 U.S.C. § 1401(3)], and the educational needs of the child, or, in case of a reevaluation of a child, whether the child continues to have such a disability and such educational needs;

(ii) the present levels of academic achievement and related developmental needs of the child;

(iii) whether the child needs special education and related services, or in the case of a reevaluation of a child, whether the child continues to need special education and related services; and

(iv) whether any additions or modifications to the special education and related services are needed to enable the child to meet the measurable annual goals set out in the individualized education program of the child and to participate, as appropriate, in the general education curriculum.

(2) Source of data. The local educational agency shall administer such assessments and other evaluation measures as may be needed to produce the data identified by the IEP Team under paragraph (1)(B).

(3) Parental consent. Each local educational agency shall obtain informed parental consent, in accordance with subsection (a)(1)(D), prior to conducting any reevaluation of a child with a disability, except that such informed parental consent need not be obtained if the local educational agency can demonstrate that it had taken reasonable measures to obtain such consent and the child's parent has failed to respond.

(4) Requirements if additional data are not needed. If the IEP Team and other qualified professionals, as appropriate, determine that no additional data are needed to determine whether the child continues to be a child with a disability and to determine the child's educational needs, the local educational agency —

(A) shall notify the child's parents of —

(i) that determination and the reasons for the determination; and

(ii) the right of such parents to request an assessment to determine whether the child continues to be a child with a disability and to determine the child's educational needs; and

(B) shall not be required to conduct such an assessment unless requested to by the child's parents.

(5) Evaluations before change in eligibility.

(A) In general. Except as provided in subparagraph (B), a local educational agency shall evaluate a child with a disability in accordance with this section before determining that the child is no longer a child with a disability.

(B) Exception.

(i) In general. The evaluation described in subparagraph (A) shall not be required before the termination of a child's eligibility under this part [20 U.S.C. §§ 1411 et seq.] due to graduation from secondary school with a regular diploma, or due to exceeding the age eligibility for a free appropriate public education under State law.

(ii) Summary of performance. For a child whose eligibility under this part [20 U.S.C. §§ 1411 et seq.] terminates under circumstances described in clause (i), a local educational agency shall provide the child with a summary of the child's academic achievement and functional performance, which shall include recommendations on how to assist the child in meeting the child's postsecondary goals.

(d) Individualized education programs.

(1) Definitions. In this title [20 U.S.C. §§ 1400 et seq.]:

(A) Individualized education program.

(i) In general. The term "individualized education program" or "IEP" means a written statement for each child with a disability that is developed, reviewed, and revised in accordance with this section and that includes —

(I) a statement of the child's present levels of academic achievement and functional performance, including —

(aa) how the child's disability affects the child's involvement and progress in the general education curriculum;

(bb) for preschool children, as appropriate, how the disability affects the child's participation in appropriate activities; and

(cc) for children with disabilities who take alternate assessments aligned to alternate achievement standards, a description of benchmarks or short-term objectives;

(II) a statement of measurable annual goals, including academic and functional goals, designed to —

(aa) meet the child's needs that result from the child's disability to enable the child to be involved in and make progress in the general education curriculum; and

(bb) meet each of the child's other educational needs that result from the child's disability;

(III) a description of how the child's progress toward meeting the annual goals described in subclause (II) will be measured and when periodic reports on the progress the child is making toward meeting the annual goals (such as through the use of quarterly or other periodic reports, concurrent with the issuance of report cards) will be provided;

(IV) a statement of the special education and related services and supplementary aids and services, based on peer-reviewed research to the extent practicable, to be provided to the child, or on behalf of the child, and a statement of the program modifications or supports for school personnel that will be provided for the child —

(aa) to advance appropriately toward attaining the annual goals;

(bb) to be involved in and make progress in the general education curriculum in accordance with subclause (I) and to participate in extracurricular and other nonacademic activities; and

(cc) to be educated and participate with other children with disabilities and nondisabled children in the activities described in this subparagraph;

(V) an explanation of the extent, if any, to which the child will not participate with nondisabled children in the regular class and in the activities described in subclause (IV)(cc);

(VI)

(aa) a statement of any individual appropriate accommodations that are necessary to measure the academic achievement and functional performance of the child on State and districtwide assessments consistent with section 612(a)(16)(A) [20 U.S.C. § 1412(a)(16)(A)]; and

(bb) if the IEP Team determines that the child shall take an alternate assessment on a particular State or districtwide assessment of student achievement, a statement of why —

(AA) the child cannot participate in the regular assessment; and

(BB) the particular alternate assessment selected is appropriate for the child;

(VII) the projected date for the beginning of the services and modifications described in subclause (IV), and the anticipated frequency, location, and duration of those services and modifications; and

(VIII) beginning not later than the first IEP to be in effect when the child is 16, and updated annually thereafter —

(aa) appropriate measurable postsecondary goals based upon age appropriate transition assessments related to training, education, employment, and, where appropriate, independent living skills;

(bb) the transition services (including courses of study) needed to assist the child in reaching those goals; and

(cc) beginning not later than 1 year before the child reaches the age of majority under State law, a statement that the child has been informed of the child's rights under this title [20 U.S.C. §§ 1400 et seq.], if any, that will transfer to the child on reaching the age of majority under section 615(m) [20 U.S.C. § 1415(m)].

(ii) Rule of construction. Nothing in this section shall be construed to require —

(I) that additional information be included in a child's IEP beyond what is explicitly required in this section; and

(II) the IEP Team to include information under 1 component of a child's IEP that is already contained under another component of such IEP.

(B) Individualized education program team. The term "individualized education program team" or "IEP Team" means a group of individuals composed of —

(i) the parents of a child with a disability;

(ii) not less than 1 regular education teacher of such child (if the child is, or may be, participating in the regular education environment);

(iii) not less than 1 special education teacher, or where appropriate, not less than 1 special education provider of such child;

(iv) a representative of the local educational agency who —

(I) is qualified to provide, or supervise the provision of, specially designed instruction to meet the unique needs of children with disabilities;

(II) is knowledgeable about the general education curriculum; and

(III) is knowledgeable about the availability of resources of the local educational agency;

(v) an individual who can interpret the instructional implications of evaluation results, who may be a member of the team described in clauses (ii) through (vi);

(vi) at the discretion of the parent or the agency, other individuals who have knowledge or special expertise regarding the child, including related services personnel as appropriate; and

(vii) whenever appropriate, the child with a disability.

(C) IEP team attendance.

(i) Attendance not necessary. A member of the IEP Team shall not be required to attend an IEP meeting, in whole or in part, if the parent of a child with a disability and the local educational agency agree that the attendance of such member is not necessary because the member's area of the curriculum or related services is not being modified or discussed in the meeting.

(ii) Excusal. A member of the IEP Team may be excused from attending an IEP meeting, in whole or in part, when the meeting involves a modification to or discussion of the member's area of the curriculum or related services, if —

(I) the parent and the local educational agency consent to the excusal; and

(II) the member submits, in writing to the parent and the IEP Team, input into the development of the IEP prior to the meeting.

(iii) Written agreement and consent required. A parent's agreement under clause (i) and consent under clause (ii) shall be in writing.

(D) IEP team transition. In the case of a child who was previously served under part C [20 U.S.C. §§ 1431 et seq.], an invitation to the initial IEP meeting shall, at the request of the parent, be sent to the part C service coordinator or other representatives of the part C system to assist with the smooth transition of services.

(2) Requirement that program be in effect.

(A) In general. At the beginning of each school year, each local educational agency, State educational agency, or other State agency, as the case may be, shall have in effect, for each child with a disability in the agency's jurisdiction, an individualized education program, as defined in paragraph (1)(A).

(B) Program for child aged 3 through 5. In the case of a child with a disability aged 3 through 5 (or, at the discretion of the State educational agency, a 2-year-old child with a disability who will turn age 3 during the school year), the IEP Team shall consider the individualized family service plan that contains the material described in section 636 [20 U.S.C. § 1436], and that is developed in accordance with this section, and the individualized family service plan may serve as the IEP of the child if using that plan as the IEP is —

(i) consistent with State policy; and

(ii) agreed to by the agency and the child's parents.

(C) Program for children who transfer school districts.

(i) In general.

(I) Transfer within the same State. In the case of a child with a disability who transfers school districts within the same academic year, who enrolls in a new school, and who had an IEP that was in effect in the same State, the local educational agency shall provide such child with a free appropriate public education, including services comparable to those described in the previously held IEP, in consultation with the parents until such time as the local educational agency adopts the previously held IEP or develops, adopts, and implements a new IEP that is consistent with Federal and State law.

(II) Transfer outside State. In the case of a child with a disability who transfers school districts within the same academic year, who enrolls in a new school, and who had an IEP that was in effect in another State, the local educational agency shall provide such child with a free appropriate public education, including services comparable to those described in the previously held IEP, in consultation with the parents until such time as the local educational agency conducts an evaluation pursuant to subsection (a)(1), if determined to be necessary by such agency, and develops a new IEP, if appropriate, that is consistent with Federal and State law.

(ii) Transmittal of records. To facilitate the transition for a child described in clause (i) —

(I) the new school in which the child enrolls shall take reasonable steps to promptly obtain the child's records, including the IEP and supporting documents and any other records relating to the provision of special education or related services to the child, from the previous school in which the child was enrolled, pursuant to section 99.31(a)(2) of title 34, Code of Federal Regulations; and

(II) the previous school in which the child was enrolled shall take reasonable steps to promptly respond to such request from the new school.

(3) Development of IEP.

(A) In general. In developing each child's IEP, the IEP Team, subject to subparagraph (C), shall consider —

(i) the strengths of the child;

(ii) the concerns of the parents for enhancing the education of their child;

(iii) the results of the initial evaluation or most recent evaluation of the child; and

(iv) the academic, developmental, and functional needs of the child.

(B) Consideration of special factors. The IEP Team shall —

(i) in the case of a child whose behavior impedes the child's learning or that of others, consider the use of positive behavioral interventions and supports, and other strategies, to address that behavior;

(ii) in the case of a child with limited English proficiency, consider the language needs of the child as such needs relate to the child's IEP;

(iii) in the case of a child who is blind or visually impaired, provide for instruction in Braille and the use of Braille unless the IEP Team determines, after an evaluation of the child's reading and writing skills, needs, and appropriate reading and writing media (including an evaluation of the child's future needs for instruction in Braille or the use of Braille), that instruction in Braille or the use of Braille is not appropriate for the child;

(iv) consider the communication needs of the child, and in the case of a child who is deaf or hard of hearing, consider the child's language and communication needs, opportunities for direct communications with peers and professional personnel in the child's language and communication mode, academic level, and full range of needs, including opportunities for direct instruction in the child's language and communication mode; and

(v) consider whether the child needs assistive technology devices and services.

(C) Requirement with respect to regular education teacher. A regular education teacher of the child, as a member of the IEP Team, shall, to the extent appropriate, participate in the development of the IEP of the child, including the determination of appropriate positive behavioral interventions and supports, and other strategies, and the determination of supplementary aids and services, program modifications, and support for school personnel consistent with paragraph (1)(A)(i)(IV).

(D) Agreement. In making changes to a child's IEP after the annual IEP meeting for a school year, the parent of a child with a disability and the local educational agency may agree not to convene an IEP meeting for the purposes of making such changes, and instead may develop a written document to amend or modify the child's current IEP.

(E) Consolidation of IEP team meetings. To the extent possible, the local educational agency shall encourage the consolidation of reevaluation meetings for the child and other IEP Team meetings for the child.

(F) Amendments. Changes to the IEP may be made either by the entire IEP Team or, as provided in subparagraph (D), by amending the IEP rather than by redrafting the entire IEP. Upon request, a parent shall be provided with a revised copy of the IEP with the amendments incorporated.

(4) Review and revision of IEP.

(A) In general. The local educational agency shall ensure that, subject to subparagraph (B), the IEP Team —

(i) reviews the child's IEP periodically, but not less frequently than annually, to determine whether the annual goals for the child are being achieved; and

(ii) revises the IEP as appropriate to address —

(I) any lack of expected progress toward the annual goals and in the general education curriculum, where appropriate;

(II) the results of any reevaluation conducted under this section;

(III) information about the child provided to, or by, the parents, as described in subsection (c)(1)(B);

(IV) the child's anticipated needs; or

(V) other matters.

(B) Requirement with respect to regular education teacher. A regular education teacher of the child, as a member of the IEP Team, shall, consistent with paragraph (1)(C), participate in the review and revision of the IEP of the child.

(5) Multi-year IEP demonstration. [Specifics of this subsection omitted by authors.]

(6) Failure to meet transition objectives. If a participating agency, other than the local educational agency, fails to provide the transition services described in the IEP in accordance with paragraph (1)(A)(i)(VIII), the local educational agency shall reconvene the IEP Team to identify alternative strategies to meet the transition objectives for the child set out in the IEP.

(7) Children with disabilities in adult prisons.

(A) In general. The following requirements shall not apply to children with disabilities who are convicted as adults under State law and incarcerated in adult prisons:

(i) The requirements contained in section 612(a)(16) [20 U.S.C. § 1412(a)(16)] and paragraph (1)(A)(i)(VI) (relating to participation of children with disabilities in general assessments).

(ii) The requirements of items (aa) and (bb) of paragraph (1)(A)(i)(VIII) (relating to transition planning and transition services), do not apply with respect to such children whose eligibility under this part [20 U.S.C. §§ 1411 et seq.] will end, because of such children's age, before such children will be released from prison.

(B) Additional requirement. If a child with a disability is convicted as an adult under State law and incarcerated in an adult prison, the child's IEP Team may modify the child's IEP or placement notwithstanding the requirements of sections 612(a)(5)(A) [20 U.S.C. § 1412(a)(5)(A)] and paragraph (1)(A) if the State has demonstrated a bona fide security or compelling penological interest that cannot otherwise be accommodated.

(e) Educational placements. Each local educational agency or State educational agency shall ensure that the parents of each child with a disability are members of any group that makes decisions on the educational placement of their child.

(f) Alternative means of meeting participation. When conducting IEP team meetings and placement meetings pursuant to this section, section 615(e) [20 U.S.C. § 1415(e)], and section 615(f)(1)(B) [20 U.S.C. § 1415(f)(1)(B)], and carrying out administrative matters under section 615 [20 U.S.C. § 1415] (such as scheduling, exchange of witness lists, and status conferences), the parent of a child with a disability and a local educational agency may agree to use alternative means of meeting participation, such as video conferences and conference calls.

1415. Procedural safeguards

(a) Establishment of procedures. Any State educational agency, State agency, or local educational agency that receives assistance under this part [20 U.S.C. §§ 1411 et seq.] shall establish and maintain procedures in accordance with this section to ensure that children with disabilities and their parents are guaranteed procedural safeguards with respect to the provision of a free appropriate public education by such agencies.

(b) Types of procedures. The procedures required by this section shall include the following:

(1) An opportunity for the parents of a child with a disability to examine all records relating to such child and to participate in meetings with respect to the identification, evaluation, and educational placement of the child, and the provision of a free appropriate public education to such child, and to obtain an independent educational evaluation of the child.

(2)

(A) Procedures to protect the rights of the child whenever the parents of the child are not known, the agency cannot, after reasonable efforts, locate the parents, or the child is a ward of the State, including the assignment of an individual to act as a surrogate for the parents, which surrogate shall not be an employee of the State educational agency, the local educational agency, or any other agency that is involved in the education or care of the child. In the case of —

(i) a child who is a ward of the State, such surrogate may alternatively be appointed by the judge overseeing the child's care provided that the surrogate meets the requirements of this paragraph; and

(ii) an unaccompanied homeless youth as defined in section 725(6) of the McKinney-Vento Homeless Assistance Act (42 U.S.C. 11434a(6)), the local educational agency shall appoint a surrogate in accordance with this paragraph.

(B) The State shall make reasonable efforts to ensure the assignment of a surrogate not more than 30 days after there is a determination by the agency that the child needs a surrogate.

(3) Written prior notice to the parents of the child, in accordance with subsection (c)(1), whenever the local educational agency —

(A) proposes to initiate or change; or

(B) refuses to initiate or change, the identification, evaluation, or educational placement of the child, or the provision of a free appropriate public education to the child.

(4) Procedures designed to ensure that the notice required by paragraph (3) is in the native language of the parents, unless it clearly is not feasible to do so.

(5) An opportunity for mediation, in accordance with subsection (e).

(6) An opportunity for any party to present a complaint —

(A) with respect to any matter relating to the identification, evaluation, or educational placement of the child, or the provision of a free appropriate public education to such child; and

(B) which sets forth an alleged violation that occurred not more than 2 years before the date the parent or public agency knew or should have known about the alleged action that forms the basis of the complaint, or, if the State has an explicit time limitation for presenting such a complaint under this part [20 U.S.C. §§ 1411 et seq.], in such time as the State law allows, except that the exceptions to the timeline described in subsection (f)(3)(D) shall apply to the timeline described in this subparagraph.

(7)

(A) Procedures that require either party, or the attorney representing a party, to provide due process complaint notice in accordance with subsection (c)(2) (which shall remain confidential) —

(i) to the other party, in the complaint filed under paragraph (6), and forward a copy of such notice to the State educational agency; and

(ii) that shall include —

(I) the name of the child, the address of the residence of the child (or available contact information in the case of a homeless child), and the name of the school the child is attending;

(II) in the case of a homeless child or youth (within the meaning of section 725(2) of the McKinney-Vento Homeless Assistance Act (42 U.S.C. 11434a(2)), available contact information for the child and the name of the school the child is attending;

(III) a description of the nature of the problem of the child relating to such proposed initiation or change, including facts relating to such problem; and

(IV) a proposed resolution of the problem to the extent known and available to the party at the time.

(B) A requirement that a party may not have a due process hearing until the party, or the attorney representing the party, files a notice that meets the requirements of subparagraph (A)(ii).

(8) Procedures that require the State educational agency to develop a model form to assist parents in filing a complaint and due process complaint notice in accordance with paragraphs (6) and (7), respectively.

(c) Notification requirements.

(1) Content of prior written notice. The notice required by subsection (b)(3) shall include —

(A) a description of the action proposed or refused by the agency;

(B) an explanation of why the agency proposes or refuses to take the action and a description of each evaluation procedure, assessment, record, or report the agency used as a basis for the proposed or refused action;

(C) a statement that the parents of a child with a disability have protection under the procedural safeguards of this part [20 U.S.C. §§ 1411 et seq.] and, if this notice is not an initial referral for evaluation, the means by which a copy of a description of the procedural safeguards can be obtained;

(D) sources for parents to contact to obtain assistance in understanding the provisions of this part [20 U.S.C. §§ 1411 et seq.];

(E) a description of other options considered by the IEP Team and the reason why those options were rejected; and

(F) a description of the factors that are relevant to the agency's proposal or refusal.

(2) Due process complaint notice.

(A) Complaint. The due process complaint notice required under subsection (b)(7)(A) shall be deemed to be sufficient unless the party receiving the notice notifies the hearing officer and the other party in writing that the receiving party believes the notice has not met the requirements of subsection (b)(7)(A).

(B) Response to complaint.

(i) Local educational agency response.

(I) In general. If the local educational agency has not sent a prior written notice to the parent regarding the subject matter contained in the parent's due process complaint notice, such local educational agency shall, within 10 days of receiving the complaint, send to the parent a response that shall include —

(aa) an explanation of why the agency proposed or refused to take the action raised in the complaint;

(bb) a description of other options that the IEP Team considered and the reasons why those options were rejected;

(cc) a description of each evaluation procedure, assessment, record, or report the agency used as the basis for the proposed or refused action; and

(dd) a description of the factors that are relevant to the agency's proposal or refusal.

(II) Sufficiency. A response filed by a local educational agency pursuant to subclause (I) shall not be construed to preclude such local educational agency from asserting that the parent's due process complaint notice was insufficient where appropriate.

(ii) Other party response. Except as provided in clause (i), the non-complaining party shall, within 10 days of receiving the complaint, send to the complaint a response that specifically addresses the issues raised in the complaint.

(C) Timing. The party providing a hearing officer notification under subparagraph (A) shall provide the notification within 15 days of receiving the complaint.

(D) Determination. Within 5 days of receipt of the notification provided under subparagraph (C), the hearing officer shall make a determination on the face of the notice of whether the notification meets the requirements of subsection (b)(7)(A), and shall immediately notify the parties in writing of such determination.

(E) Amended complaint notice.

(i) In general. A party may amend its due process complaint notice only if —

(I) the other party consents in writing to such amendment and is given the opportunity to resolve the complaint through a meeting held pursuant to subsection (f)(1)(B); or

(II) the hearing officer grants permission, except that the hearing officer may only grant such permission at any time not later than 5 days before a due process hearing occurs.

(ii) Applicable timeline. The applicable timeline for a due process hearing under this part [20 U.S.C. §§ 1411 et seq.] shall recommence at the time the party files an amended notice, including the timeline under subsection (f)(1)(B).

(d) Procedural safeguards notice.

(1) In general.

(A) Copy to parents. A copy of the procedural safeguards available to the parents of a child with a disability shall be given to the parents only 1 time a year, except that a copy also shall be given to the parents —

(i) upon initial referral or parental request for evaluation;

(ii) upon the first occurrence of the filing of a complaint under subsection (b)(6); and

(iii) upon request by a parent.

(B) Internet website. A local educational agency may place a current copy of the procedural safeguards notice on its Internet website if such website exists.

(2) Contents. The procedural safeguards notice shall include a full explanation of the procedural safeguards, written in the native language of the parents (unless it clearly is not feasible to do so) and written in an easily understandable manner, available under this section and under regulations promulgated by the Secretary relating to —

(A) independent educational evaluation;

(B) prior written notice;

(C) parental consent;

(D) access to educational records;

(E) the opportunity to present and resolve complaints, including —

    (i) the time period in which to make a complaint;

    (ii) the opportunity for the agency to resolve the complaint; and

    (iii) the availability of mediation;

(F) the child's placement during pendency of due process proceedings;

(G) procedures for students who are subject to placement in an interim alternative educational setting;

(H) requirements for unilateral placement by parents of children in private schools at public expense;

(I) due process hearings, including requirements for disclosure of evaluation results and recommendations;

(J) State-level appeals (if applicable in that State);

(K) civil actions, including the time period in which to file such actions; and

(L) attorneys' fees.

(e) Mediation.

(1) In general. Any State educational agency or local educational agency that receives assistance under this part [20 U.S.C. §§ 1411 et seq.] shall ensure that procedures are established and implemented to allow parties to disputes involving any matter, including matters arising prior to the filing of a complaint pursuant to subsection (b)(6), to resolve such disputes through a mediation process.

(2) Requirements. Such procedures shall meet the following requirements:

(A) The procedures shall ensure that the mediation process —

    (i) is voluntary on the part of the parties;

    (ii) is not used to deny or delay a parent's right to a due process hearing under subsection (f), or to deny any other rights afforded under this part [20 U.S.C. §§ 1411 et seq.]; and

    (iii) is conducted by a qualified and impartial mediator who is trained in effective mediation techniques.

(B) Opportunity to meet with a disinterested party. A local educational agency or a State agency may establish procedures to offer to parents and schools that choose not to use the mediation process, an opportunity to meet, at a time and location convenient to the parents, with a disinterested party who is under contract with —

    (i) a parent training and information center or community parent resource center in the State established under section 671 or 672 [20 U.S.C. § 1471 or 1472]; or

(ii) an appropriate alternative dispute resolution entity, to encourage the use, and explain the benefits, of the mediation process to the parents.

(C) List of qualified mediators. The State shall maintain a list of individuals who are qualified mediators and knowledgeable in laws and regulations relating to the provision of special education and related services.

(D) Costs. The State shall bear the cost of the mediation process, including the costs of meetings described in subparagraph (B).

(E) Scheduling and location. Each session in the mediation process shall be scheduled in a timely manner and shall be held in a location that is convenient to the parties to the dispute.

(F) Written agreement. In the case that a resolution is reached to resolve the complaint through the mediation process, the parties shall execute a legally binding agreement that sets forth such resolution and that —

(i) states that all discussions that occurred during the mediation process shall be confidential and may not be used as evidence in any subsequent due process hearing or civil proceeding;

(ii) is signed by both the parent and a representative of the agency who has the authority to bind such agency; and

(iii) is enforceable in any State court of competent jurisdiction or in a district court of the United States.

(G) Mediation discussions. Discussions that occur during the mediation process shall be confidential and may not be used as evidence in any subsequent due process hearing or civil proceeding.

(f) Impartial due process hearing.

(1) In general.

(A) Hearing. Whenever a complaint has been received under subsection (b)(6) or (k), the parents or the local educational agency involved in such complaint shall have an opportunity for an impartial due process hearing, which shall be conducted by the State educational agency or by the local educational agency, as determined by State law or by the State educational agency.

(B) Resolution session.

(i) Preliminary meeting. Prior to the opportunity for an impartial due process hearing under subparagraph (A), the local educational agency shall convene a meeting with the parents and the relevant member or members of the IEP Team who have specific knowledge of the facts identified in the complaint —

(I) within 15 days of receiving notice of the parents' complaint;

(II) which shall include a representative of the agency who has decisionmaking authority on behalf of such agency;

(III) which may not include an attorney of the local educational agency unless the parent is accompanied by an attorney; and

(IV) where the parents of the child discuss their complaint, and the facts that form the basis of the complaint, and the local educational agency is provided the opportunity to resolve the complaint, unless the parents and the local educational agency agree in writing to waive such meeting, or agree to use the mediation process described in subsection (e).

(ii) Hearing. If the local educational agency has not resolved the complaint to the satisfaction of the parents within 30 days of the receipt of the complaint, the due process hearing may occur, and all of the applicable timelines for a due process hearing under this part [20 U.S.C. §§ 1411 et seq.] shall commence.

(iii) Written settlement agreement. In the case that a resolution is reached to resolve the complaint at a meeting described in clause (i), the parties shall execute a legally binding agreement that is —

(I) signed by both the parent and a representative of the agency who has the authority to bind such agency; and

(II) enforceable in any State court of competent jurisdiction or in a district court of the United States.

(iv) Review period. If the parties execute an agreement pursuant to clause (iii), a party may void such agreement within 3 business days of the agreement's execution.

(2) Disclosure of evaluations and recommendations.

(A) In general. Not less than 5 business days prior to a hearing conducted pursuant to paragraph (1), each party shall disclose to all other parties all evaluations completed by that date, and recommendations based on the offering party's evaluations, that the party intends to use at the hearing.

(B) Failure to disclose. A hearing officer may bar any party that fails to comply with subparagraph (A) from introducing the relevant evaluation or recommendation at the hearing without the consent of the other party.

(3) Limitations on hearing.

(A) Person conducting hearing. A hearing officer conducting a hearing pursuant to paragraph (1)(A) shall, at a minimum —

(i) not be —

(I) an employee of the State educational agency or the local educational agency involved in the education or care of the child; or

(II) a person having a personal or professional interest that conflicts with the person's objectivity in the hearing;

(ii) possess knowledge of, and the ability to understand, the provisions of this title [20 U.S.C. §§ 1400 et seq.], Federal and State regulations pertaining to this title [20 U.S.C. §§ 1400 et seq.], and legal interpretations of this title [20 U.S.C. §§ 1400 et seq.] by Federal and State courts;

(iii) possess the knowledge and ability to conduct hearings in accordance with appropriate, standard legal practice; and

(iv) possess the knowledge and ability to render and write decisions in accordance with appropriate, standard legal practice.

(B) Subject matter of hearing. The party requesting the due process hearing shall not be allowed to raise issues at the due process hearing that were not raised in the notice filed under subsection (b)(7), unless the other party agrees otherwise.

(C) Timeline for requesting hearing. A parent or agency shall request an impartial due process hearing within 2 years of the date the parent or agency knew or should have known about the alleged action that forms the basis of the complaint, or, if the State has an explicit time limitation for requesting such a hearing under this part [20 U.S.C. §§ 1411 et seq.], in such time as the State law allows.

(D) Exceptions to the timeline. The timeline described in subparagraph (C) shall not apply to a parent if the parent was prevented from requesting the hearing due to —

(i) specific misrepresentations by the local educational agency that it had resolved the problem forming the basis of the complaint; or

(ii) the local educational agency's withholding of information from the parent that was required under this part [20 U.S.C. §§ 1411 et seq.] to be provided to the parent.

(E) Decision of hearing officer.

(i) In general. Subject to clause (ii), a decision made by a hearing officer shall be made on substantive grounds based on a determination of whether the child received a free appropriate public education.

(ii) Procedural issues. In matters alleging a procedural violation, a hearing officer may find that a child did not receive a free appropriate public education only if the procedural inadequacies —

(I) impeded the child's right to a free appropriate public education;

(II) significantly impeded the parents' opportunity to participate in the decisionmaking process regarding the provision of a free appropriate public education to the parents' child; or

(III) caused a deprivation of educational benefits.

(iii) Rule of construction. Nothing in this subparagraph shall be construed to preclude a hearing officer from ordering a local educational agency to comply with procedural requirements under this section.

(F) Rule of construction. Nothing in this paragraph shall be construed to affect the right of a parent to file a complaint with the State educational agency.

(g) Appeal.

(1) In general. If the hearing required by subsection (f) is conducted by a local educational agency, any party aggrieved by the findings and decision rendered in such a hearing may appeal such findings and decision to the State educational agency.

(2) Impartial review and independent decision. The State educational agency shall conduct an impartial review of the findings and decision appealed under paragraph (1). The officer conducting such review shall make an independent decision upon completion of such review.

(h) Safeguards. Any party to a hearing conducted pursuant to subsection (f) or (k), or an appeal conducted pursuant to subsection (g), shall be accorded —

(1) the right to be accompanied and advised by counsel and by individuals with special knowledge or training with respect to the problems of children with disabilities;

(2) the right to present evidence and confront, cross-examine, and compel the attendance of witnesses;

(3) the right to a written, or, at the option of the parents, electronic verbatim record of such hearing; and

(4) the right to written, or, at the option of the parents, electronic findings of fact and decisions, which findings and decisions —

(A) shall be made available to the public consistent with the requirements of section 617(b) [20 U.S.C. § 1417(b)] (relating to the confidentiality of data, information, and records); and

(B) shall be transmitted to the advisory panel established pursuant to section 612(a)(21) [20 U.S.C. § 1412(a)(21)].

(i) Administrative procedures.

(1) In general.

(A) Decision made in hearing. A decision made in a hearing conducted pursuant to subsection (f) or (k) shall be final, except that any party involved in such hearing may appeal such decision under the provisions of subsection (g) and paragraph (2).

(B) Decision made at appeal. A decision made under subsection (g) shall be final, except that any party may bring an action under paragraph (2).

(2) Right to bring civil action.

(A) In general. Any party aggrieved by the findings and decision made under subsection (f) or (k) who does not have the right to an appeal under subsection (g), and any party aggrieved by the findings and decision made under this subsection, shall have the right to bring a civil action with respect to the complaint presented pursuant to this section, which action may be brought in any State court of competent jurisdiction or in a district court of the United States, without regard to the amount in controversy.

(B) Limitation. The party bringing the action shall have 90 days from the date of the decision of the hearing officer to bring such an action, or, if the State has an explicit time limitation for bringing such action under this part [20 U.S.C. §§ 1411 et seq.], in such time as the State law allows.

(C) Additional requirements. In any action brought under this paragraph, the court —

(i) shall receive the records of the administrative proceedings;

(ii) shall hear additional evidence at the request of a party; and

(iii) basing its decision on the preponderance of the evidence, shall grant such relief as the court determines is appropriate.

(3) Jurisdiction of district courts; attorneys' fees.

(A) In general. The district courts of the United States shall have jurisdiction of actions brought under this section without regard to the amount in controversy.

(B) Award of attorneys' fees.

(i) In general. In any action or proceeding brought under this section, the court, in its discretion, may award reasonable attorneys' fees as part of the costs —

(I) to a prevailing party who is the parent of a child with a disability;

(II) to a prevailing party who is a State educational agency or local educational agency against the attorney of a parent who files a complaint or subsequent cause of action that is frivolous, unreasonable, or without foundation, or against the attorney of a parent who continued to litigate after the litigation clearly became frivolous, unreasonable, or without foundation; or

(III) to a prevailing State educational agency or local educational agency against the attorney of a parent, or against the parent, if the parent's complaint or subsequent cause of action was presented for any improper purpose, such as to harass, to cause unnecessary delay, or to needlessly increase the cost of litigation.

(ii) Rule of construction. Nothing in this subparagraph shall be construed to affect section 327 of the District of Columbia Appropriations Act, 2005.

(C) Determination of amount of attorneys' fees. Fees awarded under this paragraph shall be based on rates prevailing in the community in which the action or proceeding arose for the kind and quality of services furnished. No bonus or multiplier may be used in calculating the fees awarded under this subsection.

(D) Prohibition of attorneys' fees and related costs for certain services.

(i) In general. Attorneys' fees may not be awarded and related costs may not be reimbursed in any action or proceeding under this section for services performed subsequent to the time of a written offer of settlement to a parent if —

(I) the offer is made within the time prescribed by Rule 68 of the Federal Rules of Civil Procedure or, in the case of an administrative proceeding, at any time more than 10 days before the proceeding begins;

(II) the offer is not accepted within 10 days; and

(III) the court or administrative hearing officer finds that the relief finally obtained by the parents is not more favorable to the parents than the offer of settlement.

(ii) IEP team meetings. Attorneys' fees may not be awarded relating to any meeting of the IEP Team unless such meeting is convened as a result of an administrative proceeding or judicial action, or, at the discretion of the State, for a mediation described in subsection (e).

(iii) Opportunity to resolve complaints. A meeting conducted pursuant to subsection (f)(1)(B)(i) shall not be considered —

(I) a meeting convened as a result of an administrative hearing or judicial action; or

(II) an administrative hearing or judicial action for purposes of this paragraph.

(E) Exception to prohibition on attorneys' fees and related costs. Notwithstanding subparagraph (D), an award of attorneys' fees and related costs may be made to a parent who is the prevailing party and who was substantially justified in rejecting the settlement offer.

(F) Reduction in amount of attorneys' fees. Except as provided in subparagraph (G), whenever the court finds that —

(i) the parent, or the parent's attorney, during the course of the action or proceeding, unreasonably protracted the final resolution of the controversy;

(ii) the amount of the attorneys' fees otherwise authorized to be awarded unreasonably exceeds the hourly rate prevailing in the community for similar services by attorneys of reasonably comparable skill, reputation, and experience;

(iii) the time spent and legal services furnished were excessive considering the nature of the action or proceeding; or

(iv) the attorney representing the parent did not provide to the local educational agency the appropriate information in the notice of the complaint described in subsection (b)(7)(A), the court shall reduce, accordingly, the amount of the attorneys' fees awarded under this section.

(G) Exception to reduction in amount of attorneys' fees. The provisions of subparagraph (F) shall not apply in any action or proceeding if the court finds that the State or local educational agency unreasonably protracted the final resolution of the action or proceeding or there was a violation of this section.

(j) Maintenance of current educational placement. Except as provided in subsection (k)(4), during the pendency of any proceedings conducted pursuant to this section, unless the State or local educational agency and the parents otherwise agree, the child shall remain in the then-current educational placement of the child, or, if applying for initial admission to a public school, shall, with the consent of the parents, be placed in the public school program until all such proceedings have been completed.

(k) Placement in alternative educational setting.

(1) Authority of school personnel.

(A) Case-by-case determination. School personnel may consider any unique circumstances on a case-by-case basis when determining whether to order a change in placement for a child with a disability who violates a code of student conduct.

(B) Authority. School personnel under this subsection may remove a child with a disability who violates a code of student conduct from their current placement to an appropriate interim alternative educational setting, another setting, or suspension, for not more than 10 school days (to the extent such alternatives are applied to children without disabilities).

(C) Additional authority. If school personnel seek to order a change in placement that would exceed 10 school days and the behavior that gave rise to the violation of the school code is determined not to be a manifestation of the child's disability pursuant to subparagraph (E), the relevant disciplinary procedures applicable to children without disabilities may be applied to the child in the same manner and for the same duration in which the procedures would be applied to children without disabilities, except as provided in section 612(a)(1) [20 U.S.C. § 1412(a)(1)] although it may be provided in an interim alternative educational setting.

(D) Services. A child with a disability who is removed from the child's current placement under subparagraph (G) (irrespective of whether the behavior is determined to be a manifestation of the child's disability) or subparagraph (C) shall —

(i) continue to receive educational services, as provided in section 612(a)(1) [20 U.S.C. § 1412(a)(1)], so as to enable the child to continue to participate in the general education curriculum, although in another setting, and to progress toward meeting the goals set out in the child's IEP; and

(ii) receive, as appropriate, a functional behavioral assessment, behavioral intervention services and modifications, that are designed to address the behavior violation so that it does not recur.

(E) Manifestation determination.

(i) In general. Except as provided in subparagraph (B), within 10 school days of any decision to change the placement of a child with a disability because of a violation of a code of student conduct, the local educational agency, the parent, and relevant members of the IEP Team (as determined by the parent and the local educational agency) shall review all relevant information in the student's file, including the child's IEP, any teacher observations, and any relevant information provided by the parents to determine —

(I) if the conduct in question was caused by, or had a direct and substantial relationship to, the child's disability; or

(II) if the conduct in question was the direct result of the local educational agency's failure to implement the IEP.

(ii) Manifestation. If the local educational agency, the parent, and relevant members of the IEP Team determine that either subclause (I) or (II) of clause (i) is applicable for the child, the conduct shall be determined to be a manifestation of the child's disability.

(F) Determination that behavior was a manifestation. If the local educational agency, the parent, and relevant members of the IEP Team make the determination that the conduct was a manifestation of the child's disability, the IEP Team shall —

(i) conduct a functional behavioral assessment, and implement a behavioral intervention plan for such child, provided that the local educational agency had not conducted such assessment prior to such determination before the behavior that resulted in a change in placement described in subparagraph (C) or (G);

(ii) in the situation where a behavioral intervention plan has been developed, review the behavioral intervention plan if the child already has such a behavioral intervention plan, and modify it, as necessary, to address the behavior; and

(iii) except as provided in subparagraph (G), return the child to the placement from which the child was removed, unless the parent and the local educational agency agree to a change of placement as part of the modification of the behavioral intervention plan.

(G) Special circumstances. School personnel may remove a student to an interim alternative educational setting for not more than 45 school days without regard to whether the behavior is determined to be a manifestation of the child's disability, in cases where a child —

(i) carries or possesses a weapon to or at school, on school premises, or to or at a school function under the jurisdiction of a State or local educational agency;

(ii) knowingly possesses or uses illegal drugs, or sells or solicits the sale of a controlled substance, while at school, on school premises, or at a school function under the jurisdiction of a State or local educational agency; or

(iii) has inflicted serious bodily injury upon another person while at school, on school premises, or at a school function under the jurisdiction of a State or local educational agency.

(H) Notification. Not later than the date on which the decision to take disciplinary action is made, the local educational agency shall notify the parents of that decision, and of all procedural safeguards accorded under this section.

(2) Determination of setting. The interim alternative educational setting in subparagraphs (C) and (G) of paragraph (1) shall be determined by the IEP Team.

(3) Appeal.

(A) In general. The parent of a child with a disability who disagrees with any decision regarding placement, or the manifestation determination under this subsection, or a local educational agency that believes that maintaining the current placement of the child is substantially likely to result in injury to the child or to others, may request a hearing.

(B) Authority of hearing officer.

(i) In general. A hearing officer shall hear, and make a determination regarding, an appeal requested under subparagraph (A).

(ii) Change of placement order. In making the determination under clause (i), the hearing officer may order a change in placement of a child with a disability. In such situations, the hearing officer may —

(I) return a child with a disability to the placement from which the child was removed; or

(II) order a change in placement of a child with a disability to an appropriate interim alternative educational setting for not more than 45 school days if the hearing officer determines that maintaining the current placement of such child is substantially likely to result in injury to the child or to others.

(4) Placement during appeals. When an appeal under paragraph (3) has been requested by either the parent or the local educational agency —

(A) the child shall remain in the interim alternative educational setting pending the decision of the hearing officer or until the expiration of the time period provided for in paragraph (1)(C), whichever occurs first, unless the parent and the State or local educational agency agree otherwise; and

(B) the State or local educational agency shall arrange for an expedited hearing, which shall occur within 20 school days of the date the hearing is requested and shall result in a determination within 10 school days after the hearing.

(5) Protections for children not yet eligible for special education and related services.

(A) In general. A child who has not been determined to be eligible for special education and related services under this part [20 U.S.C. §§ 1411 et seq.] and who has engaged in behavior that violates a code of student conduct, may assert any of the protections provided for in this part [20 U.S.C. §§ 1411 et seq.] if the local educational agency had knowledge (as determined in accordance with this paragraph) that the child was a child with a disability before the behavior that precipitated the disciplinary action occurred.

(B) Basis of knowledge. A local educational agency shall be deemed to have knowledge that a child is a child with a disability if, before the behavior that precipitated the disciplinary action occurred —

(i) the parent of the child has expressed concern in writing to supervisory or administrative personnel of the appropriate educational agency, or a teacher of the child, that the child is in need of special education and related services;

(ii) the parent of the child has requested an evaluation of the child pursuant to section 614(a)(1)(B) [20 U.S.C. § 1414(a)(1)(B)]; or

(iii) the teacher of the child, or other personnel of the local educational agency, has expressed specific concerns about a pattern of behavior demonstrated by the child, directly to the director of special education of such agency or to other supervisory personnel of the agency.

(C) Exception. A local educational agency shall not be deemed to have knowledge that the child is a child with a disability if the parent of the child has not allowed an evaluation of the child pursuant to section 614 [20 U.S.C. § 1414] or has refused services under this part [20 U.S.C. §§ 1411 et seq.] or the child has been evaluated and it was determined that the child was not a child with a disability under this part [20 U.S.C. §§ 1411 et seq.].

(D) Conditions that apply if no basis of knowledge.

(i) In general. If a local educational agency does not have knowledge that a child is a child with a disability (in accordance with subparagraph (B) or (C)) prior to taking disciplinary measures against the child, the child may be subjected to disciplinary measures applied to children without disabilities who engaged in comparable behaviors consistent with clause (ii).

(ii) Limitations. If a request is made for an evaluation of a child during the time period in which the child is subjected to disciplinary measures under this subsection, the evaluation shall be conducted in an expedited manner. If the child is determined to be a child with a disability, taking into consideration information from the evaluation conducted by the agency and information provided by the parents, the agency shall provide special education and related services in accordance with this part [20 U.S.C. §§ 1411 et seq.], except that, pending the results of the evaluation, the child shall remain in the educational placement determined by school authorities.

(6) Referral to and action by law enforcement and judicial authorities.

(A) Rule of construction. Nothing in this part [20 U.S.C. §§ 1411 et seq.] shall be construed to prohibit an agency from reporting a crime committed by a child with a disability to appropriate authorities or to prevent State law enforcement and judicial authorities from exercising their responsibilities with regard to the application of Federal and State law to crimes committed by a child with a disability.

(B) Transmittal of records. An agency reporting a crime committed by a child with a disability shall ensure that copies of the special education and disciplinary records of the child are transmitted for consideration by the appropriate authorities to whom the agency reports the crime.

(7) Definitions. In this subsection:

(A) Controlled substance. The term "controlled substance" means a drug or other substance identified under schedule I, II, III, IV, or V in section 202(c) of the Controlled Substances Act (21 U.S.C. 812(c)).

(B) Illegal drug. The term "illegal drug" means a controlled substance but does not include a controlled substance that is legally possessed or used under the supervision of a licensed health-care professional or that is legally possessed or used under any other authority under that Act or under any other provision of Federal law.

(C) Weapon. The term "weapon" has the meaning given the term "dangerous weapon" under section 930(g)(2) of title 18, United States Code.

(D) Serious bodily injury. The term "serious bodily injury" has the meaning given the term "serious bodily injury" under paragraph (3) of subsection (h) of section 1365 of title 18, United States Code.

(l) Rule of construction. Nothing in this title [20 U.S.C. §§ 1400 et seq.] shall be construed to restrict or limit the rights, procedures, and remedies available under the Constitution, the Americans with Disabilities Act of 1990, title V of the Rehabilitation Act of 1973 [29 U.S.C. §§ 790 et seq.], or other Federal laws protecting the rights of children with disabilities, except that before the filing of a civil action under such laws seeking relief that is also available under this part [20 U.S.C. §§ 1411 et seq.], the procedures under subsections (f) and (g) shall be exhausted to the same extent as would be required had the action been brought under this part [20 U.S.C. §§ 1411 et seq.].

(m) Transfer of parental rights at age of majority.

(1) In general. A State that receives amounts from a grant under this part [20 U.S.C. §§ 1411 et seq.] may provide that, when a child with a disability reaches the age of majority under State law (except for a child with a disability who has been determined to be incompetent under State law) —

(A) the agency shall provide any notice required by this section to both the individual and the parents;

(B) all other rights accorded to parents under this part [20 U.S.C. §§ 1411 et seq.] transfer to the child;

(C) the agency shall notify the individual and the parents of the transfer of rights; and

(D) all rights accorded to parents under this part [20 U.S.C. §§ 1411 et seq.] transfer to children who are incarcerated in an adult or juvenile Federal, State, or local correctional institution.

(2) Special rule. If, under State law, a child with a disability who has reached the age of majority under State law, who has not been determined to be

incompetent, but who is determined not to have the ability to provide informed consent with respect to the educational program of the child, the State shall establish procedures for appointing the parent of the child, or if the parent is not available, another appropriate individual, to represent the educational interests of the child throughout the period of eligibility of the child under this part [20 U.S.C. §§ 1411 et seq.].

(n) Electronic mail. A parent of a child with a disability may elect to receive notices required under this section by an electronic mail (e-mail) communication, if the agency makes such option available.

(o) Separate complaint. Nothing in this section shall be construed to preclude a parent from filing a separate due process complaint on an issue separate from a due process complaint already filed.

1416-1427 [Omitted from Statutory Supplement.]

1431 Findings and policy

(a) Findings. Congress finds that there is an urgent and substantial need —

(1) to enhance the development of infants and toddlers with disabilities, to minimize their potential for developmental delay, and to recognize the significant brain development that occurs during a child's first 3 years of life;

(2) to reduce the educational costs to our society, including our Nation's schools, by minimizing the need for special education and related services after infants and toddlers with disabilities reach school age;

(3) to maximize the potential for individuals with disabilities to live independently in society;

(4) to enhance the capacity of families to meet the special needs of their infants and toddlers with disabilities; and

(5) to enhance the capacity of State and local agencies and service providers to identify, evaluate, and meet the needs of all children, particularly minority, low-income, inner city, and rural children, and infants and toddlers in foster care.

(b) Policy. It is the policy of the United States to provide financial assistance to States —

(1) to develop and implement a statewide, comprehensive, coordinated, multi-disciplinary, interagency system that provides early intervention services for infants and toddlers with disabilities and their families;

(2) to facilitate the coordination of payment for early intervention services from Federal, State, local, and private sources (including public and private insurance coverage);

(3) to enhance State capacity to provide quality early intervention services and expand and improve existing early intervention services being provided to infants and toddlers with disabilities and their families; and

(4) to encourage States to expand opportunities for children under 3 years of age who would be at risk of having substantial developmental delay if they did not receive early intervention services.

1432 Definitions

In this part [20 U.S.C. §§ 1431 et seq.]:

(1) At-risk infant or toddler. The term "at-risk infant or toddler" means an individual under 3 years of age who would be at risk of experiencing a substantial developmental delay if early intervention services were not provided to the individual.

(2) Council. The term "council" means a State interagency coordinating council established under section 641 [20 U.S.C. § 1441].

(3) Developmental delay. The term "developmental delay", when used with respect to an individual residing in a State, has the meaning given such term by the State under section 635(a)(1) [20 U.S.C. § 1435(a)(1)].

(4) Early intervention services. The term "early intervention services" means developmental services that —

(A) are provided under public supervision;

(B) are provided at no cost except where Federal or State law provides for a system of payments by families, including a schedule of sliding fees;

(C) are designed to meet the developmental needs of an infant or toddler with a disability, as identified by the individualized family service plan team, in any 1 or more of the following areas:

(i) physical development;

(ii) cognitive development;

(iii) communication development;

(iv) social or emotional development; or

(v) adaptive development;

(D) meet the standards of the State in which the services are provided, including the requirements of this part [20 U.S.C. §§ 1431 et seq.];

(E) include —

(i) family training, counseling, and home visits;

(ii) special instruction;

(iii) speech-language pathology and audiology services, and sign language and cued language services;

(iv) occupational therapy;

(v) physical therapy;

(vi) psychological services;

(vii) service coordination services;

(viii) medical services only for diagnostic or evaluation purposes;

(ix) early identification, screening, and assessment services;

(x) health services necessary to enable the infant or toddler to benefit from the other early intervention services;

(xi) social work services;

(xii) vision services;

(xiii) assistive technology devices and assistive technology services; and

(xiv) transportation and related costs that are necessary to enable an infant or toddler and the infant's or toddler's family to receive another service described in this paragraph;

(F) are provided by qualified personnel, including —

(i) special educators;

(ii) speech-language pathologists and audiologists;

(iii) occupational therapists;

(iv) physical therapists;

(v) psychologists;

(vi) social workers;

(vii) nurses;

(viii) registered dietitians;

(ix) family therapists;

(x) vision specialists, including ophthalmologists and optometrists;

(xi) orientation and mobility specialists; and

(xii) pediatricians and other physicians;

(G) to the maximum extent appropriate, are provided in natural environments, including the home, and community settings in which children without disabilities participate; and

(H) are provided in conformity with an individualized family service plan adopted in accordance with section 636 [20 U.S.C. § 1436].

(5) Infant or toddler with a disability. The term "infant or toddler with a disability" —

(A) means an individual under 3 years of age who needs early intervention services because the individual —

(i) is experiencing developmental delays, as measured by appropriate diagnostic instruments and procedures in 1 or more of the areas of cognitive development, physical development, communication development, social or emotional development, and adaptive development; or

(ii) has a diagnosed physical or mental condition that has a high probability of resulting in developmental delay; and

(B) may also include, at a State's discretion —

(i) at-risk infants and toddlers; and

(ii) children with disabilities who are eligible for services under section 619 [20 U.S.C. § 1419] and who previously received services under this part [20 U.S.C. §§ 1431 et seq.] until such children enter, or are eligible under State law to enter, kindergarten or elementary school, as appropriate, provided that any programs under this part [20 U.S.C. §§ 1431 et seq.] serving such children shall include —

(I) an educational component that promotes school readiness and incorporates pre-literacy, language, and numeracy skills; and

(II) a written notification to parents of their rights and responsibilities in determining whether their child will continue to receive services under this part [20 U.S.C. §§ 1431 et seq.] or participate in preschool programs under section 619 [20 U.S.C. § 1419].

1433 General authority

The Secretary shall, in accordance with this part [20 U.S.C. §§ 1431 et seq.], make grants to States (from their allotments under section 643 [20 U.S.C. § 1443]) to assist each State to maintain and implement a statewide, comprehensive, coordinated, multidisciplinary, interagency system to provide early intervention services for infants and toddlers with disabilities and their families.

1434 Eligibility

In order to be eligible for a grant under section 633 [20 U.S.C. § 1433], a State shall provide assurances to the Secretary that the State —

(1) has adopted a policy that appropriate early intervention services are available to all infants and toddlers with disabilities in the State and their families, including Indian infants and toddlers with disabilities and their families residing on a reservation geographically located in the State, infants and toddlers with disabilities who are homeless children and their families, and infants and toddlers with disabilities who are wards of the State; and

(2) has in effect a statewide system that meets the requirements of section 635 [20 U.S.C. § 1435].

1435 Requirements for statewide system

[Omitted from Statutory Supplement.]

1436 Individualized family service plan

(a) Assessment and program development. A statewide system described in section 633 [20 U.S.C. § 1433] shall provide, at a minimum, for each infant or toddler with a disability, and the infant's or toddler's family, to receive —

(1) a multidisciplinary assessment of the unique strengths and needs of the infant or toddler and the identification of services appropriate to meet such needs;

(2) a family-directed assessment of the resources, priorities, and concerns of the family and the identification of the supports and services necessary to enhance the family's capacity to meet the developmental needs of the infant or toddler; and

(3) a written individualized family service plan developed by a multidisciplinary team, including the parents, as required by subsection (e), including a description of the appropriate transition services for the infant or toddler.

(b) Periodic review. The individualized family service plan shall be evaluated once a year and the family shall be provided a review of the plan at 6-month intervals (or more often where appropriate based on infant or toddler and family needs).

(c) Promptness after assessment. The individualized family service plan shall be developed within a reasonable time after the assessment required by subsection (a)(1) is completed. With the parents' consent, early intervention services may commence prior to the completion of the assessment.

(d) Content of plan. The individualized family service plan shall be in writing and contain —

(1) a statement of the infant's or toddler's present levels of physical development, cognitive development, communication development, social or emotional development, and adaptive development, based on objective criteria;

(2) a statement of the family's resources, priorities, and concerns relating to enhancing the development of the family's infant or toddler with a disability;

(3) a statement of the measurable results or outcomes expected to be achieved for the infant or toddler and the family, including pre-literacy and language skills, as developmentally appropriate for the child, and the criteria, procedures, and timelines used to determine the degree to which progress toward achieving the results or outcomes is being made and whether modifications or revisions of the results or outcomes or services are necessary;

(4) a statement of specific early intervention services based on peer-reviewed research, to the extent practicable, necessary to meet the unique needs of the infant or toddler and the family, including the frequency, intensity, and method of delivering services;

(5) a statement of the natural environments in which early intervention services will appropriately be provided, including a justification of the extent, if any, to which the services will not be provided in a natural environment;

(6) the projected dates for initiation of services and the anticipated length, duration, and frequency of the services;

(7) the identification of the service coordinator from the profession most immediately relevant to the infant's or toddler's or family's needs (or who is otherwise qualified to carry out all applicable responsibilities under this part)

who will be responsible for the implementation of the plan and coordination with other agencies and persons, including transition services; and

(8) the steps to be taken to support the transition of the toddler with a disability to preschool or other appropriate services.

(e) Parental consent. The contents of the individualized family service plan shall be fully explained to the parents and informed written consent from the parents shall be obtained prior to the provision of early intervention services described in such plan. If the parents do not provide consent with respect to a particular early intervention service, then only the early intervention services to which consent is obtained shall be provided,

1437 State application and assurances

[Omitted from Statutory Supplement.]

1438 Uses of funds

[Omitted from Statutory Supplement.]

1439 Procedural safeguards

(a) Minimum procedures. The procedural safeguards required to be included in a statewide system under section 635(a)(13) [20 U.S.C. § 1435(a)(13)] shall provide, at a minimum, the following:

(1) The timely administrative resolution of complaints by parents. Any party aggrieved by the findings and decision regarding an administrative complaint shall have the right to bring a civil action with respect to the complaint in any State court of competent jurisdiction or in a district court of the United States without regard to the amount in controversy. In any action brought under this paragraph, the court shall receive the records of the administrative proceedings, shall hear additional evidence at the request of a party, and, basing its decision on the preponderance of the evidence, shall grant such relief as the court determines is appropriate.

(2) The right to confidentiality of personally identifiable information, including the right of parents to written notice of and written consent to the exchange of such information among agencies consistent with Federal and State law.

(3) The right of the parents to determine whether they, their infant or toddler, or other family members will accept or decline any early intervention service under this part [20 U.S.C. §§ 1431 et seq.] in accordance with State law without jeopardizing other early intervention services under this part [20 U.S.C. §§ 1431 et seq.].

(4) The opportunity for parents to examine records relating to assessment, screening, eligibility determinations, and the development and implementation of the individualized family service plan.

(5) Procedures to protect the rights of the infant or toddler whenever the parents of the infant or toddler are not known or cannot be found or the infant or toddler is a ward of the State, including the assignment of an individual (who

shall not be an employee of the State lead agency, or other State agency, and who shall not be any person, or any employee of a person, providing early intervention services to the infant or toddler or any family member of the infant or toddler) to act as a surrogate for the parents.

(6) Written prior notice to the parents of the infant or toddler with a disability whenever the State agency or service provider proposes to initiate or change, or refuses to initiate or change, the identification, evaluation, or placement of the infant or toddler with a disability, or the provision of appropriate early intervention services to the infant or toddler.

(7) Procedures designed to ensure that the notice required by paragraph (6) fully informs the parents, in the parents' native language, unless it clearly is not feasible to do so, of all procedures available pursuant to this section.

(8) The right of parents to use mediation in accordance with section 615 [20 U.S.C. § 1415], except that —

     (A) any reference in the section to a State educational agency shall be considered to be a reference to a State's lead agency established or designated under section 635(a)(10) [20 U.S.C. § 1435(a)(10)];

     (B) any reference in the section to a local educational agency shall be considered to be a reference to a local service provider or the State's lead agency under this part [20 U.S.C. §§ 1431 et seq.], as the case may be; and

     (C) any reference in the section to the provision of a free appropriate public education to children with disabilities shall be considered to be a reference to the provision of appropriate early intervention services to infants and toddlers with disabilities.

(b) Services during pendency of proceedings. During the pendency of any proceeding or action involving a complaint by the parents of an infant or toddler with a disability, unless the State agency and the parents otherwise agree, the infant or toddler shall continue to receive the appropriate early intervention services currently being provided or, if applying for initial services, shall receive the services not in dispute.

1440   Payor of last resort

(a) Nonsubstitution. Funds provided under section 643 [20 U.S.C. § 1443] may not be used to satisfy a financial commitment for services that would have been paid for from another public or private source, including any medical program administered by the Secretary of Defense, but for the enactment of this part [20 U.S.C. §§ 1431 et seq.], except that whenever considered necessary to prevent a delay in the receipt of appropriate early intervention services by an infant, toddler, or family in a timely fashion, funds provided under section 643 [20 U.S.C. § 1443] may be used to pay the provider of services pending reimbursement from the agency that has ultimate responsibility for the payment.

(b) Obligations related to and methods of ensuring services.

     (1) Establishing financial responsibility for services.

(A) In general. The Chief Executive Officer of a State or designee of the officer shall ensure that an interagency agreement or other mechanism for interagency coordination is in effect between each public agency and the designated lead agency, in order to ensure —

(i) the provision of, and financial responsibility for, services provided under this part [20 U.S.C. §§ 1431 et seq.]; and

(ii) such services are consistent with the requirements of section 635 [20 U.S.C. § 1435] and the State's application pursuant to section 637 [20 U.S.C. § 1437], including the provision of such services during the pendency of any such dispute.

(B) Consistency between agreements or mechanisms under part B. The Chief Executive Officer of a State or designee of the officer shall ensure that the terms and conditions of such agreement or mechanism are consistent with the terms and conditions of the State's agreement or mechanism under section 612(a)(12) [20 U.S.C. § 1412(a)(12)], where appropriate.

(2) Reimbursement for services by public agency.

(A) In general. If a public agency other than an educational agency fails to provide or pay for the services pursuant to an agreement required under paragraph (1), the local educational agency or State agency (as determined by the Chief Executive Officer or designee) shall provide or pay for the provision of such services to the child.

(B) Reimbursement. Such local educational agency or State agency is authorized to claim reimbursement for the services from the public agency that failed to provide or pay for such services and such public agency shall reimburse the local educational agency or State agency pursuant to the terms of the interagency agreement or other mechanism required under paragraph (1).

(3) Special rule. The requirements of paragraph (1) may be met through —

(A) State statute or regulation;

(B) signed agreements between respective agency officials that clearly identify the responsibilities of each agency relating to the provision of services; or

(C) other appropriate written methods as determined by the Chief Executive Officer of the State or designee of the officer and approved by the Secretary through the review and approval of the State's application pursuant to section 637 [20 U.S.C. § 1437].

(c) Reduction of other benefits. Nothing in this part [20 U.S.C. §§ 1431 et seq.] shall be construed to permit the State to reduce medical or other assistance available or to alter eligibility under title V of the Social Security Act [42 U.S.C. §§ 701 et seq.] (relating to maternal and child health) or title XIX of the Social Security Act [42 U.S.C. §§ 1396 et seq.] (relating to medicaid for infants or toddlers with disabilities) within the State.

1441-1482   [Omitted from Statutory Supplement.]

Chapter 10
REHABILITATION ACT

Rehabilitation Act
29 U.S.C. §§ 706, 791-794

705. Definitions

For the purposes of this Act:

(1) Administrative costs. [Omitted from this Statutory Supplement]

(2) Assessment for determining eligibility and vocational rehabilitation needs. The term "assessment for determining eligibility and vocational rehabilitation needs" means, as appropriate in each case —

(A)

(i) a review of existing data —

(I) to determine whether an individual is eligible for vocational rehabilitation services; and

(II) to assign priority for an order of selection described in section 101(a)(5)(A) [29 U.S.C. § 721(a)(5)(A)] in the States that use an order of selection pursuant to section 101(a)(5)(A) [29 U.S.C. § 721(a)(5)(A)]; and

(ii) to the extent necessary, the provision of appropriate assessment activities to obtain necessary additional data to make such determination and assignment;

(B) to the extent additional data is necessary to make a determination of the employment outcomes, and the nature and scope of vocational rehabilitation services, to be included in the individualized plan for employment of an eligible individual, a comprehensive assessment to determine the unique strengths, resources, priorities, concerns, abilities, capabilities, interests, and informed choice, including the need for supported employment, of the eligible individual, which comprehensive assessment —

(i) is limited to information that is necessary to identify the rehabilitation needs of the individual and to develop the individualized plan for employment of the eligible individual;

(ii) uses, as a primary source of such information, to the maximum extent possible and appropriate and in accordance with confidentiality requirements —

(I) existing information obtained for the purposes of determining the eligibility of the individual and assigning priority for an order of selection described in section 101(a)(5)(A) [29 U.S.C. § 721(a)(5)(A)] for the individual; and

(II) such information as can be provided by the individual and, where appropriate, by the family of the individual;

(iii) may include, to the degree needed to make such a determination, an assessment of the personality, interests, interpersonal skills, intelligence and related functional capacities, educational achievements, work experience, vocational aptitudes, personal and social adjustments, and employment opportunities of the individual, and the medical, psychiatric, psychological, and other pertinent vocational, educational, cultural, social, recreational, and environmental factors, that affect the employment and rehabilitation needs of the individual; and

(iv) may include, to the degree needed, an appraisal of the patterns of work behavior of the individual and services needed for the individual to acquire occupational skills, and to develop work attitudes, work habits, work tolerance, and social and behavior patterns necessary for successful job performance, including the utilization of work in real job situations to assess and develop the capacities of the individual to perform adequately in a work environment;

(C) referral, for the provision of rehabilitation technology services to the individual, to assess and develop the capacities of the individual to perform in a work environment; and

(D) an exploration of the individual's abilities, capabilities, and capacity to perform in work situations, which shall be assessed periodically during trial work experiences, including experiences in which the individual is provided appropriate supports and training.

(3) Assistive technology device. The term "assistive technology device" has the meaning given such term in section 3 of the Assistive Technology Act of 1998 [29 U.S.C. § 3002], except that the reference in such section to the term "individuals with disabilities" shall be deemed to mean more than one individual with a disability as defined in paragraph (20)(A).

(4) Assistive technology service. The term "assistive technology service" has the meaning given such term in section 3 of the Assistive Technology Act of 1998 [29 U.S.C. § 3002], except that the reference in such section —

(A) to the term "individual with a disability" shall be deemed to mean an individual with a disability, as defined in paragraph (20)(A); and

(B) to the term "individuals with disabilities" shall be deemed to mean more than one such individual.

(5) Community rehabilitation program. The term "community rehabilitation program" means a program that provides directly or facilitates the provision of vocational rehabilitation services to individuals with disabilities, and that provides, singly or in combination, for an individual with a disability to enable the individual to maximize opportunities for employment, including career advancement —

(A) medical, psychiatric, psychological, social, and vocational services that are provided under one management;

(B) testing, fitting, or training in the use of prosthetic and orthotic devices;

(C) recreational therapy;

(D) physical and occupational therapy;

(E) speech, language, and hearing therapy;

(F) psychiatric, psychological, and social services, including positive behavior management;

(G) assessment for determining eligibility and vocational rehabilitation needs;

(H) rehabilitation technology;

(I) job development, placement, and retention services;

(J) evaluation or control of specific disabilities;

(K) orientation and mobility services for individuals who are blind;

(L) extended employment;

(M) psychosocial rehabilitation services;

(N) supported employment services and extended services;

(O) services to family members when necessary to the vocational rehabilitation of the individual;

(P) personal assistance services; or

(Q) services similar to the services described in one of subparagraphs (A) through (P).

(6) Construction; cost of construction.

(A) Construction. The term "construction" means —

(i) the construction of new buildings;

(ii) the acquisition, expansion, remodeling, alteration, and renovation of existing buildings; and

(iii) initial equipment of buildings described in clauses (i) and (ii).

(B) Cost of construction. The term "cost of construction" includes architects" fees and the cost of acquisition of land in connection with construction but does not include the cost of offsite improvements.

(7) [Deleted]

(8) Designated State agency; designated State unit.

(A) Designated State agency. The term "designated State agency" means an agency designated under section 101(a)(2)(A) [29 U.S.C. § 721(a)(2)(A)].

(B) Designated State unit. The term "designated State unit" means —

(i) any State agency unit required under section 101(a)(2)(B)(ii) [29 U.S.C. § 721(a)(2)(B)(ii)]; or

(ii) in cases in which no such unit is so required, the State agency described in section 101(a)(2)(B)(i) [29 U.S.C. § 721(a)(2)(B)(i)].

(9) Disability. The term "disability" means —

(A) except as otherwise provided in subparagraph (B), a physical or mental impairment that constitutes or results in a substantial impediment to employment; or

(B) for purposes of sections 2, 14, and 15, and titles II, IV, V, and VII [29 U.S.C. §§ 701, 713, 714, 760 et seq., 780 et seq., 791 et seq., 796 et seq.], the meaning given it in section 3 of the Americans with Disabilities Act of 1990 (42 U.S.C. 12102).

(10) Drug and illegal use of drugs.

(A) Drug. The term "drug" means a controlled substance, as defined in schedules I through V of section 202 of the Controlled Substances Act (21 U.S.C. 812).

(B) Illegal use of drugs. The term "illegal use of drugs" means the use of drugs, the possession or distribution of which is unlawful under the Controlled Substances Act [21 U.S.C. §§ 801 et seq.]. Such term does not include the use of a drug taken under supervision by a licensed health care professional, or other uses authorized by the Controlled Substances Act [21 U.S.C. §§ 801 et seq.] or other provisions of Federal law.

(11) Employment outcome. The term "employment outcome" means, with respect to an individual —

(A) entering or retaining full-time or, if appropriate, part-time competitive employment in the integrated labor market;

(B) satisfying the vocational outcome of supported employment; or

(C) satisfying any other vocational outcome the Secretary may determine to be appropriate (including satisfying the vocational outcome of self-employment, telecommuting, or business ownership), in a manner consistent with this Act.

(12) Establishment of a community rehabilitation program. The term "establishment of a community rehabilitation program" includes the acquisition, expansion, remodeling, or alteration of existing buildings necessary to adapt them to community rehabilitation program purposes or to increase their effectiveness for such purposes (subject, however, to such limitations as the Secretary may determine, in accordance with regulations the Secretary shall prescribe, in order to prevent impairment of the objectives of, or duplication of, other Federal laws providing Federal assistance in the construction of facilities for community rehabilitation programs), and may include such additional equipment and staffing as the Commissioner considers appropriate.

(13) Extended services. The term "extended services" means ongoing support services and other appropriate services, needed to support and maintain an individual with a most significant disability in supported employment, that —

(A) are provided singly or in combination and are organized and made available in such a way as to assist an eligible individual in maintaining supported employment;

(B) are based on a determination of the needs of an eligible individual, as specified in an individualized plan for employment; and

(C) are provided by a State agency, a nonprofit private organization, employer, or any other appropriate resource, after an individual has made the transition from support provided by the designated State unit.

(14) Federal share. [Omitted from this Statutory Supplement] (15) Governor.[Omitted from this Statutory Supplement] (16) Impartial hearing officer. [Omitted from this Statutory Supplement]

(17) Independent living core services. The term "independent living core services" means —

(A) information and referral services;

(B) independent living skills training;

(C) peer counseling (including cross-disability peer counseling); and

(D) individual and systems advocacy.

(18) Independent living services. The term "independent living services" includes —

(A) independent living core services; and

(B)

(i) counseling services, including psychological, psychotherapeutic, and related services;

(ii) services related to securing housing or shelter, including services related to community group living, and supportive of the purposes of this Act and of the titles of this Act, and adaptive housing services (including appropriate accommodations to and modifications of any space used to serve, or occupied by, individuals with disabilities);

(iii) rehabilitation technology;

(iv) mobility training;

(v) services and training for individuals with cognitive and sensory disabilities, including life skills training, and interpreter and reader services;

(vi) personal assistance services, including attendant care and the training of personnel providing such services;

(vii) surveys, directories, and other activities to identify appropriate housing, recreation opportunities, and accessible transportation, and other support services;

(viii) consumer information programs on rehabilitation and independent living services available under this Act, especially for minorities and other individuals with disabilities who have traditionally been unserved or underserved by programs under this Act;

(ix) education and training necessary for living in a community and participating in community activities;

(x) supported living;

(xi) transportation, including referral and assistance for such transportation and training in the use of public transportation vehicles and systems;

(xii) physical rehabilitation;

(xiii) therapeutic treatment;

(xiv) provision of needed prostheses and other appliances and devices;

(xv) individual and group social and recreational services;

(xvi) training to develop skills specifically designed for youths who are individuals with disabilities to promote self-awareness and esteem, develop advocacy and self-empowerment skills, and explore career options;

(xvii) services for children;

(xviii) services under other Federal, State, or local programs designed to provide resources, training, counseling, or other assistance, of substantial benefit in enhancing the independence, productivity, and quality of life of individuals with disabilities;

(xix) appropriate preventive services to decrease the need of individuals assisted under this Act for similar services in the future;

(xx) community awareness programs to enhance the understanding and integration into society of individuals with disabilities; and

(xxi) such other services as may be necessary and not inconsistent with the provisions of this Act.

(19) Indian; American Indian; Indian American; Indian tribe.

(A) In general. The terms "Indian", "American Indian", and "Indian American" mean an individual who is a member of an Indian tribe.

(B) Indian tribe. The term "Indian tribe" means any Federal or State Indian tribe, band, rancheria, pueblo, colony, or community, including any Alaskan native village or regional village corporation (as defined in or established pursuant to the Alaska Native Claims Settlement Act [43 U.S.C. §§ 1601 et seq.]).

(20) Individual with a disability.

(A) In general. Except as otherwise provided in subparagraph (B), the term "individual with a disability" means any individual who —

(i) has a physical or mental impairment which for such individual constitutes or results in a substantial impediment to employment; and

(ii) can benefit in terms of an employment outcome from vocational rehabilitation services provided pursuant to title I, III, or VI [29 U.S.C. §§ 720 et seq., 771 et seq., or 795 et seq.].

(B) Certain programs; limitations on major life activities. Subject to subparagraphs (C), (D), (E), and (F), the term "individual with a disability" means, for purposes of sections 2, 14, and 15, and titles II, IV, V, and VII of this Act [29 U.S.C. §§ 701, 714, 715, 760 et seq., 780 et seq., 791 et seq., 796 et seq.], any person who has a disability as defined in section 3 of the Americans with Disabilities Act of 1990 (42 U.S.C. 12102).

(C) Rights and advocacy provisions.

(i) In general; exclusion of individuals engaging in drug use. For purposes of title V [29 U.S.C. §§ 791 et seq.], the term "individual with a disability" does not include an individual who is currently engaging in the illegal use of drugs, when a covered entity acts on the basis of such use.

(ii) Exception for individuals no longer engaging in drug use. Nothing in clause (i) shall be construed to exclude as an individual with a disability an individual who —

(I) has successfully completed a supervised drug rehabilitation program and is no longer engaging in the illegal use of drugs, or has otherwise been rehabilitated successfully and is no longer engaging in such use;

(II) is participating in a supervised rehabilitation program and is no longer engaging in such use; or

(III) is erroneously regarded as engaging in such use, but is not engaging in such use; except that it shall not be a violation of this Act for a covered entity to adopt or administer reasonable policies or procedures, including but not limited to drug testing, designed to ensure that an individual described in subclause (I) or (II) is no longer engaging in the illegal use of drugs.

(iii) Exclusion for certain services. Notwithstanding clause (i), for purposes of programs and activities providing health services and services provided under titles I, II, and III [29 U.S.C. §§ 720 et seq., 760 et seq., 771 et seq.], an individual shall not be excluded from the benefits of such programs or activities on the basis of his or her current illegal use of drugs if he or she is otherwise entitled to such services.

(iv) Disciplinary action. For purposes of programs and activities providing educational services, local educational agencies may take disciplinary action pertaining to the use or possession of illegal drugs or alcohol against any student who is an individual with a disability and who currently is engaging in the illegal use of drugs or in the use of alcohol to the same extent that such disciplinary action is taken against students who are not individuals with disabilities. Furthermore, the due process procedures at section 104.36 of title 34, Code of Federal Regulations (or any corresponding similar regulation or ruling) shall not apply to such disciplinary actions.

(v) Employment; exclusion of alcoholics. For purposes of sections 503 and 504 [29 U.S.C. §§ 793, 794] as such sections relate to employment, the term "individual with a disability" does not include any individual who is an alcoholic whose current use of alcohol prevents such individual from performing the duties of the job in question or whose employment, by reason of such current alcohol abuse, would constitute a direct threat to property or the safety of others.

(D) Employment; exclusion of individuals with certain diseases or infections. For the purposes of sections 503 and 504 [29 U.S.C. §§ 793, 794], as such sections relate to employment, such term does not include an individual who has a currently contagious disease or infection and who, by reason of such disease or infection, would constitute a direct threat to the health or safety of other individuals or who, by reason of the currently contagious disease or infection, is unable to perform the duties of the job.

(E) Rights provisions; exclusion of individuals on basis of homosexuality or bisexuality. For the purposes of sections 501, 503, and 504 [29 U.S.C. §§ 791, 793, 794] —

(i) for purposes of the application of subparagraph (B) to such sections, the term "impairment" does not include homosexuality or bisexuality; and

(ii) therefore the term "individual with a disability" does not include an individual on the basis of homosexuality or bisexuality.

(F) Rights provisions; exclusion of individuals on basis of certain disorders. For the purposes of sections 501, 503, and 504 [29 U.S.C. §§ 791, 793, 794], the term "individual with a disability" does not include an individual on the basis of —

(i) transvestism, transsexualism, pedophilia, exhibitionism, voyeurism, gender identity disorders not resulting from physical impairments, or other sexual behavior disorders;

(ii) compulsive gambling, kleptomania, or pyromania; or

(iii) psychoactive substance use disorders resulting from current illegal use of drugs.

(G) Individuals with disabilities. The term "individuals with disabilities" means more than one individual with a disability.

(21) Individual with a significant disability.

(A) In general. Except as provided in subparagraph (B) or (C), the term "individual with a significant disability" means an individual with a disability —

(i) who has a severe physical or mental impairment which seriously limits one or more functional capacities (such as mobility, communication, self-care, self-direction, interpersonal skills, work tolerance, or work skills) in terms of an employment outcome;

(ii) whose vocational rehabilitation can be expected to require multiple vocational rehabilitation services over an extended period of time; and

(iii) who has one or more physical or mental disabilities resulting from amputation, arthritis, autism, blindness, burn injury, cancer, cerebral palsy, cystic fibrosis, deafness, head injury, heart disease, hemiplegia, hemophilia, respiratory or pulmonary dysfunction, intellectual disability, mental illness, multiple sclerosis, muscular dystrophy, musculo-skeletal disorders, neuro-logical disorders (including stroke and epilepsy), paraplegia, quadriplegia, and other spinal cord conditions, sickle cell anemia, specific learning disability, end-stage renal disease, or another disability or combination of disabilities determined on the basis of an assessment for determining eligibility and vocational rehabilitation needs described in subparagraphs (A) and (B) of paragraph (2) to cause comparable substantial functional limitation.

(B) Independent living services and centers for independent living. For purposes of title VII [29 U.S.C. §§ 796 et seq.], the term "individual with a significant disability" means an individual with a severe physical or mental impairment whose ability to function independently in the family or commu-nity or whose ability to obtain, maintain, or advance in employment is substantially limited and for whom the delivery of independent living services will improve the ability to function, continue functioning, or move toward functioning independently in the family or community or to continue in employment, respectively.

(C) Research and training. For purposes of title II [29 U.S.C. §§ 760 et seq.], the term "individual with a significant disability" includes an individual described in subparagraph (A) or (B).

(D) Individuals with significant disabilities. The term "individuals with significant disabilities" means more than one individual with a significant disability.

(E) Individual with a most significant disability.

(i) In general. The term "individual with a most significant disability", used with respect to an individual in a State, means an individual with a significant disability who meets criteria established by the State under section 101(a)(5)(C) [29 U.S.C. § 721(a)(5)(C)].

(ii) Individuals with the most significant disabilities. The term "individuals with the most significant disabilities" means more than one individual with a most significant disability.

(22) Individual's representative; applicant's representative. The terms "indi-vidual's representative" and "applicant's representative" mean a parent, a family member, a guardian, an advocate, or an authorized representative of an individual or applicant, respectively.

(23) Institution of higher education. The term "institution of higher education" has the meaning given the term in section 101 of the Higher Education Act of 1965 [20 U.S.C. § 1001].

(24) Local agency. The term "local agency" means an agency of a unit of general local government or of an Indian tribe (or combination of such units or

tribes) which has an agreement with the designated State agency to conduct a vocational rehabilitation program under the supervision of such State agency in accordance with the State plan approved under section 101 [29 U.S.C. § 721]. Nothing in the preceding sentence of this paragraph or in section 101 shall be construed to prevent the local agency from arranging to utilize another local public or nonprofit agency to provide vocational rehabilitation services if such an arrangement is made part of the agreement specified in this paragraph.

(25) Local workforce investment board. The term "local workforce investment board" means a local workforce investment board established under section 117 of the Workforce Investment Act of 1998 [29 U.S.C. § 2832].

(26) Nonprofit. The term "nonprofit", when used with respect to a community rehabilitation program, means a community rehabilitation program carried out by a corporation or association, no part of the net earnings of which inures, or may lawfully inure, to the benefit of any private shareholder or individual and the income of which is exempt from taxation under section 501(c)(3) of the Internal Revenue Code of 1986 [26 U.S.C. § 501(c)(3)].

(27) Ongoing support services. The term "ongoing support services" means services —

(A) provided to individuals with the most significant disabilities;

(B) provided, at a minimum, twice monthly —

(i) to make an assessment, regarding the employment situation, at the worksite of each such individual in supported employment, or, under special circumstances, especially at the request of the client, off site; and

(ii) based on the assessment, to provide for the coordination or provision of specific intensive services, at or away from the worksite, that are needed to maintain employment stability; and

(C) consisting of —

(i) a particularized assessment supplementary to the comprehensive assessment described in paragraph (2)(B);

(ii) the provision of skilled job trainers who accompany the individual for intensive job skill training at the worksite;

(iii) job development, job retention, and placement services;

(iv) social skills training;

(v) regular observation or supervision of the individual;

(vi) followup services such as regular contact with the employers, the individuals, the individuals" representatives, and other appropriate individuals, in order to reinforce and stabilize the job placement;

(vii) facilitation of natural supports at the worksite;

(viii) any other service identified in section 103; or

(ix) a service similar to another service described in this subparagraph.

(28) Personal assistance services. The term "personal assistance services" means a range of services, provided by one or more persons, designed to assist an individual with a disability to perform daily living activities on or off the job that the individual would typically perform if the individual did not have a disability. Such services shall be designed to increase the individual's control in life and ability to perform everyday activities on or off the job.

(29) Public or nonprofit. The term "public or nonprofit", used with respect to an agency or organization, includes an Indian tribe.

(30) Rehabilitation technology. The term "rehabilitation technology" means the systematic application of technologies, engineering methodologies, or scientific principles to meet the needs of and address the barriers confronted by individuals with disabilities in areas which include education, rehabilitation, employment, transportation, independent living, and recreation. The term includes rehabilitation engineering, assistive technology devices, and assistive technology services.

(31) Secretary. The term "Secretary", except when the context otherwise requires, means the Secretary of Education.

(32) State. The term "State" includes, in addition to each of the several States of the United States, the District of Columbia, the Commonwealth of Puerto Rico, the United States Virgin Islands, Guam, American Samoa, and the Commonwealth of the Northern Mariana Islands.

(33) State workforce investment board. The term "State workforce investment board" means a State workforce investment board established under section 111 of the Workforce Investment Act of 1998 [29 U.S.C. § 2821].

(34) Statewide workforce investment system. The term "statewide workforce investment system" means a system described in section 111(d)(2) of the Workforce Investment Act of 1998 [29 U.S.C. § 2821(d)(2)].

(35) Supported employment.

(A) In general. The term "supported employment" means competitive work in integrated work settings, or employment in integrated work settings in which individuals are working toward competitive work, consistent with the strengths, resources, priorities, concerns, abilities, capabilities, interests, and informed choice of the individuals, for individuals with the most significant disabilities —

(i)

(I) for whom competitive employment has not traditionally occurred; or

(II) for whom competitive employment has been interrupted or intermittent as a result of a significant disability; and

(ii) who, because of the nature and severity of their disability, need intensive supported employment services for the period, and any extension, described in paragraph (36)(C) and extended services after the transition described in paragraph (13)(C) in order to perform such work.

(B) Certain transitional employment. Such term includes transitional employment for persons who are individuals with the most significant disabilities due to mental illness.

(36) Supported employment services. The term "supported employment services" means ongoing support services and other appropriate services needed to support and maintain an individual with a most significant disability in supported employment, that —

(A) are provided singly or in combination and are organized and made available in such a way as to assist an eligible individual to achieve competitive employment;

(B) are based on a determination of the needs of an eligible individual, as specified in an individualized plan for employment; and

(C) are provided by the designated State unit for a period of time not to extend beyond 18 months, unless under special circumstances the eligible individual and the rehabilitation counselor or coordinator involved jointly agree to extend the time in order to achieve the employment outcome identified in the individualized plan for employment.

(37) Transition services. The term "transition services" means a coordinated set of activities for a student, designed within an outcome-oriented process, that promotes movement from school to post school activities, including postsecondary education, vocational training, integrated employment (including supported employment), continuing and adult education, adult services, independent living, or community participation. The coordinated set of activities shall be based upon the individual student's needs, taking into account the student's preferences and interests, and shall include instruction, community experiences, the development of employment and other post school adult living objectives, and, when appropriate, acquisition of daily living skills and functional vocational evaluation.

(38) Vocational rehabilitation services. The term "vocational rehabilitation services" means those services identified in section 103 [29 U.S.C. § 723] which are provided to individuals with disabilities under this Act.

(39) Workforce investment activities. The term "workforce investment activities" means workforce investment activities, as defined in section 101 of the Workforce Investment Act of 1998 [29 U.S.C. § 2801], that are carried out under that Act.

791. Employment of individuals with disabilities

[Omitted from Statutory Supplement.]

793. Employment under Federal contracts

(a) Amount of contracts or subcontracts; provision for employment and advancement of qualified individuals with disabilities; regulations. Any contract in excess of $ 10,000 entered into by any Federal department or agency for the procurement of personal property and nonpersonal services (including construction) for the United States shall contain a provision requiring that the party contracting with the United

States shall take affirmative action to employ and advance in employment qualified individuals with disabilities. The provisions of this section shall apply to any subcontract in excess of $ 10,000 entered into by a prime contractor in carrying out any contract for the procurement of personal property and nonpersonal services (including construction) for the United States. The President shall implement the provisions of this section by promulgating regulations within ninety days after the date of enactment of this section [enacted Sept. 26, 1973].

(b) Administrative enforcement; complaints; investigations; departmental action. If any individual with a disability believes any contractor has failed or refused to comply with the provisions of a contract with the United States, relating to employment of individuals with disabilities, such individual may file a complaint with the Department of Labor. The Department shall promptly investigate such complaint and shall take such action thereon as the facts and circumstances warrant, consistent with the terms of such contract and the laws and regulations applicable thereto.

(c) Waiver by President; national interest special circumstances for waiver of particular agreements; waiver by Secretary of Labor of affirmative action requirements.

(1) The requirements of this section may be waived, in whole or in part, by the President with respect to a particular contract or subcontract, in accordance with guidelines set forth in regulations which the President shall prescribe, when the President determines that special circumstances in the national interest so require and states in writing the reasons for such determination.

(2)

(A) The Secretary of Labor may waive the requirements of the affirmative action clause required by regulations promulgated under subsection (a) with respect to any of a prime contractor's or subcontractor's facilities that are found to be in all respects separate and distinct from activities of the prime contractor or subcontractor related to the performance of the contract or subcontract, if the Secretary of Labor also finds that such a waiver will not interfere with or impede the effectuation of this Act.

(B) Such waivers shall be considered only upon the request of the contractor or subcontractor. The Secretary of Labor shall promulgate regulations that set forth the standards used for granting such a waiver.

(d) Standards used in determining violation of section. The standards used to determine whether this section has been violated in a complaint alleging nonaffirmative action employment discrimination under this section shall be the standards applied under title I of the Americans with Disabilities Act of 1990 (42 U.S.C. 12111 et seq.) and the provisions of sections 501 through 504, and 510, of the Americans with Disabilities Act of 1990 (42 U.S.C. 12201-12204 and 12210), as such sections relate to employment.

(e) Avoidance of duplicative efforts and inconsistencies. [Omitted from Statutory Supplement.]

794. Nondiscrimination under Federal grants and programs

(a) Promulgation of rules and regulations. No otherwise qualified individual with a disability in the United States, as defined in section 7(20) [29 U.S.C. § 705(20)], shall, solely by reason of her or his disability, be excluded from the participation in, be denied the benefits of, or be subjected to discrimination under any program or activity receiving Federal financial assistance or under any program or activity conducted by any Executive agency or by the United States Postal Service. The head of each such agency shall promulgate such regulations as may be necessary to carry out the amendments to this section made by the Rehabilitation, Comprehensive Services, and Developmental Disabilities Act of 1978. Copies of any proposed regulation shall be submitted to appropriate authorizing committees of the Congress, and such regulation may take effect no earlier than the thirtieth day after the date on which such regulation is so submitted to such committees.

(b) "Program or activity" defined. For the purposes of this section, the term "program or activity" means all of the operations of —

(1)

(A) a department, agency, special purpose district, or other instrumentality of a State or of a local government; or

(B) the entity of such State or local government that distributes such assistance and each such department or agency (and each other State or local government entity) to which the assistance is extended, in the case of assistance to a State or local government;

(2)

(A) a college, university, or other postsecondary institution, or a public system of higher education; or

(B) a local educational agency (as defined in section 9101 of the Elementary and Secondary Education Act of 1965 [20 U.S.C. § 7801]), system of vocational education, or other school system;

(3)

(A) an entire corporation, partnership, or other private organization, or an entire sole proprietorship —

(i) if assistance is extended to such corporation, partnership, private organization, or sole proprietorship as a whole; or

(ii) which is principally engaged in the business of providing education, health care, housing, social services, or parks and recreation; or

(B) the entire plant or other comparable, geographically separate facility to which Federal financial assistance is extended, in the case of any other corporation, partnership, private organization, or sole proprietorship; or

(4) any other entity which is established by two or more of the entities described in paragraph (1), (2), or (3); any part of which is extended Federal financial assistance.

(c) Significant structural alterations by small providers. Small providers are not required by subsection (a) to make significant structural alterations to their existing facilities for the purpose of assuring program accessibility, if alternative means of providing the services are available. The terms used in this subsection shall be construed with reference to the regulations existing on the date of the enactment of this subsection [enacted March 22, 1988].

(d) Standards used in determining violation of section. The standards used to determine whether this section has been violated in a complaint alleging employment discrimination under this section shall be the standards applied under title I of the Americans with Disabilities Act of 1990 (42 U.S.C. 12111 et seq.) and the provisions of sections 501 through 504, and 510, of the Americans with Disabilities Act of 1990 (42 U.S.C. 12201-12204 and 12210), as such sections relate to employment.

794a. Remedies and attorney's fees

(a)

(1) The remedies, procedures, and rights set forth in section 717 of the Civil Rights Act of 1964 (42 U.S.C. 2000e-16), including the application of sections 706(f) through 706(k) (42 U.S.C. 2000e-5(f) through (k)) (and the application of section 706(e)(3) (42 U.S.C. 2000e-5(e)(3)) to claims of discrimination in compensation), shall be available, with respect to any complaint under section 501 of this Act [29 U.S.C. § 791], to any employee or applicant for employment aggrieved by the final disposition of such complaint, or by the failure to take final action on such complaint. In fashioning an equitable or affirmative action remedy under such section, a court may take into account the reasonableness of the cost of any necessary work place accommodation, and the availability of alternatives therefor or other appropriate relief in order to achieve an equitable and appropriate remedy.

(2) The remedies, procedures, and rights set forth in title VI of the Civil Rights Act of 1964 (42 U.S.C. 2000d et seq.) (and in subsection (e)(3) of section 706 of such Act (42 U.S.C. 2000e-5), applied to claims of discrimination in compensation) shall be available to any person aggrieved by any act or failure to act by any recipient of Federal assistance or Federal provider of such assistance under section 504 of this Act [29 U.S.C. § 794].

(b) In any action or proceeding to enforce or charge a violation of a provision of this title [29 U.S.C. §§ 790 et seq.], the court, in its discretion, may allow the prevailing party, other than the United States, a reasonable attorney's fee as part of the costs.

Chapter 11

MODEL REGULATIONS IMPLEMENTING SECTION 504 OF THE REHABILITATION ACT

Model Regulations Implementing
Section 504 of the Rehabilitation Act
34 C.F.R. Part 104

Editor's Note on Model Regulations: Each federal agency is required to have regulations to implement Section 504 for its agency. The model regulations that are to be guidance for those agencies were promulgated in 1978, 47 Fed. Reg. 2132 (January 13, 1978), and are included in this chapter. These serve as the framework for all agencies.

Note: The term "handicap" is used instead of the preferred term of "disability" in most federal statutes and regulations.

104.1 Purpose

The purpose of this part is to effectuate section 504 of the Rehabilitation Act of 1973, which is designed to eliminate discrimination on the basis of handicap in any program or activity receiving Federal financial assistance.

104.2 Application

This part applies to each recipient of Federal financial assistance from the Department of Education and to the program or activity that receives such assistance.

104.3 Definitions

As used in this part, the term:

(a) The Act means the Rehabilitation Act of 1973, Pub. L. 93-112, as amended by the Rehabilitation Act Amendments of 1974, Pub. L. 93-516, 29 U.S.C. 794.

(b) Section 504 means section 504 of the Act.

(c) Education of the Handicapped Act means that statute as amended by the Education for all Handicapped Children Act of 1975, Pub. L. 94-142, 20 U.S.C. 1401 et seq.

(d) Department means the Department of Education.

(e) Assistant Secretary means the Assistant Secretary for Civil Rights of the Department of Education.

(f) Recipient means any state or its political subdivision, any instrumentality of a state or its political subdivision, any public or private agency, institution, organization, or other entity, or any person to which Federal financial assistance is extended directly or through another recipient, including any successor, assignee, or transferee of a recipient, but excluding the ultimate beneficiary of the assistance.

(g) Applicant for assistance means one who submits an application, request, or

271

plan required to be approved by a Department official or by a recipient as a condition to becoming a recipient.

(h) Federal financial assistance means any grant, loan, contract (other than a procurement contract or a contract of insurance or guaranty), or any other arrangement by which the Department provides or otherwise makes available assistance in the form of:

(1) Funds;

(2) Services of Federal personnel; or

(3) Real and personal property or any interest in or use of such property, including:

(i) Transfers or leases of such property for less than fair market value or for reduced consideration; and

(ii) Proceeds from a subsequent transfer or lease of such property if the Federal share of its fair market value is not returned to the Federal Government.

(i) Facility means all or any portion of buildings, structures, equipment, roads, walks, parking lots, or other real or personal property or interest in such property.

(j) Handicapped person —

(1) Handicapped persons means any person who (i) has a physical or mental impairment which substantially limits one or more major life activities, (ii) has a record of such an impairment, or (iii) is regarded as having such an impairment.

(2) As used in paragraph (j)(1) of this section, the phrase:

(i) Physical or mental impairment means (A) any physiological disorder or condition, cosmetic disfigurement, or anatomical loss affecting one or more of the following body systems: neurological; musculoskeletal; special sense organs; respiratory, including speech organs; cardiovascular; reproductive, digestive, genito-urinary; hemic and lymphatic; skin; and endocrine; or (B) any mental or psychological disorder, such as mental retardation, organic brain syndrome, emotional or mental illness, and specific learning disabilities.

(ii) Major life activities means functions such as caring for one's self, performing manual tasks, walking, seeing, hearing, speaking, breathing, learning, and working.

(iii) Has a record of such an impairment means has a history of, or has been misclassified as having, a mental or physical impairment that substantially limits one or more major life activities.

(iv) Is regarded as having an impairment means (A) has a physical or mental impairment that does not substantially limit major life activities but that is treated by a recipient as constituting such a limitation; (B) has a physical or mental impairment that substantially limits major life activities only as a result of the attitudes of others toward such impairment; or (C) has none of the impairments defined in paragraph (j)(2)(i) of this section but is treated by a recipient as having such an impairment.

(k) Program or activity means all of the operations of —

(1)

(i) A department, agency, special purpose district, or other instrumentality of a State or of a local government; or

(ii) The entity of such State or local government that distributes such assistance and each such department or agency (and each other State or local government entity) to which the assistance is extended, in the case of assistance to a State or local government;

(2)

(i) A college, university, or other postsecondary institution, or a public system of higher education; or

(ii) A local educational agency (as defined in 20 U.S.C. 8801), system of vocational education, or other school system;

(3)

(i) An entire corporation, partnership, or other private organization, or an entire sole proprietorship —

(A) If assistance is extended to such corporation, partnership, private organization, or sole proprietorship as a whole; or

(B) Which is principally engaged in the business of providing education, health care, housing, social services, or parks and recreation; or

(ii) The entire plant or other comparable, geographically separate facility to which Federal financial assistance is extended, in the case of any other corporation, partnership, private organization, or sole proprietorship; or

(4) Any other entity which is established by two or more of the entities described in paragraph (k)(1), (2), or (3) of this section; any part of which is extended Federal financial assistance. (Authority: 29 U.S.C. 794(b))

(l) Qualified handicapped person means:

(1) With respect to employment, a handicapped person who, with reasonable accommodation, can perform the essential functions of the job in question;

(2) With respect to public preschool elementary, secondary, or adult educational services, a handicappped person (i) of an age during which nonhandicapped persons are provided such services, (ii) of any age during which it is mandatory under state law to provide such services to handicapped persons, or (iii) to whom a state is required to provide a free appropriate public education under section 612 of the Education of the Handicapped Act; and

(3) With respect to postsecondary and vocational education services, a handicapped person who meets the academic and technical standards requisite to admission or participation in the recipient's education program or activity;

(4) With respect to other services, a handicapped person who meets the essential eligibility requirements for the receipt of such services.

(m) Handicap means any condition or characteristic that renders a person a handicapped person as defined in paragraph (j) of this section.

104.4 Discrimination prohibited

(a) General. No qualified handicapped person shall, on the basis of handicap, be excluded from participation in, be denied the benefits of, or otherwise be subjected to discrimination under any program or activitiy which receives Federal financial assistance.

(b) Discriminatory actions prohibited.

(1) A recipient, in providing any aid, benefit, or service, may not, directly or through contractual, licensing, or other arrangements, on the basis of handicap:

(i) Deny a qualified handicapped person the opportunity to participate in or benefit from the aid, benefit, or service;

(ii) Afford a qualified handicapped person an opportunity to participate in or benefit from the aid, benefit, or service that is not equal to that afforded others;

(iii) Provide a qualified handicapped person with an aid, benefit, or service that is not as effective as that provided to others;

(iv) Provide different or separate aid, benefits, or services to handicapped persons or to any class of handicapped persons unless such action is necessary to provide qualified handicapped persons with aid, benefits, or services that are as effective as those provided to others;

(v) Aid or perpetuate discrimination against a qualified handicapped person by providing significant assistance to an agency, organization, or person that discriminates on the basis of handicap in providing any aid, benefit, or service to beneficiaries of the recipients program or activity;

(vi) Deny a qualified handicapped person the opportunity to participate as a member of planning or advisory boards; or

(vii) Otherwise limit a qualified handicapped person in the enjoyment of any right, privilege, advantage, or opportunity enjoyed by others receiving an aid, benefit, or service.

(2) For purposes of this part, aids, benefits, and services, to be equally effective, are not required to produce the identical result or level of achievement for handicapped and nonhandicapped persons, but must afford handicapped persons equal opportunity to obtain the same result, to gain the same benefit, or to reach the same level of achievement, in the most integrated setting appropriate to the person's needs.

(3) Despite the existence of separate or different aid, benefits, or services provided in accordance with this part, a recipient may not deny a qualified handicapped person the opportunity to participate in such aid, benefits, or services that are not separate or different.

(4) A recipient may not, directly or through contractual or other arrangements, utilize criteria or methods of administration (i) that have the effect of subjecting qualified handicapped persons to discrimination on the basis of handicap, (ii) that have the purpose or effect of defeating or substantially impairing accomplishment of the objectives of the recipient's program or activity with respect to handicapped persons, or (iii) that perpetuate the discrimination of another recipient if both recipients are subject to common administrative control or are agencies of the same State.

(5) In determining the site or location of a facility, an applicant for assistance or a recipient may not make selections (i) that have the effect of excluding handicapped persons from, denying them the benefits of, or otherwise subjecting them to discrimination under any program or activity that receives Federal financial assistance or (ii) that have the purpose or effect of defeating or substantially impairing the accomplishment of the objectives of the program or activity with respect to handicapped persons.

(6) As used in this section, the aid, benefit, or service provided under a program or activity receiving Federal financial assistance includes any aid, benefit, or service provided in or through a facility that has been constructed, expanded, altered, leased or rented, or otherwise acquired, in whole or in part, with Federal financial assistance.

(c) Aid, benefits, or services limited by Federal law. The exclusion of nonhandicapped persons from aid, benefits, or services limited by Federal statute or executive order to handicapped persons or the exclusion of a specific class of handicapped persons from aid, benefits, or services limited by Federal statute or executive order to a different class of handicapped persons is not prohibited by this part.

104.5   Assurances required

[Omitted from Statutory Supplement.]

104.6   Remedial action, voluntary action, and self-evaluation

(a) Remedial action.

(1) If the Assistant Secretary finds that a recipient has discriminated against persons on the basis of handicap in violation of section 504 or this part, the recipient shall take such remedial action as the Assistant Secretary deems necessary to overcome the effects of the discrimination.

(2) Where a recipient is found to have discriminated against persons on the basis of handicap in violation of section 504 or this part and where another recipient exercises control over the recipient that has discriminated, the Assistant Secretary, where appropriate, may require either or both recipients to take remedial action.

(3) The Assistant Secretary may, where necessary to overcome the effects of discrimination in violation of section 504 or this part, require a recipient to take remedial action (i) with respect to handicapped persons who are no longer participants in the recipient's program or activity but who were participants in

the program or activity when such discrimination occurred or (ii) with respect to handicapped persons who would have been participants in the program or activity had the discrimination not occurred.

(b) Voluntary action. A recipient may take steps, in addition to any action that is required by this part, to overcome the effects of conditions that resulted in limited participation in the recipient's program or activity by qualified handicapped persons.

(c) Self-evaluation.

(1) A recipient shall, within one year of the effective date of this part:

(i) Evaluate, with the assistance of interested persons, including handicapped persons or organizations representing handicapped persons, its current policies and practices and the effects thereof that do not or may not meet the requirements of this part;

(ii) Modify, after consultation with interested persons, including handicapped persons or organizations representing handicapped persons, any policies and practices that do not meet the requirements of this part; and

(iii) Take, after consultation with interested persons, including handicapped persons or organizations representing handicapped persons, appropriate remedial steps to eliminate the effects of any discrimination that resulted from adherence to these policies and practices.

(2) A recipient that employs fifteen or more persons shall, for at least three years following completion of the evaluation required under paragraph (c)(1) of this section, maintain on file, make available for public inspection, and provide to the Assistant Secretary upon request:

(i) A list of the interested persons consulted,

(ii) A description of areas examined and any problems identified, and

(iii) A description of any modifications made and of any remedial steps taken.

104.7 Designation of responsible employee and adoption of grievance procedures

[Omitted from Statutory Supplement.]

104.8 Notice

[Omitted from Statutory Supplement.]

104.9 Administrative requirements for small recipients

[Omitted from Statutory Supplement.]

104.10 Effect of state or local law or other requirements and effect of employment opportunities

(a) The obligation to comply with this part is not obviated or alleviated by the existence of any state or local law or other requirement that, on the basis of handicap, imposes prohibitions or limits upon the eligibility of qualified handicapped persons to receive services or to practice any occupation or profession.

(b) The obligation to comply with this part is not obviated or alleviated because employment opportunities in any occupation or profession are or may be more limited for handicapped persons than for nonhandicapped persons.

104.11   Discrimination prohibited

(a) General.

(1) No qualified handicapped person shall, on the basis of handicap, be subjected to discrimination in employment under any program or activity to which this part applies.

(2) A recipient that receives assistance under the Education of the Handicapped Act shall take positive steps to employ and advance in employment qualified handicapped persons in programs or activities assisted under that Act.

(3) A recipient shall make all decisions concerning employment under any program or activity to which this part applies in a manner which ensures that discrimination on the basis of handicap does not occur and may not limit, segregate, or classify applicants or employees in any way that adversely affects their opportunities or status because of handicap.

(4) A recipient may not participate in a contractual or other relationship that has the effect of subjecting qualified handicapped applicants or employees to discrimination prohibited by this subpart. The relationships referred to in this paragraph include relationships with employment and referral agencies, with labor unions, with organizations providing or administering fringe benefits to employees of the recipient, and with organizations providing training and apprenticeships.

(b) Specific activities. The provisions of this subpart apply to:

(1) Recruitment, advertising, and the processing of applications for employment;

(2) Hiring, upgrading, promotion, award of tenure, demotion, transfer, layoff, termination, right of return from layoff and rehiring;

(3) Rates of pay or any other form of compensation and changes in compensation;

(4) Job assignments, job classifications, organizational structures, position descriptions, lines of progression, and seniority lists;

(5) Leaves of absence, sick leave, or any other leave;

(6) Fringe benefits available by virtue of employment, whether or not administered by the recipient;

(7) Selection and financial support for training, including apprenticeship, professional meetings, conferences, and other related activities, and selection for leaves of absence to pursue training;

(8) Employer sponsored activities, including those that are social or recre-

ational; and

(9) Any other term, condition, or privilege of employment.

(c) A recipient's obligation to comply with this subpart is not affected by any inconsistent term of any collective bargaining agreement to which it is a party.

104.12   Reasonable accommodation

(a) A recipient shall make reasonable accommodation to the known physical or mental limitations of an otherwise qualified handicapped applicant or employee unless the recipient can demonstrate that the accommodation would impose an undue hardship on the operation of its program or activity.

(b) Reasonable accommodation may include:

(1) Making facilities used by employees readily accessible to and usable by handicapped persons, and

(2) Job restructuring, part-time or modified work schedules, acquisition or modification of equipment or devices, the provision of readers or interpreters, and other similar actions.

(c) In determining pursuant to paragraph (a) of this section whether an accommodation would impose an undue hardship on the operation of a recipient's program or activity, factors to be considered include:

(1) The overall size of the recipient's program or activity with respect to number of employees, number and type of facilities, and size of budget;

(2) The type of the recipient's operation, including the composition and structure of the recipient's workforce; and

(3) The nature and cost of the accommodation needed.

(d) A recipient may not deny any employment opportunity to a qualified handicapped employee or applicant if the basis for the denial is the need to make reasonable accommodation to the physical or mental limitations of the employee or applicant.

104.13   Employment criteria

(a) A recipient may not make use of any employment test or other selection criterion that screens out or tends to screen out handicapped persons or any class of handicapped persons unless:

(1) The test score or other selection criterion, as used by the recipient, is shown to be job-related for the position in question, and

(2) Alternative job-related tests or criteria that do not screen out or tend to screen out as many handicapped persons are not shown by the Director to be available.

(b) A recipient shall select and administer tests concerning employment so as best to ensure that, when administered to an applicant or employee who has a handicap that impairs sensory, manual, or speaking skills, the test results accurately reflect the applicant's or employee's job skills, aptitude, or whatever other factor the test purports to measure, rather than reflecting the applicant's or employee's impaired sensory, manual, or speaking skills (except where those skills are the factors that the test purports to measure).

104.14   Preemployment inquiries

(a) Except as provided in paragraphs (b) and (c) of this section, a recipient may not conduct a preemployment medical examination or may not make preemployment inquiry of an applicant as to whether the applicant is a handicapped person or as to the nature or severity of a handicap. A recipient may, however, make preemployment inquiry into an applicant's ability to perform job-related functions.

(b) When a recipient is taking remedial action to correct the effects of past discrimination pursuant to § 104.6 (a), when a recipient is taking voluntary action to overcome the effects of conditions that resulted in limited participation in its federally assisted program or activity pursuant to § 104.6(b), or when a recipient is taking affirmative action pursuant to section 503 of the Act, the recipient may invite applicants for employment to indicate whether and to what extent they are handicapped, Provided, That:

(1) The recipient states clearly on any written questionnaire used for this purpose or makes clear orally if no written questionnaire is used that the information requested is intended for use solely in connection with its remedial action obligations or its voluntary or affirmative action efforts; and

(2) The recipient states clearly that the information is being requested on a voluntary basis, that it will be kept confidential as provided in paragraph (d) of this section, that refusal to provide it will not subject the applicant or employee to any adverse treatment, and that it will be used only in accordance with this part.

(c) Nothing in this section shall prohibit a recipient from conditioning an offer of employment on the results of a medical examination conducted prior to the employee's entrance on duty, Provided, That:

(1) All entering employees are subjected to such an examination regardless of handicap, and

(2) The results of such an examination are used only in accordance with the requirements of this part.

(d) Information obtained in accordance with this section as to the medical condition or history of the applicant shall be collected and maintained on separate forms that shall be accorded confidentiality as medical records, except that:

(1) Supervisors and managers may be informed regarding restrictions on the work or duties of handicapped persons and regarding necessary accommodations;

(2) First aid and safety personnel may be informed, where appropriate, if the condition might require emergency treatment; and

(3) Government officials investigating compliance with the Act shall be

provided relevant information upon request.

104.21 Discrimination prohibited

No qualified handicapped person shall, because a recipient's facilities are inaccessible to or unusable by handicapped persons, be denied the benefits of, be excluded from participation in, or otherwise be subjected to discrimination under any program or activity to which this part applies.

104.22 Existing facilities

(a) Accessibility. A recipient shall operate its program or activity so that when each part is viewed in its entirety, it is readily accessible to handicapped persons. This paragraph does not require a recipient to make each of its existing facilities or every part of a facility accessible to and usable by handicapped persons.

(b) Methods. A recipient may comply with the requirements of paragraph (a) of this section through such means as redesign of equipment, reassignment of classes or other services to accessible buildings, assignment of aides to beneficiaries, home visits, delivery of health, welfare, or other social services at alternate accessible sites, alteration of existing facilities and construction of new facilities in conformance with the requirements of § 104.23, or any other methods that result in making its program or activity accessible to handicapped persons. A recipient is not required to make structural changes in existing facilities where other methods are effective in achieving compliance with paragraph (a) of this section. In choosing among available methods for meeting the requirement of paragraph (a) of this section, a recipient shall give priority to those methods that serve handicapped persons in the most integrated setting appropriate.

(c) Small health, welfare, or other social service providers. If a recipient with fewer than fifteen employees that provides health, welfare, or other social services finds, after consultation with a handicapped person seeking its services, that there is no method of complying with paragraph (a) of this section other than making a significant alteration in its existing facilities, the recipient may, as an alternative, refer the handicapped person to other providers of those services that are accessible.

(d) Time period. A recipient shall comply with the requirement of paragraph (a) of this section within sixty days of the effective date of this part except that where structural changes in facilities are necessary, such changes shall be made within three years of the effective date of this part, but in any event as expeditiously as possible.

(e) Transition plan. In the event that structural changes to facilities are necessary to meet the requirement of paragraph (a) of this section, a recipient shall develop, within six months of the effective date of this part, a transition plan setting forth the steps necessary to complete such changes. The plan shall be developed with the assistance of interested persons, including handicapped persons or organizations representing handicapped persons. A copy of the transition plan shall be made available for public inspection. The plan shall, at a minimum:

(1) Identify physical obstacles in the recipient's facilities that limit the

accessibility of its program or activity to handicappped persons;

(2) Describe in detail the methods that will be used to make the facilities accessible;

(3) Specify the schedule for taking the steps necessary to achieve full accessibility in order to comply with paragraph (a) of this section and, if the time period of the transition plan is longer than one year, identify the steps of that will be taken during each year of the transition period; and

(4) Indicate the person responsible for implementation of the plan.

(f) Notice. The recipient shall adopt and implement procedures to ensure that interested persons, including persons with impaired vision or hearing, can obtain information as to the existence and location of services, activities, and facilities that are accessible to and usable by handicapped persons.

104.23   New construction

(a) Design and construction. Each facility or part of a facility constructed by, on behalf of, or for the use of a recipient shall be designed and constructed in such manner that the facility or part of the facility is readily accessible to and usable by handicapped persons, if the construction was commenced after the effective date of this part.

(b) Alteration. Each facility or part of a facility which is altered by, on behalf of, or for the use of a recipient after the effective date of this part in a manner that affects or could affect the usability of the facility or part of the facility shall, to the maximum extent feasible, be altered in such manner that the altered portion of the facility is readily accessible to and usable by handicapped persons.

(c) Conformance with Uniform Federal Accessibility Standards.

(1) Effective as of January 18, 1991, design, construction, or alteration of buildings in conformance with sections 3-8 of the Uniform Federal Accessibility Standards (UFAS) (Appendix A to 41 CFR subpart 101-19.6) shall be deemed to comply with the requirements of this section with respect to those buildings. Departures from particular technical and scoping requirements of UFAS by the use of other methods are permitted where substantially equivalent or greater access to and usability of the building is provided.

(2) For purposes of this section, section 4.1.6(1)(g) of UFAS shall be interpreted to exempt from the requirements of UFAS only mechanical rooms and other spaces that, because of their intended use, will not require accessibility to the public or beneficiaries or result in the employment or residence therein of persons with physical handicaps.

(3) This section does not require recipients to make building alterations that have little likelihood of being accomplished without removing or altering a load-bearing structural member.

104.31   Application of this subpart

Subpart D applies to preschool, elementary, secondary, and adult education programs or activities that receive Federal financial assistance and to recipients that operate, or that receive Federal financial assistance for the operation of, such programs or activities.

104.32   Location and notification

A recipient that operates a public elementary or secondary education program or activity shall annually:

(a) Undertake to identify and locate every qualified handicapped person residing in the recipient's jurisdiction who is not receiving a public education; and

(b) Take appropriate steps to notify handicapped persons and their parents or guardians of the recipient's duty under this subpart.

104.33   Free appropriate public education

(a) General. A recipient that operates a public elementary or secondary education program or activity shall provide a free appropriate public education to each qualified handicapped person who is in the recipient's jurisdiction, regardless of the nature or severity of the person's handicap.

(b) Appropriate education.

(1) For the purpose of this subpart, the provision of an appropriate education is the provision of regular or special education and related aids and services that (i) are designed to meet individual educational needs of handicapped persons as adequately as the needs of nonhandicapped persons are met and (ii) are based upon adherence to procedures that satisfy the requirements of §§ 104.34, 104.35, and 104.36.

(2) Implementation of an Individualized Education Program developed in accordance with the Education of the Handicapped Act is one means of meeting the standard established in paragraph (b)(1)(i) of this section.

(3) A recipient may place a handicapped person or refer such a person for aid, benefits, or services other than those that it operates or provides as its means of carrying out the requirements of this subpart. If so, the recipient remains responsible for ensuring that the requirements of this subpart are met with respect to any handicapped person so placed or referred.

(c) Free education —

(1) General. For the purpose of this section, the provision of a free education is the provision of educational and related services without cost to the handicapped person or to his or her parents or guardian, except for those fees that are imposed on non-handicapped persons or their parents or guardian. It may consist either of the provision of free services or, if a recipient places a handicapped person or refers such person for aid, benefits, or services not operated or provided by the recipient as its means of carrying out the requirements of this subpart, of payment for the costs of the aid, benefits, or services. Funds available from any public or private agency may be used to meet the requirements of this subpart. Nothing in this section shall be construed to relieve an insurer or similar third party from an otherwise valid obligation to provide or pay for services

provided to a handicapped person.

(2) Transportation. If a recipient places a handicapped person or refers such person for aid, benefits, or services not operated or provided by the recipient as its means of carrying out the requirements of this subpart, the recipient shall ensure that adequate transportation to and from the aid, benefits, or services is provided at no greater cost than would be incurred by the person or his or her parents or guardian if the person were placed in the aid, benefits, or services operated by the recipient.

(3) Residential placement. If a public or private residential placement is necessary to provide a free appropriate public education to a handicapped person because of his or her handicap, the placement, including non-medical care and room and board, shall be provided at no cost to the person or his or her parents or guardian.

(4) Placement of handicapped persons by parents. If a recipient has made available, in conformance with the requirements of this section and § 104.34, a free appropriate public education to a handicapped person and the person's parents or guardian choose to place the person in a private school, the recipient is not required to pay for the person's education in the private school. Disagreements between a parent or guardian and a recipient regarding whether the recipient has made a free appropriate public education available or otherwise regarding the question of financial responsibility are subject to the due process procedures of § 104.36.

(d) Compliance. A recipient may not exclude any qualified handicapped person from a public elementary or secondary education after the effective date of this part. A recipient that is not, on the effective date of this regulation, in full compliance with the other requirements of the preceding paragraphs of this section shall meet such requirements at the earliest practicable time and in no event later than September 1, 1978.

104.34   Educational setting

(a) Academic setting. A recipient to which this subpart applies shall educate, or shall provide for the education of, each qualified handicapped person in its jurisdiction with persons who are not handicapped to the maximum extent appropriate to the needs of the handicapped person. A recipient shall place a handicapped person in the regular educational environment operated by the recipient unless it is demonstrated by the recipient that the education of the person in the regular environment with the use of supplementary aids and services cannot be achieved satisfactorily. Whenever a recipient places a person in a setting other than the regular educational environment pursuant to this paragraph, it shall take into account the proximity of the alternate setting to the person's home.

(b) Nonacademic settings. In providing or arranging for the provision of nonacademic and extracurricular services and activities, including meals, recess periods, and the services and activities set forth in § 104.37(a)(2), a recipient shall ensure that handicapped persons participate with nonhandicapped persons in such activities and services to the maximum extent appropriate to the needs of the handicapped person in question.

(c) Comparable facilities. If a recipient, in compliance with paragraph (a) of this section, operates a facility that is identifiable as being for handicapped persons, the recipient shall ensure that the facility and the services and activities provided therein are comparable to the other facilities, services, and activities of the recipient.

104.35   Evaluation and placement

(a) Preplacement evaluation. A recipient that operates a public elementary or secondary education program or activity shall conduct an evaluation in accordance with the requirements of paragraph (b) of this section of any person who, because of handicap, needs or is believed to need special education or related services before taking any action with respect to the initial placement of the person in regular or special education and any subsequent significant change in placement.

(b) Evaluation procedures. A recipient to which this subpart applies shall establish standards and procedures for the evaluation and placement of persons who, because of handicap, need or are believed to need special education or related services which ensure that:

(1) Tests and other evaluation materials have been validated for the specific purpose for which they are used and are administered by trained personnel in conformance with the instructions provided by their producer;

(2) Tests and other evaluation materials include those tailored to assess specific areas of educational need and not merely those which are designed to provide a single general intelligence quotient; and

(3) Tests are selected and administered so as best to ensure that, when a test is administered to a student with impaired sensory, manual, or speaking skills, the test results accurately reflect the student's aptitude or achievement level or whatever other factor the test purports to measure, rather than reflecting the student's impaired sensory, manual, or speaking skills (except where those skills are the factors that the test purports to measure).

(c) Placement procedures. In interpreting evaluation data and in making placement decisions, a recipient shall (1) draw upon information from a variety of sources, including aptitude and achievement tests, teacher recommendations, physical condition, social or cultural background, and adaptive behavior, (2) establish procedures to ensure that information obtained from all such sources is documented and carefully considered, (3) ensure that the placement decision is made by a group of persons, including persons knowledgeable about the child, the meaning of the evaluation data, and the placement options, and (4) ensure that the placement decision is made in conformity with § 104.34.

(d) Reevaluation. A recipient to which this section applies shall establish procedures, in accordance with paragraph (b) of this section, for periodic reevaluation of students who have been provided special education and related services. A reevaluation procedure consistent with the Education for the Handicapped Act is one means of meeting this requirement.

104.36   Procedural safeguards

A recipient that operates a public elementary or secondary education program or activity shall establish and implement, with respect to actions regarding the identification, evaluation, or educational placement of persons who, because of handicap, need or are believed to need special instruction or related services, a system of procedural safeguards that includes notice, an opportunity for the parents or guardian of the person to examine relevant records, an impartial hearing with opportunity for participation by the person's parents or guardian and representation by counsel, and a review procedure. Compliance with the procedural safeguards of section 615 of the Education of the Handicapped Act is one means of meeting this requirement.

104.37   Nonacademic services

(a) General.

(1) A recipient to which this subpart applies shall provide non-academic and extracurricular services and activities in such manner as is necessary to afford handicapped students an equal opportunity for participation in such services and activities.

(2) Nonacademic and extracurricular services and activities may include counseling services, physical recreational athletics, transportation, health services, recreational activities, special interest groups or clubs sponsored by the recipients, referrals to agencies which provide assistance to handicapped persons, and employment of students, including both employment by the recipient and assistance in making available outside employment.

(b) Counseling services. A recipient to which this subpart applies that provides personal, academic, or vocational counseling, guidance, or placement services to its students shall provide these services without discrimination on the basis of handicap. The recipient shall ensure that qualified handicapped students are not counseled toward more restrictive career objectives than are nonhandicapped students with similar interests and abilities.

(c) Physical education and athletics.

(1) In providing physical education courses and athletics and similar aid, benefits, or services to any of its students, a recipient to which this subpart applies may not discriminate on the basis of handicap. A recipient that offers physical education courses or that operates or sponsors interscholastic, club, or intramural athletics shall provide to qualified handicapped students an equal opportunity for participation.

(2) A recipient may offer to handicapped students physical education and athletic activities that are separate or different from those offered to nonhandicapped students only if separation or differentiation is consistent with the requirements of § 104.34 and only if no qualified handicapped student is denied the opportunity to compete for teams or to participate in courses that are not separate or different.

104.38   Preschool and adult education

A recipient to which this subpart applies that provides preschool education or day care or adult education may not, on the basis of handicap, exclude qualified handicapped persons and shall take into account the needs of such persons in determining the aid, benefits or services to be provided.

104.39   Private education

(a) A recipient that provides private elementary or secondary education may not, on the basis of handicap, exclude a qualified handicapped person if the person can, with minor adjustments, be provided an appropriate education, as defined in § 104.33(b)(1), within that recipient's program or activity.

(b) A recipient to which this section applies may not charge more for the provision of an appropriate education to handicapped persons than to nonhandicapped persons except to the extent that any additional charge is justified by a substantial increase in cost to the recipient.

(c) A recipient to which this section applies that provides special education shall do so in accordance with the provisions of §§ 104.35 and 104.36. Each recipient to which this section applies is subject to the provisions of §§ 104.34, 104.37, and 104.38.

104.41   Application of this subpart

Subpart E applies to postsecondary education programs or activities, including postsecondary vocational education programs or activities, that receive Federal financial assistance and to recipients that operate, or that receive Federal financial assistance for the operation of, such programs or activities.

104.42   Admissions and recruitment

(a) General. Qualified handicapped persons may not, on the basis of handicap, be denied admission or be subjected to discrimination in admission or recruitment by a recipient to which this subpart applies.

(b) Admissions. In administering its admission policies, a recipient to which this subpart applies:

(1) May not apply limitations upon the number or proportion of handicapped persons who may be admitted;

(2) May not make use of any test or criterion for admission that has a disproportionate, adverse effect on handicapped persons or any class of handicapped persons unless (i) the test or criterion, as used by the recipient, has been validated as a predictor of success in the education program or activity in question and (ii) alternate tests or criteria that have a less disproportionate, adverse effect are not shown by the Assistant Secretary to be available.

(3) Shall assure itself that (i) admissions tests are selected and administered so as best to ensure that, when a test is administered to an applicant who has a handicap that impairs sensory, manual, or speaking skills, the test results accurately reflect the applicant's aptitude or achievement level or whatever other factor the test purports to measure, rather than reflecting the applicant's impaired sensory, manual, or speaking skills (except where those skills are the factors that the test purports to measure); (ii) admissions tests that are designed

for persons with impaired sensory, manual, or speaking skills are offered as often and in as timely a manner as are other admissions tests; and (iii) admissions tests are administered in facilities that, on the whole, are accessible to handicapped persons; and

(4) Except as provided in paragraph (c) of this section, may not make preadmission inquiry as to whether an applicant for admission is a handicapped person but, after admission, may make inquiries on a confidential basis as to handicaps that may require accommodation.

(c) Preadmission inquiry exception. When a recipient is taking remedial action to correct the effects of past discrimination pursuant to § 104.6(a) or when a recipient is taking voluntary action to overcome the effects of conditions that resulted in limited participation in its federally assisted program or activity pursuant to § 104.6(b), the recipient may invite applicants for admission to indicate whether and to what extent they are handicapped, Provided, That:

(1) The recipient states clearly on any written questionnaire used for this purpose or makes clear orally if no written questionnaire is used that the information requested is intended for use solely in connection with its remedial action obligations or its voluntary action efforts; and

(2) The recipient states clearly that the information is being requested on a voluntary basis, that it will be kept confidential, that refusal to provide it will not subject the applicant to any adverse treatment, and that it will be used only in accordance with this part.

(d) Validity studies. For the purpose of paragraph (b)(2) of this section, a recipient may base prediction equations on first year grades, but shall conduct periodic validity studies against the criterion of overall success in the education program or activity in question in order to monitor the general validity of the test scores.

104.43   Treatment of students; general

(a) No qualified handicapped student shall, on the basis of handicap, be excluded from participation in, be denied the benefits of, or otherwise be subjected to discrimination under any academic, research, occupational training, housing, health insurance, counseling, financial aid, physical education, athletics, recreation, transportation, other extracurricular, or other postsecondary education aid, benefits, or services to which this subpart applies.

(b) A recipient to which this subpart applies that considers participation by students in education programs or activities not operated wholly by the recipient as part of, or equivalent to, and education program or activity operated by the recipient shall assure itself that the other education program or activity, as a whole, provides an equal opportunity for the participation of qualified handicapped persons.

(c) A recipient to which this subpart applies may not, on the basis of handicap, exclude any qualified handicapped student from any course, course of study, or other part of its education program or activity.

(d) A recipient to which this subpart applies shall operate its program or activity in the most integrated setting appropriate.

104.44   Academic adjustments

(a) *Academic requirements.* A recipient to which this subpart applies shall make such modifications to its academic requirements as are necessary to ensure that such requirements do not discriminate or have the effect of discriminating, on the basis of handicap, against a qualified handicapped applicant or student. Academic requirements that the recipient can demonstrate are essential to the instruction being pursued by such student or to any directly related licensing requirement will not be regarded as discriminatory within the meaning of this section. Modifications may include changes in the length of time permitted for the completion of degree requirements, substitution of specific courses required for the completion of degree requirements, and adaptation of the manner in which specific courses are conducted.

(b) *Other rules.* A recipient to which this subpart applies may not impose upon handicapped students other rules, such as the prohibition of tape recorders in classrooms or of dog guides in campus buildings, that have the effect of limiting the participation of handicapped students in the recipient's education program or activity.

(c) *Course examinations.* In its course examinations or other procedures for evaluating students' academic achievement, a recipient to which this subpart applies shall provide such methods for evaluating the achievement of students who have a handicap that impairs sensory, manual, or speaking skills as will best ensure that the results of the evaluation represents the student's achievement in the course, rather than reflecting the student's impaired sensory, manual, or speaking skills (except where such skills are the factors that the test purports to measure).

(d) *Auxiliary aids.*

(1) A recipient to which this subpart applies shall take such steps as are necessary to ensure that no handicapped student is denied the benefits of, excluded from participation in, or otherwise subjected to discrimination because of the absence of educational auxiliary aids for students with impaired sensory, manual, or speaking skills.

(2) Auxiliary aids may include taped texts, interpreters or other effective methods of making orally delivered materials available to students with hearing impairments, readers in libraries for students with visual impairments, classroom equipment adapted for use by students with manual impairments, and other similar services and actions. Recipients need not provide attendants, individually prescribed devices, readers for personal use or study, or other devices or services of a personal nature.

104.45   Housing

(a) *Housing provided by the recipient.* A recipient that provides housing to its nonhandicapped students shall provide comparable, convenient, and accessible housing to handicapped students at the same cost as to others. At the end of the transition period provided for in Subpart C, such housing shall be available in sufficient quantity and variety so that the scope of handicapped students' choice of living accommodations is, as a whole, comparable to that of nonhandicapped students.

(b) Other housing. A recipient that assists any agency, organization, or person in making housing available to any of its students shall take such action as may be necessary to assure itself that such housing is, as a whole, made available in a manner that does not result in discrimination on the basis of handicap.

104.46   Financial and employment assistance to students

(a) Provision of financial assistance.

(1) In providing financial assistance to qualified handicapped persons, a recipient to which this subpart applies may not,

(i) On the basis of handicap, provide less assistance than is provided to nonhandicapped persons, limit eligibility for assistance, or otherwise discriminate or

(ii) Assist any entity or person that provides assistance to any of the recipient's students in a manner that discriminates against qualified handicapped persons on the basis of handicap.

(2) A recipient may administer or assist in the administration of scholarships, fellowships, or other forms of financial assistance established under wills, trusts, bequests, or similar legal instruments that require awards to be made on the basis of factors that discriminate or have the effect of discriminating on the basis of handicap only if the overall effect of the award of scholarships, fellowships, and other forms of financial assistance is not discriminatory on the basis of handicap.

(b) Assistance in making available outside employment. A recipient that assists any agency, organization, or person in providing employment opportunities to any of its students shall assure itself that such employment opportunities, as a whole, are made available in a manner that would not violate subpart B if they were provided by the recipient.

(c) Employment of students by recipients. A recipient that employs any of its students may not do so in a manner that violates subpart B.

104.47   Nonacademic services

(a) Physical education and athletics.

(1) In providing physical education courses and athletics and similar aid, benefits, or services to any of its students, a recipient to which this subpart applies may not discriminate on the basis of handicap. A recipient that offers physical education courses or that operates or sponsors intercollegiate, club, or intramural athletics shall provide to qualified handicapped students an equal opportunity for participation in these activities.

(2) A recipient may offer to handicapped students physical education and athletic activities that are separate or different only if separation or differentiation is consistent with the requirements of § 104.43(d) and only if no qualified

handicapped student is denied the opportunity to compete for teams or to participate in courses that are not separate or different.

(b) Counseling and placement services. A recipient to which this subpart applies that provides personal, academic, or vocational counseling, guidance, or placement services to its students shall provide these services without discrimination on the basis of handicap. The recipient shall ensure that qualified handicapped students are not counseled toward more restrictive career objectives than are nonhandicapped students with similar interests and abilities. This requirement does not preclude a recipient from providing factual information about licensing and certification requirements that may present obstacles to handicapped persons in their pursuit of particular careers.

(c) Social organizations. A recipient that provides significant assistance to fraternities, sororities, or similar organizations shall assure itself that the membership practices of such organizations do not permit discrimination otherwise prohibited by this subpart.

104.51   Application of this subpart

Subpart F applies to health, welfare, and other social service programs or activities that receive Federal financial assistance and to recipients that operate, or that receive Federal financial assistance for the operation of, such programs or activities.

104.52   Health, welfare, and other social services

(a) General. In providing health, welfare, or other social services or benefits, a recipient may not, on the basis of handicap:

(1) Deny a qualified handicapped person these benefits or services;

(2) Afford a qualified handicapped person an opportunity to receive benefits or services that is not equal to that offered nonhandicapped persons;

(3) Provide a qualified handicapped person with benefits or services that are not as effective (as defined in § 104.4(b)) as the benefits or services provided to others;

(4) Provide benefits or services in a manner that limits or has the effect of limiting the participation of qualified handicapped persons; or

(5) Provide different or separate benefits or services to handicapped persons except where necessary to provide qualified handicapped persons with benefits and services that are as effective as those provided to others.

(b) Notice. A recipient that provides notice concerning benefits or services or written material concerning waivers of rights or consent to treatment shall take such steps as are necessary to ensure that qualified handicapped persons, including those with impaired sensory or speaking skills, are not denied effective notice because of their handicap.

(c) Emergency treatment for the hearing impaired. A recipient hospital that provides health services or benefits shall establish a procedure for effective communication with persons with impaired hearing for the purpose of providing emergency health care.

(d) Auxiliary aids.

(1) A recipient to which this subpart applies that employs fifteen or more persons shall provide appropriate auxiliary aids to persons with impaired sensory, manual, or speaking skills, where necessary to afford such persons an equal opportunity to benefit from the service in question.

(2) The Assistant Secretary may require recipients with fewer than fifteen employees to provide auxiliary aids where the provision of aids would not significantly impair the ability of the recipient to provide its benefits or services.

(3) For the purpose of this paragraph, auxiliary aids may include brailled and taped material, interpreters, and other aids for persons with impaired hearing or vision.

104.53   Drug and alcohol addicts

A recipient to which this subpart applies that operates a general hospital or outpatient facility may not discriminate in admission or treatment against a drug or alcohol abuser or alcoholic who is suffering from a medical condition, because of the person's drug or alcohol abuse or alcoholism.

104.54   Education of institutionalized persons

A recipient to which this subpart applies and that operates or supervises a program or activity that provides aid, benefits or services for persons who are institutionalized because of handicap shall ensure that each qualified handicapped person, as defined in § 104.3(k)(2), in its program or activity is provided an appropriate education, as defined in § 104.33(b). Nothing in this section shall be interpreted as altering in any way the obligations of recipients under subpart D.

104.61   Procedures

The procedural provisions applicable to title VI of the Civil Rights Act of 1964 apply to this part. These procedures are found in §§ 100.6-100.10 and part 101 of this title.